ROYALTY UNVEILED

Women Trailblazers in Church Of God In Christ International Missions 1920 – 1970

Pioneer International Missionary Mary Beth Kennedy returning to Wissikeh

Glenda Williams Goodson

HCM PUBLISHING
Lancaster, Texas

HCM PUBLISHING
Lancaster, Texas

Copyright 2011 Glenda Williams Goodson

Photo credits constitute a continuation of this copyright page.

Royalty Unveiled: Women Trailblazers in Church Of God In Christ International Missions 1920 -1970 is published by HCM Publishing

All quotations and references to Scripture, unless otherwise indicated, have been taken from the King James Version of the Bible.

Royalty Unveiled: Women Trailblazers in Church Of God In Christ International Missions 1920 – 1970. Copyright © 2011. All rights reserved. Printed in the United States of America. Because of the dynamic nature of the Internet, any web addresses or links contained in this book may have changed since publication and may not longer be valid. The views expressed are the author's only. No part of this book may be used or reproduced in any manner whatsoever without written permission except in case of brief quotations. For information address inquiries to HCM Publishing, P.O. Box 36, Lancaster, TX 75146

Cover design by Halo Graphics

First Edition

ISBN 0975334247
ISBN 978-0-975-3342-4-9

The tenacious passion that Glenda Williams Goodson displays to "walk in her calling" is admirable. She exemplifies the fact that God uses ordinary individuals to accomplish extraordinary achievements. Glenda's latest scripted offering *Royalty Unveiled: Women Trailblazers in Church Of God In Christ International Missions 1920 – 1970*, is a profound statement of dedication and commitment to expose readers to knowledge.

It has been said that "leaders build while critics destroy." *Royalty* affords its readers the opportunity to learn about the paramount sacrifices that were made by COGIC's International Missionaries who were willing to build upon the foundation that Jesus Christ laid. They were determined to impact those who had not heard the Pentecostal message.

Bishop J. Neaul Haynes, Prelate
Texas Northeast First Ecclesiastical Jurisdiction
Member of the General Board, Church Of God In Christ, Inc.

Once again, Evangelist Glenda Goodson showcases her passion of unveiling courageous women whose labor established the foundation on which we now stand. This writing presents a historical analysis of the Mission Department, specifically the pioneering missionaries who have for decades carried the gospel message to foreign fields. She shares their experiences, roles and many contributions. A must read for those seeking to understand the global impact of the Church Of God In Christ.

Dr. Barbara McCoo Lewis,
Jurisdictional Supervisor, Southern California One
Church Of God In Christ, Inc.

Royalty Unveiled is a thoroughly researched and inspiring work. Using new sources and bringing fresh insight to classic documents, Glenda Goodson tells the story of a group of trailblazing women who most certainly should be added to the roll call of faith.

This book is a gem and must read for anyone interested in Women's Studies, African American History, Pentecostal Studies or the history of the Church Of God In Christ.

Daniel E. Walker, PhD
Research Associate
The Center for Religion and Civic Culture
The University of Southern California

This historical book is one of a kind in that it depicts the pioneer African American missionaries who dared to go where many African Americans would not go to carry the Gospel. It shares how they gave up their lifestyles to help others receive the news of Jesus Christ, education, and provisions for their medical needs. Because of their tenacity thousands of lives have been changed. I believe this book should be part of the library of every individual interested in missions, and further, in the hands of every member of the Church Of God In Christ.

Chaplain Marva Cromartie Nyema
U.S. Air National Guard (Ret. Major)
International Missionary to Liberia

DEDICATED TO

All past and present heroes who have worked untiringly in the faith for Christ's mandate of global evangelism and missions

FOREWORD

Looking Ahead Yet Thinking Back

By Mrs. Willie Mae Rivers
Sixth International Supervisor, Department of Women
Church Of God In Christ, Inc.

Most Spirit filled individuals can probably recall when they first received the Baptism in the Holy Ghost. They may not remember exactly where they were or the exact date but they probably remember that special feeling of wonderful joy that went along with the endowment of power coming upon their sanctified life.

In 1946, long before becoming the Sixth International Supervisor of the Department of Women of the Church Of God In Christ, I received the Holy Ghost and that joy and power. As I got to know the church, the stories of early adherents of the Church Of God In Christ doctrine moving through insurmountable obstacles with might and power of great force to spread the gospel, train disciples, and build sanctuaries have been dear to my heart. This gives me the strength to hold on to the legacy that they left, endeavoring to esteem them highly.

Glenda Goodson first interviewed me for her research on the lives of Church Of God In Christ pioneers at the Women's International Convention in 1988. She told me that the work I had done for the kingdom (and those before me) had to be researched and documented. With passion she further stated that God called her to be one of the individuals to perform this research. Since that meeting I have found she is faithful in completing the projects He commissions her to do. With a willing heart, she somehow finds the time and resources to share the wonderful story of the work of the pioneering saints of the Church Of God In Christ which will be a blessing to this and oncoming generations.

In her new book, *Royalty Unveiled: Women Trailblazers in Church Of God In Christ International Missions 1920-1970* every line, every photo or copy of a document substantiating the power of the pioneers will carry the story of the early international missionaries long after we're gone. I pray that this book will find its way into the hands of a little Purity Class or older YPWW student who will be inspired to follow the legacy and continue to spread the story of sanctification or the necessity of being filled with the Baptism in the Holy Ghost. I hope that this book fires their curiosity about all of the great men and women who paved the way for thousands of individuals in this world and emerging countries to come to the saving knowledge of Jesus Christ.

It will serve as a teaching tool and catalyst to renew interest among young women and men to head out to the vital work of international missions.

Mother Willie Mae Rivers
Goose Creek, South Carolina
February 2011

PREFACE

In more than 100 years since the remarkable arrival of the Holy Ghost at Los Angeles' Bonnie Brae Street, Pentecostals have evolved. This has both good and not so good implications. It is good that Pentecostals continue to carry the marriage of justification, sanctification and Holy Ghost power outside our walls but we must be careful to nurture our prophetic voice. Pentecostalism is more than speaking in tongues. We have a lot to say about what it means to live a truly yielded life, must remain uncompromised in our cry for true holiness, and not use our gifts as schemes to gain personal wealth, power or temporal enjoyment. The empowered believer, living a life separated from the world witnesses for her Savior through the daily living out of the sanctified life. This is what individuals from all races, ethnicities and genders experienced at what became the Azusa Street Revival. Leaving Azusa these emboldened believers took the message of God's power to save, fill, heal, and deliver back to their home churches and ultimately into the everywhere. Central to the movement was the belief that Jesus was soon to return. It was this driving force that caused them to go into highways and hedges to reach the lost for Christ whether in Newport News, Virginia or the tropical forests of far away Africa. In the year 2011 the Church Of God In Christ (COGIC) celebrates 100 years of service of its Department of Women (1911-2011). Closely affiliated with the Department is Home and Foreign Missions which in less than fifteen years celebrates its centennial. These pages share recollections from pioneers who paved the way in foreign fields or those of their children and/or caretakers. As they eagerly recalled long forgotten incidents, my purpose to allow their voices to ring out sharing their sacrifice and struggle was realized. While everyone contacted thanked me for gathering their history, I was especially moved by a woman who explained that as a result of this project thousands, who never heard from a missionary's mouth, can look over their shoulders to read of the faithfulness of God in taking care of them in the midst of deprivation and danger.

Film maker and documentarian Ken Burns says "the key part of the word 'history' is its second half — story." And that's how the seeds for this COGIC international mission's history began: my paternal grandmother, "Mama 'Ma' Fannie," planted stories which were germinated through my father Elder Joseph Robert Williams and finally nourished by my mother Missionary Gladys Alexander Williams. I do not have any idea how the minds of many Black children of my generation self-identified as descendants of mighty men and women from hearing scattered references to Blacks prior to slavery but the Williams children sure did! An avid reader, during the 1950s Ma Fannie secured all types of books, including those about Africa, from untold sources and declared to the family that we were probably torn from Western Africa. She regaled us with amazing stories of African kings and queens, golden stools and tantalized our minds with stories of libraries where individuals came to study from around world.

A sanctified pastor, my father was hesitant in purchasing a TV feeling it would introduce too much worldliness to our home. However after repeated reports of his children standing near neighbor's windows, determined to enjoy this invention, he relented. Monitoring the fare offered, he informed us (as we sat enthralled as Tarzan, the king of the jungle caused fear and trembling among literally hundreds of actors portrayed as half naked savages) he dealt with Hollywood distortions by proclaiming though Africans were unlike us culturally they did not live as the writers depicted them.

Stories of strong Black COGIC women and men who ventured through high risk activities stemming from problems of disease, hostility from indigenous peoples, governments and the elements to bring hope and the Gospel of Jesus Christ to the host countries in Africa, Haiti, and other locales date to the early 1900s and offer delight in the telling. Texas native Beatrice Lott and others shared their stories and my mother further piqued my interest as she gathered clothing and other items COGIC missionaries carried to Haiti and Africa, insisting that supporting missions was vitally necessary.

Someone said that the hallmark of high quality research is that is connects well to that work that preceded it. *Royalty Unveiled: Women Trailblazers in Church Of God In Christ International Missions 1920-1970*, is an important work in that much of it is seminal. Unless research done and now in private collections, *Royalty* is the first to give definition to the work of *Church Of God In Christ* international pioneers who blazed paths in education and spreading Pentecost. With godly pride I offer their accomplishments to the world during the *100th Centennial of the Church Of God In Christ Department of Women* ministries. I pray that *Royalty* serves as a launching pad to flush out other stories of full time and short term international missionaries of the Church Of God In Christ.

Glenda Williams Goodson
Lancaster, Texas
February 2011

ACKNOWLEDGEMENTS

The history of female international missionaries in the Church Of God In Christ is art, music, medicine, education, architecture, diplomacy and story telling. To capture it in book form has been a journey which has taken me so many difficult years to complete that at times I did not think I would see it off the press. However, God indeed makes provision for vision. It was so important for these stories to be told that I leaned on many individuals. I cannot name all of those precious ones who approached me during COGIC Women's Conventions, Holy Convocations or even "April Call" to provide vital contacts and information. Nevertheless, there are some who went the distance and I take this opportunity to give them a shout out. For their transparency in providing first person accounts, indepth insight and sharing their triumphs and defeats as young COGIC women serving in non-Western countries I appreciate: Pearl Page Brown (San Jose); Naomi Lundy (Philadelphia); and Mary Beth Kennedy (Erie, PA). Bishop Abraham and Mother Jessie Brown (Philadelphia) shared photos, documents and videos. While conducting interviews in Washington State Liberian national Jeremiah Nyema and wife Marva opened their home. Jerry helped me spell names of places correctly and Marva, an international missionary since the 80s, also assisted as researcher and fact checker. A host of professionals were invaluable. I am indebted to each librarian but especially Lisa Lipton (Dallas Downtown Library) and Margaret Endress (Lancaster Veterans Memorial Library) who walked me through Worldcat, Ebsco and interlibrary loan processes. While I had to mine the field to locate sources for information on the COGICs work in nearby Haiti, I found a wealth of information coming out of Africa. Rev. Robert Kauya shared the history of the COGIC in the Republic of Congo as I attempted to understand African culture and Dr. Debey Sayndee, Liberia's National Director of the African Leadership Bible Training Center for Pastors, talked with me for hours about his country's history and people. When I wished to better understand the strength underlying the overwhelming bewilderment of ancestors kidnapped from the great continent whose progeny would return bringing Christianity and later the power of Pentecost I turned to the African American Museum in Los Angeles Middle Passage exhibit. Though shaken, I left Los Angeles stronger for the experience and appreciate the curators who readily answered questions.

The network of scholars who assisted from start to finish included: Quintin Robertson, PhD, David Hall, Sr., PhD, Goldie Wells PhD, Larry Britton, PhD, Daniel Walker, PhD and Michelle Early, PhD;. Dr. Raynard Smith always sent articles he came across to move the research forward. Arriving in Philidalphia ill and feverish with exhaustion from nonstop travel, Dr. Anthea Butler nursed me to health, lent her camcorder, and took time from duties at the University of Pennsylvania to transport me to Philadelphia interviews. Emma Clark, Founder/Curator of the McGlothen Library (Richmond, CA) allowed access to the archives and transported me. Ladrian Young, M.D., Founder, D.J. Young Foundation shared a wealth of information. Bishop Robert Asberry's long time intellectual investment and financial assistance proved invaluable. Dr. David Daniels, Chairman of COGICs Department of Education, has believed in my work since the 80s, was first to invite me to present at the Society for Pentecostal Studies and can never know the extent to which his phone calls sharing needed leads or words of encouragement were lifelines.

By the time I reached Mississippi I was almost done and now doubt about low funds begin to distract me from purpose. The arguments of those voices who asked why I sacrificed valuable time researching and writing church history when it was not financially viable began to sound very cogent. I wondered "who cares about the work of these women anyway?" God provided two angels, Supt. Curtis and Lady Margaret Cobbins, who donated the Dovie Simmons Saints College archives. Wisely, Margaret encouraged me to spend some time at the Holmes County jail cell where Bishop Mason was destined to die. In a moment of true ephipany I resolved if Bishop Mason and other pioneers were willing to sacrifice their lives for what they believed I could do no less to tell their stories!

COGIC historian Jerry Ramsey copied 1940s/50s Whole Truths and recommended me for a speaking engagement with Supt. Odell and Lady Betty Franklin (they opened their parsonage) so I didn't have to worry about gas money to continue the Mississippi trip. On a night filled with tornado warnings historian Theda Wells waited at Memphis' Department of Women offices allowing me access to her archives. The legendary Sara Jordan Powell and husband John prayed me through. Mother Page's daughter Eleanor and husband Willie Campbell gave up their room for the days I spent in San Jose. My sister-friend Earlyn McDowell's insight on her grandfather, Bishop C.H. Mason, was invaluable. Her daughters Julie and Giseila provided lodging and transportation. True yokefellow Kentucky 1st Jurisdictional Supervisor Romanetha Stallworth and her husband Everett provided funds, referrals, prayers and encouragement. My dearly beloved friend, California 1st Jurisdictional Supervisor Barbara McCoo Lewis, not only prayed for and encouraged me but assisted financially.

Northern Georgia 2nd Jurisdictional Supervisor Bertha Fitts and COGIC National Adjutant Mother Geraldine Miller (a dear supporter since the 80s) pressed money into my hands and encouragement in my ears. Periodically every individual needs an ear and two great ladies, Supervisor Edith McGrew and Evangelist Louise Patterson, were there. When I needed a distraction Pastor Eldon Williams, my sister-friend Lady Becky Williams, Pastor R.C. Beecham and Lady Janice Beecham forced me to take a breather. Stephanie Johnson and husband Gerald provided funds and getaways. Chaplain Carlos Bell's support is sustaining. Supt. Charles and Lady Lessie Beard prayed with and for me. Lady Sophronia Smith not only shared recollections but also banquet tickets, fried fish on Fridays and her husband Pastor Roy Smith shared his mouth watering barbeque. COGIC National Prayer Leader Frances Kelley and Texas historian Administrator Janis Echols helped tremendously. Once tongue in cheek Bishop C.D. Owens referred to Int'l Missions President Bishop C.L. Moody as bishop of the world. Although he has a tremendous schedule whenever I called for information he responded positively. International Supervisor Willie Mae Rivers is a true Mother in Zion, who over the years has taken time to encourage me. Shortly after experiencing the darkest hour in my life at the sudden death of my husband Mother Rivers insisted that I go on with my work.

It was less expensive to fly into Cleveland so Elder and Sis. Steve Lott made two hour round trips taking me to Pennsylvania and trusted me to borrow from their archives. I interviewed Mother Lott years ago, however, without the memories of her caretaker Dr. Lisa Peeples, her voice would not have been as rich. COGIC General Board Member Bishop J. Neaul Haynes, his wife Vivian, and sister Maxine Kyles shared memories. Supt. J.E. Hornsby and Pastor Joseph Jackson are giants I look up to and received prayer and advice during this and other projects. My pastor, Dr. Glenn Tatum, Pastor Keith Ford, and friends/prayer warriors Chris Davis, Thea Glover, Credia Simon, Charlotte Williams, Carolyn Harvey and Annie Scott covered me in prayer. My sisters Victoria, Sherron and Judith gave me space and funds. I am covered by all six of my living brothers but Elder Robert Williams drove me to the airport as early as 3am and picked me up way past midnight so many times that I don't know how I can ever repay him. No mother could have a better child than our biological son Anthony or daughter-in-law Tavisha. God gave us many spiritual children but daughters Jana Burse and Yolanda Cooper looked out for me. My brother Akin says my mom was born a saint. While that's not theologically correct when my mother Gladys Williams said I was a great woman of God who inspires her, those words from that blessed one meant more than rubies. May God richly bless my friend Houston businessman Joseph Isaac who sponsored the first printing of this book.

It is not always easy to live with a creative or writer but George Goodson was the wind beneath my wings, cheering me on in everything I attempted. Had my husband lived he would have smiled so big, proud that I reached another goal. I will love him for eternity.

God is my shield and my strength. I thank Him for allowing me to respond to the unsearchable richness of His love by ordaining and sustaining my work for His glory. And I am grateful that His love and compassion allowed the Royal Women of the Church Of God In Christ to declare His glory among all.

INTRODUCTION

The world is like a mask dancing. You cannot see it well if you stand in one place. African proverb

We as Black COGIC Pentecostals do not know enough of our history to take what God has accomplished through our human efforts seriously. The Lord ordained this work as a tool to move the work of one essential component of the church, missions, forward. We cannot afford to do disservice to upcoming generations by failing to engage in discourse about brave men and women willing to go beyond borders of comfort and convenience to represent the God of power and love wherever the call was made to go. And the women went. In fact, the heart of this project came about because, although men were at the helm of COGIC Missions since its inception, I wished to research the history of women who were dominant in providing leadership as international missionaries. Fighting against poverty, disease and illiteracy on the ground in foreign countries these symbols of religious strength involved themselves in administration, caring roles, cultural training, healthcare and teaching. Despite threats and attacks by witch doctors beginning with their entrance on foreign soils to reports of stabbings of evangelists who preached the gospel in the 1960s they persevered through tours lasting from three to thirty years. What drove them to leave known environments to face the dangers of flooding and isolation when travel was all but impossible in some locales during rainy seasons? It was because their spirits were awakened through genuine revival.

Estrelda Alexander has written "one hallmark of genuine revival is a renewed zeal for missions — a passionate desire to spread the newly rekindled faith to those who have...never heard."[1] *Royalty Unveiled: Women Trailblazers in Church Of God In Christ International Missions 1920-1970* reveals the work of female international missionaries fired up by the Holy Ghost driving them to go in the fields during the defined period. With a new found vision of who they were, the women of the COGIC transcended their environment exhibiting zeal and stamina to share their faith in the powerful Christ with those yet to believe, in America and then into worlds of new customs and challenges. While 21st century COGIC journals and DVDs are 90 percent pictorials, pre-1980 souvenir books are historical treasure troves. During over twenty five years of connecting COGIC documents and memorabilia the fascinating and impactive life stories of great women emboldened by the Holy Ghost jumped out at me. *Royalty* utilizes these documents but also includes an admiring look at records of those having the wherewithal to independently pen their stories. Mother Evangelist Jane Brown was one such woman. Describing her work in the 1922-1972 Fiftieth Year Golden Jubilee of the Emanuel Church Of God In Christ, Harrisburg, PA her narrative discloses a classic, early Pentecostal experience: her 1923 conversion, sanctification, and the Holy Ghost coming upon the sanctified life. She tells of evangelizing in her home church and city (Judea), across the United States (Samaria), then to the utmost parts of the world (Canada, Alaska, Mexico, Cuba, Jamaica, and the Bahamas).

Whether working at home or abroad, individuals having a passion for missions shared the hallmark of the effective

---

[1] Alexander, Estrelda, *The Women of Azusa Street* The Pilgrim's Press, Cleveland: 2005

spiritual revival. Within these pages a chronicling of events from old state and national souvenir journals, articles and personal interviews unfold. These share the development of the COGIC missions as actually seen and interpreted through the lens of those who lived the gospel mandate out on foreign soil or supported the work. Beginning in the 1960s International Missions magazines detail groups visiting churches in Talejero, Michoacan, Mexico, mention Holy Convocations in Jamaica, Mission Conferences in Tijuana and England, and tell of the work of the COGIC on Native American reservations. Ardent mission's supporters such as Bishop J.A. Blake of California dedicated a Spanish language church led by Pastor Timoteo Figueroa; in 1963 Sis. Lottie Crouch and the Ministers' Wives of the Emmanuel Church donated funds to build Pastor Jesus Montes' church in Obregon, Sonora, Mexico.

Chapters 1 and 2 contexualize the work of the COGIC international missionary within the larger narrative of U.S. missions' activities, the entrance of Black sending agencies and the advent of 20th century Pentecostalism. **Chapter 1**, *The Missionary Movement and Introduction of American Female Missionaries* focuses on the movement in U.S. Western territories then across the Pacific as American missionaries, first male then female, all mainly Caucasian, brought Christianity to every area they settled. The controversial American Colonization Society was established by wealthy white men in the early 19th century to support emigration by free Blacks and continued after the Emancipation Proclamation. For information on Black migraton to Haiti and Africa I borrowed heavily from the New York Library's Schomburg Center for Research in Black Culture, In Motion, The African-American Migration Experience.

It is inaccurate to assume that all Africans wished to leave the United States, if only the wherewithal was available. In researching migration patterns I found that as early as the 19th century there was no consensus for mass emigration for Africans born into bondage or Blacks born free. Those sons and daughters of Africa who felt it was God's will for them to leave the U.S. to evangelize boarded ships, not as chattel slaves bringing wealth to the Americas, but bound for Haiti or their ancestral homelands to offer eternal wealth in Jesus Christ. Blacks continued their exodus in the dawn of the 20th century in response to discrimination and intimidation on American shores. Adventurous Blacks traveled to a variety of places however, most of the information in this volume focuses on the major destination of the missionaries, Africa (Liberia) and Haiti.

Chapter 2, *The Call to Go Forth,* overviews the advent of the the 20TH century Pentecostal movement and connects it to global missions. The modern day Pentecostal revival is said to have begun in 1900 at Bethel Bible School in Topeka, KS when those seeking more of God spoke in tongues (the initial evidence of Spirit baptism called glossolalia from two Greek words for tongue and speaking). After this time Pentecostals saw speaking in tongues as a sign of Spirit baptism. These ecstatic utterances, strange carryings on of holy dancing and exorcism as well as the Pentecostal believers' claim that the Baptism in the Holy Ghost (Holy Spirit) enabled them to live lives uninterrupted by continual leanings and yielding to their sin nature, were an offense to mainline churches. Husbands and wives, single men and women as well as teams went into Asia, Africa, and the Caribbean to proclaim that the gift Jesus Christ promised had come and empowered. The revival had its hiccups with critics pointing to issues problematic to the cause (some of this new group declared linguistic training unnecessary as the Holy Ghost would speak in each hearer's language or dialect). However, none could deny that the drive to prepare for the Second Coming altered the worldwide religious landscape. Blacks in America, less than fifty years removed from enslavement, made great strides in upward mobility through their educational, political and religious institutions. *Historical Overview of the Church Of God In Christ and Women's Ministry* in **Chapter 3** sets the birth of the COGIC within this upward movement. It traces the break from the Baptist church when Rev. C.P. Jones and Rev. C.H. Mason began preaching that God called for sanctification and holiness among believers. It extends to the estrangement of the co-leaders after Mason and others received the Baptism in the Holy Ghost at Azusa, the right hand of fellowship being withdrawn and the reorganization of the Church Of God In Christ as a Holiness-Pentecostal religious organization. Shortly after the church's reorganization, Mason taps Lizzie Woods (Robinson) as the Overseer of Women's Work.

Chapter 4, *History of Evangelism and Missions in the Church Of God In Christ,* reviews the beginning of the COGIC Missions. National Mother Lizzie Robinson laid the groundwork for an official Missions Department in 1926 when she introduced Elder Searcy to the National Convocation. After its reorganization the Department had grown to such an extent that the COGIC expanded its reach to a number of Third World countries. In 1943 an appeal was made to Bishop S.M. Crouch from Ladyselborn Pretoria, South Africa for a headquarters for the work of the COGIC (see Chapter 10, The Western Voice). By the 1965 Holy Convocation the COGIC showed a strong presence in places as diverse as Nova Scotia, Cuba,

Ontario, Puerto Rico and Panama. The year 1970 found churches and missions in Mexico, Korea, the Philippines, Panama, Barbados, Colombia, Guadalajara, India and Korea.[2] *The Divine Call Was Great,* **Chapter 5**, explores reasons causing females to enter international missionary work. Why were they willing to enter a vastly different culture and assuredly experience sacrifice thousands of miles away from home? Given that the majority of early adherents in the agrarian culture of Mississippi, Tennessee and Arkansas had limited incomes, what was the message of Mason and other pioneers that caused them to act with global vision after many made the bold step of leaving the Southland and migrating North?

Midway through the book is **Chapter 6** entitled *Here Am I, Send. . .A Woman?* I pursue answers to longstanding questions concerning females in international missions work: Did COGIC female missionaries go to foreign fields as single women or missionary wives? Did working on foreign soil offer greater freedom in ministry than any subordination they may have experienced at home? Given their role as power figures in the field, how were problematic issues such as power language subordinated upon their re-entry to the States? What position in the Stateside COGIC church compared to their global missions role? Were they more successful than men? If so, why? What were their educational levels? What did the men of indigenous cultures think of women coming to the missions' field? Although they ministered to people of color did COGIC foreign missionaries experience culture shock? How did international missionaries persuade male preachers to become involved – were native

---

[2] Church Of God In Christ Home and Foreign Missions Report, 11/7/70

Christians trained or did men relocate from the states? How were they supported financially? What were the day-to-day activities of the international missionaries? If success is to be measured by the impact of what they accomplished who were some of the mission children who went on to become officials and professionals in the countries where they served? This chapter is replete with excerpts from actual interviews. I wished the reader to actually "hear" them as they describe activities of teaching children in the missions schools they built, caring for them at the orphanages they built, dispensing medicine and providing care out of the medical stations they constructed and evangelizing, transforming lives through the power of the Word of God. The question of power is discussed in **Chapter 7,** *Signs and Wonders Followed Them.* The Apostle Paul speaks frequently of power with signs and wonders. One of the strengths of the early COGIC was the confidence in the authority of God that allowed them to use the power of the Holy Ghost to cast out demons. The missionaries most likely encountered demonic forces during some COGIC deliverance services and were not overwhelmed when facing this real and perceived danger of indigenous peoples. When confronted by witch doctors or voodoo activities entrenched in the culture of host countries what risks do the missionaries expose themselves to? How do they confront the power of the culture? The chapter addresses (1) The power of God over the power of the devil, (2) The power shown through demonstrations which followed their teaching and preaching and (3) The authority of the women to perform weddings, burials, and the sacraments of the church.

Chapter 8, *The Macedonia Call – A Network of Helps* shows that official COGIC missions support began with Bishop

Mason and Mother Robinson and developed through the networks of the church. International Supervisor Lillian Brooks Coffey and her Women's International Convention, State Women's Department leaders, individual churches and youth workers brought a new dimension to fundraising efforts and laid the groundwork for international missions' expansion with continued support of subsequent International Supervisors of Women, Jurisdictional Bishops, individual churches and Youth Department involvement. **Chapter 9**, *International Trailblazers. . .Instruments of Power* includes the profiles of as many international missionaries and major supporters as possible. Traveling thousands of miles from California and Washington State to the west, Philadelphia and New York to the east, south to Louisiana and Mississippi and down the middle of America I was blessed to conduct interviews with retired foreign workers and those active in some way, (most of who are at this writing in their mid 80s to early 90s). These include Pearl Page Brown (Haiti and Liberia), Naomi Lundy (Liberia), Ivory Coast Jurisdictional Prelate Bishop Abraham Brown (a former mission student and later the superintendent of Manolu, Tugbakeh and Wissekeh), his wife Jessie Brown, (former missions student and later missions teacher) and current Supervisor of the Democratic Republic of the Congo Mary Beth Kennedy (Tugbakeh and Wissekeh). In the late 80s I interviewed Beatrice Lott, Dorothy Webster Exume at her daughter's home in Norcross, Georgia and in 2000 I interviewed Bishop B.R. Benbow in Los Angeles. Through the reflections of Exume's children—Amilcar, Fronz and Marlil—an informed picture of her early work emerged. Eleanor Campbell, daughter of Pearl Page Brown provided valuable insight as well as Elder Charles Kennedy, Jr. and Dr. Grace Kennedy. Telephone interviews were conducted with former mission students

Sam Boley (Chicago), Bernice Nah (Rochester, Minnesota) and Alexander Gbayee (Chicago). I also interviewed Dr. Sayndee Debey of Liberia as well as Dr. Lisa Peeples, caretaker for Beatrice Lott and Bernice Abrams, caretaker for Mother Emma Crouch who provided insight into their missions support. Each individual provided enlightenment on how the COGIC practices and principles affected host cultures.

As the COGIC was established, calls were made by the missionaries for assistance in the foreign field. **Chapter 10** shares articles and reports from Whole Truth newspapers on the work of the foreign missionaries which raised awareness of their activities in *Missions Beginnings and News from Whole Truth and Other Media*. While the book focuses on the major destination of COGIC international missionaries, *Church Of God In Christ International Missions and Church Plantings Prior to 1970* in **Chapter 11** shares the work of COGIC adherents going into the everywhere through 1970. In an increasingly complex America **Chapter 12,** *Where Do We Go From Here?* encourages to reader to question the lack of knowledge of COGIC mission activities. It also asks that while American society wrestles with myriad problems on the home front if the support of international missionaries, in light of Mark 16:15 is still a relevant choice or should the church turn inward? At the end of the book I have preserved the voice of the missionaries by adding material extracted from rare and out of print booklets, newspapers and other media. These are included for those researching the COGIC to conduct historical analysis.

Contents

Foreword
Preface
Acknowledgement
Introduction

Chapter One   2

The Missionary Movement and Introduction of American Missionaries, Blacks Migrate to Africa and Haiti

Chapter Two   29
The Call to Go Forth

Chapter Three   38

Historical Overview of the Church Of God In Christ and Women's Ministry

Chapter Four   56

History of Evangelism and Missions in the Church Of God In Christ

Chapter Five   64
The Divine Call Was Great

Chapter Six   77
Here Am I, Send. . .A Woman?

Chapter Seven   141
Signs and Wonders Followed Them

Chapter Eight   157
The Macedonia Call – A Network of Helps

Chapter Nine   199
   International Trailblazers...Instruments of Power

Chapter Ten   233
   *Missions Beginnings and News from Whole Truth and
               Other Media*

Chapter Eleven   243
   *Church Of God In Christ International Missions and
           Church Plantings Prior to 1970*

Chapter Twelve   261
   Where Do We Go From Here?

Appendix   273

Selected Bibliography   302

INDEX   310

CHAPTER ONE

The Missionary Movement and Introduction of American Female Missionaries, Blacks Migrate to Africa and Haiti

During the 18th and 19th century the entrance of young sciences such as botany and the emergence of free thinkers in Europe caused doubt about the origin of humankind, the Bible as literal truth, and the existence of God. Individuals now debated issues that would have been labeled heretical in earlier times. At the same time Europe immersed itself in a cloud of doubt, its global influence slowly gave way to what was still considered the new world and its continued expansion. And missionaries, operating under the banner of the Christian church, would play an integral part in the dynamic.

On the one hand the missionary has been castigated, sometimes with merit, as a cover for imperialism. On the other the missionary as saint was revered as necessary to bring light to heathens who historically were red, yellow, or brown. The true missionary offered hope, warning, and the sense that the practice of the emissary's rule of conduct was superior to what the recipient's religious order offered, sometimes having problematic consequences. From a Christian perspective, one of the first missionaries recorded in biblical text was Jonah, the reluctant missionary to the hated Ninevites.[3] Jonah did not wish to see those foreign or hostile to Israel enjoy life and eagerly anticipated their annihilation. The moral of the story is that God is sovereign and it is His desire that all align themselves with His rule and His way. Yet there must be someone willing to speak truth and offer hope to those outside the commonwealth. Whether at home or abroad Black Americans have offered little resistance when the call was made to speak the truth of God's word.

Much has been written about the lives and achievements of the majority culture called into foreign missions work. However, the story of Blacks who emigrated from American shores to work in this field is complicated. Did they go to Africa or other countries as colonists or missionaries? Were the majority sent by White sending agencies or African American organizations? Documented reports added to the oral tradition tracing the work of western Blacks, both as settlers and Christian workers emigrating offer a number of clues. In the early 1750s, English missionary Thomas Thompson persuaded his New Jersey Anglican sponsors to allow him begin a risky mission in West Africa and by 1752, he had established the first official Anglican mission at the slave-trading Gold Coast. Influenced by developments in American missionary practice — the Great Awakening had unleashed a tremendous amount of native missionary

---

[3] Jonah 1:1-2

projects in the 1740s and 1750s — Thompson immediately set out to train native peoples to serve as his assistants. Three of them were sent to England for missionary training. One of the boys died and another went insane. Philip Quaque, however, finished his training by 1765 and sailed to West Africa writing prodigiously of his experiences as a minister in the Anglican Church.[4]

George Liele is considered to be the first American overseas missionary after he moved his family to Kingston, Jamaica. He indentured himself to a British officer in 1782 to avoid re-enslavement by his former master's heirs. Within two years he repaid his indenture and devoted all his energy to preaching. With four other former American slaves, he formed the First African Baptist Church of Kingston. Four hundred and fifty men and women, known as the *Black Poor*, sailed from Britain and settled in Sierra Leone in 1787. These destitute settlers were joined by twelve hundred former U.S. bondsmen called *Black Loyalists* coming from Nova Scotia in 1792. After fighting alongside the British Army during the Revolutionary War they were dissatisfied with conditions in Nova Scotia. In the 1800s Jamaican Maroons, runaways who had been deceitfully deported to Canada after signing a peace treaty with the British, followed them.[5]

---

[4] Excerpts from Quaque's letters illuminate the importance of native African's to missionary efforts. While he lamented his countrymen's superstitions he did not force his thinking on them to convert. *Philip Quaque, Letters of the Rev. Philip Quaque of West Africa* (East Ardsley: Micro Methods Ltd. 198-85). *Philip Quaque, The letters of Philip Quaque*, 1766-1811 (East Ardsley: E.P. Microform, 1970s).

[5] *The Providence African Society's Sierra Leone Emigration Scheme, 1794-1795: Prologue to the African Colonization Movement...from The International Journal of African Historical Studies, Vol. 7, no. 2 (1974)* by George E. Brooks, Jr. "Courtesy of The New York Public Library. www.nypl.org"

Black rebellion against human oppression in Santa Doming in 1791 (what is called Haiti today) was a factor in forcing the decision of the French revolutionary government to emancipate half a million French slaves in 1794. Additionally, the passage of a bill by the English House of Commons to destroy the English slave trade caused antislavery sentiment to increase by the late 1700s. Each of these events provided fertile ground for those wishing to be free from American slavery.[6] The problem of what to do with Black former slaves was global and the early nineteenth century found a growing interest in immigration among Blacks. Sierra Leone was home to the Temne, Mandingo, Fulani, Bullom, and Kru people. These natives were soon to be joined by Blacks previously removed from African soil, becoming the location of the first known African colonization.

To understand how American Blacks entered Africa or Haiti a look at the American missionary movement is important. According to Daniels Bays for the first two thirds of the century any overseas movement was overshadowed by the focus of most American Protestant groups on the internal planting of churches on the advancing frontier, and on the Civil War."[7] By 1900, its expansion was in full bloom, and would continue well into the 20th century, with its presence on all continents characterized by a distinctive American mixture of religious and national or "civilizing" purpose.[8]

From the 1800s to the 1960s America had three major

---

[6]Nash, Dr. Gary B., Excerpt of *"The Unknown American Revolution,"* presented at the University of Pittsburgh 10/25/05

[7] Bays, Daniel H., *The Foreign Missionary Movement in the 19th and early 20th Centuries*, nationalhumanitiescenter.org/.../fmmovementcredits.htm

[8] Ibid

population shifts. The first was the migration of Native Americans. They were forced to resettle from their revered lands onto reservations maintained by their conquerors. American settlers moving westward included Christian missionaries whose purpose was to civilize indigenous people found in Native American territories and nations. In the Pacific Northwest single non-Indian missionaries or missionary teams brought their form of Christianity to the Nez Perce and other tribes. After some success with Native America conversions, Protestant missionaries began to proselytize in cities, directing their attention on individuals practicing Roman Catholicism and later Jewish immigrants. By the early 20th century American missionaries focused on journeying across the Pacific with the intent of civilizing what they considered heathen countries. The movement had its heyday from 1880 to 1930 with tens of thousands of Americans involved through settling in foreign land or supporting those who braved the danger. The profile of these missionaries was that they were male and were educated beyond college.

Blacks were legally transformed from indentured servants during the colonial period to slaves. As black gold they were increasingly torn from their ancestral homes and estranged from their tribes with little hope of freedom. Upon arrival in America the Africans found that Christianity could be used as a form of social cohesion and Blacks received Christian baptism since the colonial period in America.[9] According to the U.S. Census by 1800 the Black population was a little over 1,000,000 (18.9%)

---

[9]Frazier, E. Franklin, *The Negro Church in America*, 1963 Schocken Books, New York, 7-8

living in America of which 108,000 were free[10] and by 1860 America's free Black population had grown to 500,000. Some Blacks were able to purchase their freedom but chafed under the constant threat of re-enslavement by unscrupulous bounty hunters from the South. (A man could purchase his freedom, only to have his papers burned, and be re-enslaved on his way North.) After the Civil War the majority of Blacks remained in the South. Those migrating North discovered covert racism in discriminatory labor and housing laws. A very small number of those who remained were ministers, teachers or doctors with most working as sharecroppers or tenant farmers. Many of these blacks identified with the Presbyterian, Methodist, Baptist and Catholic Church and began organizing what came to be called the Black Church where they created spaces to worship as they saw fit.[11] Before and after their human bondage they always had a sense of the spiritual and finding refuge in the certainty of a just God, eagerly shared their faith.

Beginning in the early 19th century Black and White clergy, abolitionists, philanthropists and even some slave holders (the latter feared that the increasing number of free blacks would prove problematic by never assimilating into American society), agreed that a solution had to be addressed. Research was done in opening parts of the West or even Louisiana as a place for free Blacks to be maintained. For a short while Haiti, the first Black republic and the second country to gain independence (in 1804), was the most popular destination for American Blacks Under the leadership of François

---

[10] Source: *Statistical Abstract of the United States: 2003*, and *We, The American Blacks*, U.S. Census Bureau, 1993.

[11] Luntz, Norma Jean, *History of the Black Church*, 2001: Chelsea House Publishers, Philadelphia, 11

Dominique Toussaint L'Ouverture and second in command Jean-Jaques Dessalines, both ex-slaves, 40,000 of the French colony's 465,429 slaves revolted.[12] After defeating a French army three times their size the independent Haiti flung its door wide open as an asylum for Blacks fleeing bondage from anywhere in the Americas. This reportedly drew the wrath of the United States. Robinson notes that only three years after Haiti's independence, the British [and Americans] ended their Atlantic slave trade. This fact, plus its proximity to the United States and its history of self-liberation and Christianity, made the island attractive to Black proponents of emigration. They stressed that since it was so close, emigrants would not be abandoning their enslaved brothers and sisters. White advocates saw Haiti as another site to which undesirable free Blacks could be deported.[13] (Haiti experienced increasing problems. L'Ouverture would be kidnapped and starved to death by Napoleon and Dessalines would lead before being assassinated and replaced by Henry Christophe who declared himself the king of the world's first Black republic.[14])

In 1824, the New York Colonization Society received a commitment from Haitian President Jean-Pierre Boyer to pay the passage of U.S. emigrants. Boyer also promised to support them for their first four months and to grant them land. The same year, Black leaders, including wealthy Philadelphia businessman James Forten and

---

[12] Robinson, Randall, *Haiti: The Truth African-Americans Have Not Been Allowed to Know,* Ebony Magazine, April 2010, 78-79

[13] The Schomburg Center for Research in Black Culture, In Motion, *The African-American Migration Experience, Migration to Haiti* "Courtesy of The New York Public Library. www.nypl.org

[14] News of Haiti article *20,000 Died Building Massive Citadel,* Numero 6, January 30, 1970, 3

Bishop Richard Allen, formed the Haytian Emigration Society of Coloured People. (Richard Allen is famous as the founder of the African Methodist Episcopal Church, formed as a protest against segregation in 1787. This former slave purchased his freedom while in his twenties and settled in Philadelphia.) They arranged for the transportation of several hundred people, not only to Haiti but also to Santo Domingo, the Spanish-speaking western part of the island of Hispaniola that had been conquered by Haiti in 1822. In 1830, he helped organize the American Society of Free Persons of Color and became its first president. Allen argued for Haiti as an alternative to Liberia for emigration of Blacks in America. The African Methodist Episcopal Church developed an active mission program in Africa and the Caribbean, which continues into the present era.[15] Many Blacks and Whites, including Frederick Douglass, were opposed to Haitian immigration. Haitian supporters had an ally in the Great Emancipator President Abraham Lincoln who had for some years prior to his presidency encouraged the movement as a means of solving the "problem of Blacks." With his support more than 400 men and women were transported from Virginia - to L'Ile-à-Vache, an island off the Haitian coast. The experiment failed due to inadequate planning and poor leadership. In less than a year, the survivors returned to the United States. In the mid-nineteenth century, James Theodore Holly, a fourth generation Northern free man, was one of the strongest proponents of immigration to Haiti. As an agent of the Haitian Bureau of Emigration, he led a group of emigrants from New Haven and Canada in 1861. His wife, his mother, and two of his children died shortly after their arrival in Haiti. Although many settlers left the

---

[15] yale.edu/.../storm/AfricanAmericanMissionaries Revised.pdf

country, Holly remained on the island until his death. He became the first Episcopal bishop of Haiti in 1874.[16] Henry Highland Garner, born into slavery in Maryland, escaped to New York with his father at the age of nine and later became a leading abolitionist. Garner supported emigration and was a missionary for the United Presbyterian Church of Scotland in Jamaica in the 1850s. Due to illness Garnett was forced to return to the United States but remained active in sponsoring immigration to Haiti and Africa. He was a founding member of the African Civilization Society[17] and in 1865 became the first African American to preach a sermon in the U.S. House of Representatives.

When agreement could not be reached on how to solve the problem of Blacks, the American Colonization Society (ACS) was established (1816) by Robert Finley to offer free Blacks an opportunity to relocate to Africa. Initially many Blacks, some who did not identify with Africa, distrusted the organization believing that the ACS would attempt to deport all Blacks and saw their goals as an affront to their dignity. Martin R. Delaney was such a man. In his review of Martin Delaney's book, Benjamin Quarles, Chairman, Department of History, Morgan State College found that Delaney, a grandson of a slave, the color of jet and proud of it, was an original mind. "I thank God for making me a man simply," wrote Frederick Douglass, "but Delaney always thanks Him for making him a Black man." In a letter to Secretary of War Stanton President Abraham Lincoln introduced Martin R. Delaney as "this most extraordinary and intelligent Black man." Initially critical of immigration efforts Delaney

---

[16] ibid

[17] ibid

believed Liberia was a mere dependency of Southern slaveholders and the American Colonizationists and unworthy of any consideration. He further cautioned that "...White Americans...supposed that we are too ignorant to understand what we want; whenever they want to get rid of us, would drive us anywhere; so that we left them...[but] we will think for ourselves."[18]

Despite criticism from Delaney and other powerful Blacks the ACS moved forward. After years of lobbying the President and Congress for support founders James Monroe, Bushrod Washington, Andrew Jackson, Francis Scott Key, and Daniel Webster received $100,000 from Congress. Three groups—the American missionaries (White), the Black settler/colonists (Africans repatriated from America) and indigenous tribal people who inhabited the land—influenced the introduction of Christianity to Liberia. In 1820 the ship *Elizabeth* sailed from New York headed for West Africa with three White ACS agents and 88 emigrants.[19] Unable to find land in Liberia, the ship journeyed safely to Sierra Leone. In 1821 the ACS was successful in obtaining acreage and a ship carrying thirty-three Blacks landed at Cape Mesuardo – later to become Monrovia, named after U.S. President James Monroe. Liberia, the land of the Vai, Kru, Kissi, Grebo, Bassa, Kpelle, Mandingo, and other populations became the primary destination of American Blacks with the ACS chartering forty-one ships between 1848 and 1854 carrying over four thousand mostly free Blacks to the new land. One ship, the *Azor*, was purchased in 1878 by the Liberian Exodus Joint Stock Steamship Company

---

[18] Delaney, Martin R. *The Condition, Elevation, Emigration, and Destiny of the Colored People of the United States,* Published by the Author, 1852
[19] personal.denison.edu/~waite/liberia/history/acs.htm

and left Charleston, SC with 250 immigrants on board headed for Liberia. A few were single men but most brought their wives and children to brave the unknown in a quest to share their dreams and determine their own destiny. (See Appendix 1:3).

One of the former Christian slaves who purchased his freedom in 1813, Rev. Lott Carey, sailed for Sierra Leone in 1821. Rev. Carey relocated to Monrovia, Liberia in 1822 and established the Providence Baptist Church, reported to be the first Baptist church in the country, where he ministered to the congregation as well as to native tribes in evangelism, education and health care.[20] Black Baptists established the Lott Carey movement in 1897 to assist foreign missions efforts in Africa for the "primary objective of advancing God's mission throughout the world"[21] although Sutherland says multiple motives operated and their desire could not be categorized neatly. Further inquiry into their thinking reveals they also ventured to shores outside the United States in search of racial affinity.

> I am an African, and in this country, however meritorious my conduct, and respectable my character, I cannot receive credit due to either. I wish to go to a country where I shall be estimated by my merits, not by my complexion; and I feel bound to labor for my suffering race.[22]

On February 13, 1824 one hundred and five like minded Blacks arrived via the ship *Cyrus* and joined Lott's group.

---

[20] yale.edu/.../storm/AfricanAmericanMissionaries Revised.pdf
[21] www.lottcarey.org/history
[22] Sutherland, James W. *African American Underrepresentation in Intercultural Missions: Perceptions of Black Missionaries and the Theory of Survival/Security*, Dissertation Submitted to the Faculty in partial fulfillment of the requirements for the degree of Doctor of Philosophy, Intercultural Studies at Trinity Evangelical Divinity School, Deerfield, IL, May 1998, 34

These missionaries were the first sent by a Black organization, the Richmond African Baptist Missionary Society.

Slaveholders like Gen. Robert E. Lee freed slaves prior to the Civil War offering to pay their expenses to Liberia. Two of Lee's slaves, William and Rosabella Burke immigrated with their children to Liberia where Burke went to seminary in Monrovia and became a Presbyterian minister in 1857. Every right thinking individual in any age is endowed by his Maker with the fundamental need to control their earthly destiny and the slave was no different. Families like the Burke's had gained their personal freedom but with the prospect of gaining true freedom as humans were clear headed in their willingness to suffer hardship. A year later, he wrote a friend back home that "Persons coming to Africa should expect to go through many hardships, such as are common to the first settlement in any new country. I expected it and was not disappointed or discouraged at anything that I met with; and so far from being dissatisfied with the country, I bless the Lord that ever my lot was cast in this part of the earth."[23] Methodists, Baptists and Presbyterian churches were all involved in the missionary movement, sometimes accompanying freed slaves to Haiti and Africa.[24] Initially the Whites and not the emigrants led the new colonies lending their expertise as superintendents of schools, teachers, and missions stations builders.

---

[23] The Schomburg Center for Research in Black Culture, In Motion, *The African-American Migration Experience, The Colonization of Liberia* "Courtesy of The New York Public Library. www.nypl.org"
[24] www.phcmontreat.org/bios/Bios-Missionaries-Africa.htm

Some Pioneer Missionaries

Rev. Lott Carey

Rev. Richard Allen

Rev. Amanda Smith

Rev. John Brooke Pinney

Henry Highland Garnett

James Theodore Holly

Jane Warning Roberts

James Temple

Betsey Stockton

Illustrative of the foundational work of the first White settlers to Liberia are twenty-seven year old Presbyterian missionary, Rev. John Brooke Pinney and Rev. John L. Wilson. Pinney was appointed by the Western Foreign Missionary Society Synod of Pittsburgh, arrived in Monrovia February 16, 1833 and was the first Protestant missionary to serve in Liberia. Accompanying him were Rev. John Cloud, Rev. Matthew and Mrs. Harrier Myer who all died of dysentery four months after their arrival in Liberia.[25] Rev. John L. Wilson served as a linguist, evangelist, author, naturalist, humanitarian, and missionary statesman. He was appointed by Southern Board of Missions, auxiliary society to American Board of Commissioners for Foreign Missions, in 1833. Wilson served at Cape Palmas, Liberia with the new colony of freed slaves, travelled frequently to the interior and printed Scripture in the Greybo language. In 1842, he and his wife transferred to Gabon, opening work at Baraka, an old slave barracks near Libreville where he served until 1852 and was the author of "Western Africa, Its History, Condition & Prospects." [26]

More Colonization Societies were organized for the purpose of forming settlements and Blacks were not only emigrating to Sierra Leone but also to Liberia. Emigrants to Sierra Leone, Liberia and Haiti received financial assistance to resettle outside the United States from Blacks and Whites. With a history of civilization and nation building Blacks were eager to control their destiny as evidenced by the work of Paul Cuffee, a prosperous

---

[25] Cogswell, *6F. Thompson, 296. The Missionary Herald, Vol. 20, 1844, 222.*
[26] Hampden C. Dubose, Rev. John Leighton Wilson, D.D., Missionary to Africa and Secretary of Foreign Missions (Richmond Presbyterian Committee of Publication, 1895, John Miller Wells, Southern Presbyterian Worthies, Chapter II–John Leighton Wilson: The Foreign Missionary, Richmond, VA: Presbyterian Committee of Publication, 1936

ship owner. African-American involvement in Sierra Leone began in 1811 when England's Royal African Society invited the Quaker and lifelong campaigner for black civil rights to visit Sierra Leone. Along with nine African-American seamen he sailed from Massachusetts to Freetown. In Freetown, Cuffee decided to develop trade between Blacks in England, Sierra Leone, and the U.S. He also began to consider the possibility of relocating skilled Blacks to the colony, and founded the Friendly Society of Sierra Leone. In 1815, thirty-eight emigrants accompanied him to the colony. Among them were a Senegalese who had migrated from Haiti, and a Congolese. This would be the first migration of Blacks from the United States to Africa. [27] According to diaries and letters sent home the new emigrants felt that it would be better to live in hardship in Africa than endure oppression in America.

Black leaders, while not opposing any who made a decision to return to Africa, wished the decision to be their own. In 1830 a call was made for Blacks to meet in Philadelphia for a Negro Convention. There Negro leaders discussed identity and destiny with the consensus that they were Americans first. They desired Blacks to begin calling themselves Negro or Colored as an opposition to those who identified them as African and would expatriate them to Africa. Those who may have wished to flee Northern race riots but also desired to identify with their ancestral culture prepared to emigrate to the continent. Some of the members of the Black

---

[27] *The Providence African Society's Sierra Leone Emigration Scheme, 1794-1795: Prologue to the African Colonization Movement...* from The International Journal of African Historical Studies, Vol. 7, no. 2 (1974) by George E. Brooks, Jr. "Courtesy of The New York Public Library. www.nypl.org"

Church became the first African American international missionaries with Blacks working in overseas missions in the 18th century. (See Appendix 1:2) Entrepreneurs and artisans joined them in responding to laws meant to codify their inferior status, by expatriating from America, looking to Africa as a place that they would have the opportunity to succeed or fail on their own. James Temple, appointed by the Presbytery of Philadelphia in 1834, was listed as the "Negro assistant missionary" and arrived in Liberia on Dec. 31, 1833. Temple returned to America around the summer of 1834 after the deaths of numerous missionaries from African fever. In 1837 the Commonwealth was formed, giving virtually all power to the emigrants. The society retained only the right to choose the governor. After 1842, only Negro missionaries were sent to Liberia. Among those listed in the Presbyterian Heritage Center's biographical index of Missionaries to Africa were Washington McDonough (a black teacher in Settra Kroo), Rev. and Mrs. T. Wilson (black teacher in Settra Kroo); Cecilia Van Tyere, (Black teacher in Settra Kroo); Rev. and Mrs. H.W. Ellis (redeemed from slavery his family left for Monrovia in 1847 and were supported by churches in Alabama and Mississippi); and Louisiana A. Coke, (a colored female highly qualified for teaching Settra Kroo)."[28] By 1843 Rev. James M. Priest was among 60 American Negro missionaries in Liberia. A former Kentucky slave, he was educated by slaveholder Jane Anderson Meaux and sent to Liberia to examine the potential of the colony. On his return to the U.S., Priest received more education and was appointed a Presbyterian missionary. In 1843, he emigrated to Liberia under the auspices of the ACS and served for 40 years in King Will's Town, then Greenville.

---

[28] www.phcmontreat.org/bios/Bios-Missionaries-Africa.htm

Those Black expatriates found the task daunting but were fortified by the fact that in Liberia they would chart their own destiny.

Blacks like Lee's former slave William Burke were excited to live in a land free from oppression. However, whites in the ACS still ran Liberia's government. The settlers soon demanded control of their own affairs. By 1847 the colony established on the west coast of Africa had become the independent nation of Liberia, and in 1848, Joseph Jenkins Roberts—a Monrovian merchant who emigrated from Virginia twenty years earlier—was elected president. By 1867 the society had sent more than 13,000 emigrants Mission work in Liberia was carried out 1833–1894; in Gabon 1843–1894; and on the island of Corisco 1850–1875. In a December 17, 1873 New York Times article Rev. York Dr. Alexander, an officer of the New York Colonization Society read a report where the organization congratulated themselves on sending emigrants to Africa from Tennessee, Georgia and Florida to "repay the debt which America so unquestionably owes to Africa."[29]

Approximately one thousand Blacks immigrated to Liberia between 1890 and 1910. For many Africans, the arrival of the black Americans was, at best, a mixed blessing. Landing on African soil the expatriates were confronted with cultural adjustments and tensions between natives and Americo-Liberians, as they were called, sometimes ran high. In the early years the ACS ran Liberia's government, the newcomers spoke English and not all Liberians welcomed them with their American

---

[29] The New York Times, December 17, 1873

manners, American homes and American religion. Some immigrants exploited their new neighbors by taking thousands of acres of native Liberian lands. Native Liberians felt that the newcomers did not accept them as equals with hostilities escalating in 1843 in a revolt against the Americo-Liberians. An all-out war erupted in 1875 between the colonists and the Grebo, and violent conflicts persisted until the turn of the twentieth century.

In the U.S. the Supreme Court decision declared the Civil Rights Act of 1875 unconstitutional and upholding legal segregation sped up the process of Black subordination. By 1877 White Northerner's interest in the problems of the recently freed slaves diminished. However, the importance of colonization and emigration raised the nationalist consciousness of America's Black population. Perhaps its most enduring legacy was the Pan-African movement, which blossomed in the late nineteenth and early twentieth centuries. A concept pioneered by Martin R. Delaney, Edward Wilmot Blyden, and others, it led to the recognition that until Africa was free of oppression, Black people around the world could not become free. The visionary Black leader W. E. B. Du Bois who had never advocated emigration would spearhead Pan-Africanism throughout his lifetime. In 1961, like Henry Highland Garnett before him, Du Bois, in his old age, left the United States for Ghana, where he died on the eve of the historic 1963 March on Washington for Jobs and Freedom. Other Blacks would follow his path, immigrating to various parts of the world in search of their dream of freedom and equality.

Emigration to Africa continued on a small scale into the twentieth century. Though small in number, these efforts were not insignificant, as in most cases they represented self-initiated migrations, heavily influenced by nationalist ideas. Although individuals continued to migrate to the continent, organized movements as those led by Chief Alfred Sam or Marcus Garvey were few. In 1913, sixty Oklahomans settled in the Gold Coast under the leadership of Chief Alfred Sam.[30] Marcus Garvey would gain worldwide attention when he took the helm of the Back to Africa movement. Born in 1887 in Jamaica, Garvey was certain that Blacks could not experience equality in any country where they held minority status. He founded the Black Nationalist Negro Improvement Association in 1914 to "promote the spirit of race pride."[31] Stating that Africa was for Africans, he found that Liberia was the place to go for blacks seeking a land where they could prosper. In June 1920 President C.D.B. King invited the organization to establish headquarters there and the Liberian senate incorporated the group in January 1921.[32] Discontent against Americo-Liberian rule by native Liberians converged with a series of events causing the UNIA to soon suffer setbacks politically and religiously. Since the settling of Liberia the issue of land had been a problem and after UNIA requests for land Liberia denounced the UNIA. The UNIA began expansion into Nigeria, however, the movement was stemmed and a June 1921 "La Rome Noire," newspaper reported on Garvey, published in La Dépeche Coloniale; and circulated widely in France and French West Africa blamed African uprisings in Belgian Congo on the

---

[30] *Chief Sam's African Movement and Race Consciousness in West Africa* from Phylon, vol. 32, no. 2 (Second quarter, 1971) by J. Ayo Langley, Courtesy of New York Public Library, nypl.org

[31] The Columbia Encyclopedia. Copyright © 2001-10 Columbia University Press.

[32] Copyright © 1995-2010 The Marcus Garvey and UNIA Papers Project, UCLA "African Series Introduction: Volume VIII: October 1913--June 1921". *The Marcus Garvey and UNIA Papers Project.* UCLA. http://www.international.ucla.edu/africa/mgpp/intro08.asp. Retrieved 3 February 2010

circulation of African-American newspapers there. As the UNIA became influential in Liberia the U.S. State Department began investigating it and some African governments became reluctant to admit foreign missionaries due to the Garvey movement. Garvey's actions were seen to hinder the work of the missionaries. Bishop Charles S. Smith, AME, Detroit, wrote a letter to the British secretary of state for the colonies, denouncing Garvey and claims "... it is calculated to prompt the imposition of restrictions on the movements of colored American religious bodies conducting mission work in Africa."[33] Still missionaries moved forward in their quest to lift the standards of native Liberian communities and villages. In 1926 land in the Bassa community was granted by the Liberian government to a group of Baptists who immediately built a small house used as a maternity center. (Later the Japanese, who relations with Liberia date back to the 1950s, would expand and reopen the hospital after unknown persons destroyed it during the war in the 1980s.)

While some of the newcomers attempted to balance life in Africa with their ideas of Western culture racism developed between people of the same racial background but differing cultural values with the latter considering the indigenous populations heathen prior to their becoming Christians. The attitude that there was little to value in the Liberian culture chafed men like eighty plus Liberian native Abraham Brown. He notes that all racial problems did not have origins with the Whites and recalled initial encounters with American Blacks while working as a teenage common laborer, then houseboy, for a wealthy Americo-Liberian couple in Monrovia.

---

[33] ibid

They took over our country. What we call the negroes, yea, they invaded Liberia years ago. And they are the ones in power, they are the government, they are the rich. They are the ones we worship! Some of the blacks treated [us Africans] worst than [we heard] the whites in Alabama treated blacks there. You have to say yes, sir!

We had one lantern in the house. When I finished cooking their food and everything when they go on upstairs the whole downstairs is dark. I am in the dark until the next morning. No light downstairs. You talk about a dark country. Man! They were the civilized people and so as you say they were using this for themselves. I was servant. I was not too important to be in the light. When I cook and finish, when I take the food off that heat and they take the lantern upstairs I am to close the door. They say servant stay downstairs. They call us *natives*. My tribe *Tobou!*[34]

THE MISSIONARY MOVEMENT AND INTRODUCTION OF AMERICAN FEMALE MISSIONARIES

The Great Commission found in Mark 16:15 was a spiritual mission and since the Apostle Paul's recommendation of Phebe to the Roman churches women have played an important role in spreading the gospel. In the practical area of providing food and sustenance to those who would be won to Christ, female missionaries in the 19th and early 20th century (called the golden age of missionary expansion 1880-1920s), were poised to make a difference. Driven by the belief that American Christianity

---

[34]Interview by author with Rev. Abraham Brown, Manolu Missions Student, Missions Overseer at his Philadelphia home. September 2010

was the true faith they were eager to civilize the individuals they considered the heathen in foreign fields. Yet there would be obstacles simply because of gender restrictions to upward mobility within the church. During this period women were merely tolerated within the ranks of church leadership. Few men were like Charles G. Finney who encouraged women to pray in mixed circles. (He further created uproars when he, perhaps taking cue from his first two strong willed wives, urged them to use whatever influence they had to positively impact society outside home and hearth.)

No matter what the race or obstacle because of their gender holy women of God were determined to walk through the doors of foreign missions. Why couldn't they use their God given gifts to help build and teach in schools, orphanages and medical stations to expand the cause of Christ? The Victorian notion that respectable women operated only within narrow confines was very real and major obstacles for the women to serve on foreign fields. Women found that for each inch of victory many miles of justification of their desire to serve in the public sphere had to be trod. Haley Feuerbacher says while single men were encouraged to take a wife before leaving for foreign missions, single women were rejected outright at the beginning of the foreign missions movement. If single women were allowed to serve, they had to accompany another family and were subject to the authority of the male head of that family. Feuerbacher felt that many women married simply to follow their calling but to their dismay found themselves fulfilling the same roles they had at home of caring for the "real missionary" who was the husband. Though men were seen as the principal missionaries they found they could not speak to women due to cultural constraints. Thus, the missionary wives soon joined by single females, performed the work that the men could not do. Likewise, women were prohibited from speaking to men, and even in their work with women and children, they were often censured for "preaching" or speaking publicly and thus overstepping the bounds of feminine propriety. Women took it upon themselves to evangelize and educate local women and children as a means of uplifting the moral tone of the society. Their work in medicine, education, and social work, though frowned upon by many, led to the realization that they indeed were capable of serving in a greater capacity.[35] Eventually about half of those serving on the foreign mission field would be female — either wives of missionaries or single women who found more freedom in faraway lands than on the home front. Despite opposition against forming female missionary societies, in 1861 Sarah Doremus founded the Women's Union Missionary Society.[36] By 1881 the nondenominational Society had sent out over 100 missionaries to twelve stations. Following its success other missionary societies were founded by women along denominational lines. Women's ordination, public preaching and other religious issues as well as the hot button secular issue of women's suffrage were influenced by the growing women's missionary movement. The DNA of organizational genius among the societies may have contained the mitochondria of its downfall as later women's influence would diminish as societies merged with missions boards of the general church.

While many White female missionaries hailed from upper

---

[35] Haley Feuerbacher, *How Women's Participation in Christian Missions Over History Has Met Formidable Opposition Based on Gender Issues*, associatedcontent.com/article/58338/

[36] www.christianhistorytimeline.com/GLIMPSEF

class society and often graduates of elite universities, Black women went abroad from diverse backgrounds. Their wish to align themselves to the direction they found in Scripture to live lives according to the will of God was second only to the longing Black women and men had to see their brothers and sisters transformed in every area of their lives. While in Liberia or Sierra Leone a class system evolved with educated or freed Blacks at the top of society, mixed races in the middle and aborigines as servants, the work of the Black female international missionaries ultimately lifted the society through the founding of schools, clinics and hospitals. And women persevered! Despite arduous backbreaking work they did not give up. Free women of color, in the North as well as the South, played crucial roles in organizing emigration. The work of the following is representative of unnamed Black female global Christians who served as pioneer missionaries.

At one time working in service was prevalent among White and Black American domestic workers. In service meant that these workers actually lived with their employers providing cleaning, cooking and other chores. Betsey Stockton began her education while living in the household of Princeton College's president and used his library to educate herself. Later she was tutored by Princeton Theological Seminary students. She was appointed as a missionary to Hawaii in 1822 by the American Board of Commissioners for Foreign Missions and in 1823 accompanied thirteen white missionaries, a single man, three Hawaiian men and a Tahitian on a five month trip to the Sandwich Islands (called Hawaii today). She is recognized as the first single woman missionary to go overseas in the history of modern missions. Stockton served as domestic assistant to Rev. and Mrs. Charles S.

Stewart, who were expecting a child while concurrently conducting a school, teaching classes to the *maka'āinana* (commoners) farmers, their wives and children in Maui. After establishing schools in Hawaii and Canada, she helped to start the first Black Presbyterian Church in Princeton—now known as the Witherspoon Street Presbyterian Church. Later, Stockton founded a night school and persuaded PTS students to teach young Blacks history, English, algebra, and literature.[37]

Though not an appointed missionary, Jane Waring Roberts' life illustrates the important role of Black women in the settlement of Liberia. The daughter of a Baptist minister, Roberts immigrated to Liberia from Virginia in 1824. Twelve years later, she became the second wife of Joseph Jenkins Roberts, Liberia's first president. In 1887, she started a project to build a hospital at Monrovia.[38]

Amanda Smith (1837-1915) was an African Methodist Episcopal Church evangelist and Missionary. Born on Rachel Green's dairy farm in Long Green, Maryland in 1837 she was listed in the property of the Shadrach Green estate that he left to his wife upon his death.[39] Smith preached throughout the country, spent a year in England, two years in India, and 8 years in Monrovia, Liberia. In her 2/5/84 journal entry while in Africa she wrote "Surely the Spirit of the Lord is with us, and He is blessing us greatly. Not so much liberty in speaking, but God is with us, and we are expecting great things. Oh, Lord, for Jesus' sake, answer prayer, and send us the Holy

---

[37] yale.edu/.../storm/AfricanAmericanMissionaries Revised.pdf

[38] ibid

[39] The Story of the Lord's Dealings with Mrs. Amanda Berry Smith (Chicago: Meyer and Brother, Publishers, 1893)

Ghost to quicken and revive us." She later opened an orphanage in Illinois which was the only institution open to Negro orphans in the state.[40]

The women who would later serve as Pentecostal missionaries carried the same desire for the Holy Ghost to quicken them as they carried out their assignment to lift up humankind and share the gospel as their foremothers. They came from diverse religious communities but would identify with indigenous cultures in their worship expressions as well as the power they saw manifested in the work of the missionaries.

---

[40] yale.edu/.../storm/AfricanAmericanMissionaries Revised.pdf

CHAPTER TWO

The Call to Go Forth
20th Century Pentecostal Outpour Calls New Group to Global Missions

The U.S. Census reports that as of late 2010 there were 6,876,362,300 people on planet Earth. Upwards of two billion of these individuals identify themselves as Christian. Of these self-identifying Christians who come from a Christian culture the majority identify themselves as born again and experiencing a personal relationship with Jesus Christ. In the "World Christian Encyclopedia: A comparative survey of churches and religions - *AD 30 to 2200*," statistics estimate that as of 2000, Christians made up 33% of the world's population.[41] Because the Pentecostal quest to reach lost souls was successfully preached using Scriptures such as Mark 16:15 and Acts 1:8 many of these self-identifying Christians consider themselves Pentecostal trending with exponential growth in the emerging economies of South America and Africa.

---

[41] www.religioustolerance.org/worldrel.htm

The presence of the Holy Ghost manifesting Himself across the globe by the 20th century globe cannot be overemphasized (e.g., the Welsh Revival 1904—1905; the Keswick Convention 1905, the Korean Pentecost 1907—1908; the African revival movement 1910) and early Pentecostals saw themselves as a part of this larger worldwide revival ushering in the return of Jesus Christ. However, the foremost outpouring of the Spirit in the early 20th century can be traced to the Azusa Street revival, the most prominent center of Pentecostalism. This American led Pentecostal movement began when a group of believers (mainly female) received the baptism of the Holy Ghost with the biblical sign of speaking in tongues at a Bible School in Topeka, Kansas founded by healing evangelist Charles Parham. The fire spread to Bonnie Brae Street in a house that is said even in 2010 to be a deep wellspring from which an anointing flows. Seymour preached to the poor "colored" people who lived in the Black community surrounding Bonnie Brae Street and those arriving early climbed the steps up to the house where they were told how the Holy Ghost manifested Himself in Los Angeles.

While Parham (1873-1929) is recognized as the father of the modern day Pentecostal/Charismatic revival, it was a one-eyed Black preacher and Parham protégé, William Seymour (1870-1922), who would lead the Azusa Street Revival and become spiritual father to thousands of those leaving out from Azusa.[42] Visitors by the hundreds from across America and around the world came to see what was happening at the Azusa Street revival. The crowds grew larger and the mission was forced to move to larger quarters at 312 Azusa Street, a former African Methodist

---

[42]Synan, Vinson, *The Century of the Holy Spirit*, 2001: Thomas Nelson, Nashville, 4

Episcopal Church building and was called the Apostolic Faith Mission. Within a few days more than a thousand persons attempted to enter the small mission building, and the Azusa Street Revival was underway. All were welcomed at Azusa with ethnic minorities finding a dignity previously denied them. Anderson quotes Frank Bartleman stating "it seems everybody that had to go to 'Azusa" [and] he recorded that 'missionaries were gathered there from Africa, India, and the islands of the sea ... an irresistible drawing to Los Angeles.[43] The early Pentecostal movement was a missionary movement and those eager to receive the fullness of the Spirit came and were baptized then went out to baptize others. This new society of empowered believers rapidly evolved into an international movement with Pentecostal missionaries fanning out across the country and later to India, China, Europe and Africa. And just as females were commissioned by Jesus to bring the message of the Resurrection to the Apostles they were pivotal in spreading the gospel of Pentecost. As recipients of His inexplicable joy and emboldened by the splendor of His power an army of Pentecostal women and men braved danger to offer themselves to the cause.

Females were vital to the organization and administration of the Revival. Alexander finds it noteworthy that though William J. Seymour spoke of "a divine call that led me from Houston to Los Angeles," a woman Neely Terry, was instrumental in him being invited. Women like Terry were in the forefront of the movement. In fact, the core group consisted primarily of black female domestic

---

[43] Anderson, Allan, *The Azusa Street Revival and the Emergence of Pentecostal Missions in the Early Twentieth Century*, Transformation 23/2 April 2006, 113

workers and over a period of three years, from 1906 to 1908, the Revival drew persons of every race, nationality, culture and gender. These newly empowered believers attempted to spread the message of Pentecost in the mainline churches with varying degrees of acceptance. Disdained by mainline churches, women filled with the Spirit and zeal to win converts preached on the streets, in storefronts and in churches that opened their doors. Initially not only did the color line seem washed away in the blood but women were treated with equality playing an integral role in the movement through its boards and media. In Seymour's words, "the work began among the colored people. God baptized several sanctified women with the Holy Ghost, who have been much used of Him."[44] Seymour's periodical *The Apostolic Faith* reached an international circulation of 50,000 at its peak in 1908 and the world owes much to this media in the telling of the entire Azusa story including the experience and work of females.

The revival lasted for years but after the initial outpour what would the newly filled Azusa Street believers do with this *dunamis* power? The Azusa Street Revival was destined to change the world's religious landscape but how would the Spirit manifest Himself in this new season? Having experienced Pentecost at Azusa these newly empowered saints viewed the world as their parish and were bound and determined to conquer territory from the vise of Satan. While Pentecostal worship was an offense to mainline churches with its ecstatic and strange carryings on of holy dancing or speaking in tongues, they

---

[44]Cyberjournal for Pentecostal-Charismatic Research, 1996 PCCNA National Conference Memphis, Tennessee, October 1, 1996, *"History of Women in the Pentecostal Movement"*, Dr. Cheryl J. Sanders, Howard University School of Divinity, http://www.fullnet.net/np/archives/cyberj/sanders.html

spread the fire of Pentecost throughout California and the Western States to the Midwest and South with at least twenty-six different denominations tracing their Pentecostal origins to Azusa Street, including the Church Of God In Christ. Influential females including Aimee Sempson McPherson, founder of the Foursquare Gospel Church, later affiliated with the Assemblies of God which traces its roots to the Azusa Street Mission. Pentecostal believers and their churches entered mainstream America. This was hard work. They battled past obstacles, days were filled with itinerant travel and marginalized meetings in brush arbors, fields, converted barns and storefront churches.

Jesus said to Peter and the disciples, "I will build my church." (Matthew 16:18a) In light of this truth, as they matured in their new found understanding Pentecostals learned the essential task was to establish fellowships of believers where none were found. It was now time to move beyond America. This Pentecostal afterglow caused a new group to enter the foreign missions field and this group is said to have begun the most significant global expansion of the Christian movement in the history of Christianity. Believing that "this was that" prophesied by the prophet Joel (Joel 2:28) and that the same Spirit caused Peter to show courage in preaching on Pentecost (Acts 2), they fanned out from the United States into Egypt, Sweden, France, Brazil and Japan. Pentecostal missionaries sent out from Azusa Street reached over twenty-five nations in two years.[45]

The idea of a new dimension in God exploded with men and women eager to find hungry souls to share the

---

[45] Henri Gooren: *Review of An Introduction to Pentecostalism:* Global Charismatic Christianity

experience of Pentecost. The healing evangelist John Graham Lake is an example of the transnational spread of Pentecost. Synan says that the work of the newly Spirit baptized Lake whose wife had been miraculously healed of tuberculosis, caused him to leave the United States with a team, arriving in Johannesburg, South Africa in 1908. Two churches would become large and influential...The Apostolic Faith Mission established as the White branch, 1910 and the Black branch, Zion Christian Church, with a reported six million members in 2000.[46]

Alexander further observes that females, important to carrying the gospel in foreign fields under the auspices of mainline churches, now eagerly returned to Africa and other countries sharing their Pentecostal experience. Well armed with the knowledge of how to subsist in lean times as a farm wife Ardella "Ardie" Mead accompanied her missionary husband Samuel to Angola where they taught the Bible as well as agriculture and other areas to assist the self sufficiency of the African. Allan Anderson reports that missionaries, many female and African American, went out from Azusa into foreign fields only five months after the revival had begun in teams as large as a dozen.[47] Lucy Farrow, the niece of the abolitionist Frederick Douglas, was one of the women leaving Azusa to work in Liberian missions in 1906. The prior year William Seymour attended Farrow's Houston, Texas church and heard her speak in tongues. Harvey Cox, author of *Fire From Heaven* notes that [Seymour] heard a woman pray aloud in a language...that no one could understand [and] was touched to the core. After the meeting he asked

---

[46] Ibid, 6
[47] Anderson, Allan, *The Azusa Street Revival and the Emergence of Pentecostal Missions in the Early Twentieth Century*, Transformation 23/2 April 2006, 112

Farrow...more about her remarkable gift.[48] The remaining female team members were Julia Hutchins and Daisy Batman. G.W. and Daisy Batman left Azusa with their three children bound for Liberia. Daisy Batman's account of the Lord's call is excerpted from the 1906 edition of the Apostolic Faith: "The Lord gave us the call to Africa. At first I thought I would stay and let my husband go, but He said, 'No, you must go too.' And three months after we received our baptism, He said, 'Now go to Africa.' O glory to God, I am so glad I got to the place where the blessed Lord's will is my will."[49] Daisy along with her husband and three children all died while in Africa.

Believing that the return of Christ was imminent, Pentecostal Churches embraced global inclusion with zeal and sent the Batman's and other disciples into every nation. The Assemblies of God (AG) was organized in Hot Springs, Arkansas in 1914 and would become the world's largest Pentecostal denomination largely through its mission's efforts. At their Second General Council held in Chicago in November 1914, the AG committed to their involvement in ""the greatest evangelism that the world has ever seen."[50] As Pentecost spread, their journeys took AG missionaries to China, Japan, Africa and beyond. Reaching the unreached meant that like the Apostle Paul early Pentecostals had to adjust to the dynamics of the host culture because all customs of the countries were not

---

[48] Carter, Jessica F., *Known and Yet Unknown, Women of Color and the Assemblies of God,* Assemblies of God Heritage, 2008, Vol 28, 40

[49] Alexander, Estrelda, *The Women of Azusa Street,* 2005: The Pilgrim's Press, Cleveland, 119

[50] McGee, Gary and Darrin J. Rodgers, *The Assemblies of God: Our Heritage in Perspective* www.ifphc.org/index.cfm?fuseaction=history.main

negative. While temporal assistance or a rise in literacy was important, to make a case for Jesus the gospel had to make sense in order to reach the culture. There were some stumbles along the way. Wishing to have as many receive this blessing of God as manifested at Azusa, some taught there was no need for linguistic training. The new missionaries felt that the Holy Ghost would speak through them to carry the message to the so called heathen. (This was later recanted.) Other Pentecostal missionaries, like the Baptists or Presbyterians before them, were confronted with cultural differences that sometimes hindered the expansion of Pentecost. For example, rather than attempting to understand customs of men marrying multiple wives to facilitate enlightenment based on the word of God, some early missionaries condemned the practice outright.

A returned nonCOGIC missionary told the following story of how cultural differences affected the message of the missionaries: As the missionaries brought clothing, learning materials and foodstuffs including rice, canned meat and canned corn from the United States the natives of the country welcomed them. After a while the natives ceased meeting ships and assisting in offloading containers destined for the missions. Knowing the poverty of the villages and how the material could help the missionaries repeatedly asked the leaders what was wrong. Finally, one elder told them that when they brought canned yams a picture of yams was on the can; when they received canned corn, a picture of corn was on the label and so forth. So when the missionaries attempted to give the women baby food and the label showed a baby the elders instructed the villagers to refuse all help from the American "heathens." Once the missionaries overcame these kinds of cultural miscues, the gospel took root through spiritual direction provided by Bible study, preaching and teaching. They also understood that in order to win souls and shape the society they must value collaborative efforts made by those Africans who identified as Africans but first and foremost considered themselves Christians. African scholars consider these leaders both understanding the language and culture hybrid in that the international missionaries trained them to successfully fuse Western and African cultural interaction. This caused the work to flourish. From that base all kinds of good works flowed from the church to help transform the society for good (Eph. 2:10). Increasingly, the entrance of Black foreign missionaries also helped the cause of missions and evangelism.

The COGIC soon joined other Pentecostals leaving America's shores. One COGIC foreign worker, an Elder Sullivan who was believed to be White, served for a time in Sierra Leone, however, for the most part early COGIC missionaries settled in Liberia and Haiti. Elizabeth White, the first official COGIC missionary to Africa, male or female, began her work under the banner of the Assemblies of God in the 1920s.

CHAPTER THREE

Historical Overview of the Church Of God In Christ and Women's Ministry

In an address entitled "Beyond Discovery, Love" Dr. Martin L. King, Jr. stated that the church is "the chief moral guardian of the community and...must broaden horizons, challenge the status quo, and break the mores when necessary." Dialogue regarding the relevance of the Black Church in the 21st century sometimes discounts that churches have served as anchors of the community since the first converts organized. During bondage the Black Church was a meeting place for spiritual direction, safe places for guidance to those who would escape slavery and a gathering where, after a time, Blacks were able to escape the watchful eye of the master. The first Black banks, normal schools and later universities had their beginnings in the Black Church as well as havens, however nebulous in light of increasing brutality, for Civil Rights meetings beginning in the 1950s. Historically, Black churches have served the community well, including the rapidly growing COGIC. In fact, Billingsley says that by the end of the 80's the Black Church in the United States had approximately 75,000 congregations and twenty percent of these congregations were Church Of God In Christ.[51] The COGIC was born in the pain of conflict and has a legacy of great achievement amidst turmoil and challenge. Some thirty two years after the American Civil War, the Church was born (1897) under the leadership of former Baptist ministers Rev. C.P. Jones and Rev. Charles Harrison Mason. Jones and Mason, believing that sanctification was important to the Christian life, preached the second blessing and were later joined by other Baptist ministers including Rev. John Jeter and Rev. W.S. Pleasant. Tensions grew as these militant preachers espoused holiness and sanctification resulting in the right hand of fellowship being withdrawn by their Baptist brethren. Those excommunicated believers formed the COGIC as a holiness church in Jackson, Mississippi. As a result of doctrinal differences between groups led by Rev. C.P. Jones and others led by Rev. C.H. Mason, the COGIC would later reorganize as a Holiness-Pentecostal organization.

Much was happening in the United States leading up to the reorganization of the COGIC: the radio came into its own with American innovators making the first radio broadcast in history. (Later Mason would use radio as an effective tool to acquaint listeners with Pentecost through broadcasting annual COGIC holy convocation sessions on Memphis' WDIA); in 1906 an earthquake almost totally destroyed San Francisco then in January 1907 another earthquake hit Kingston, Jamaica killing more than 1,000

---

[51]Troutman, Joseph E., Editor, *The Journal of the Interdenominational Theological Center,* 1987: ITC Press, Atlanta, 6, 7

people; death would again visit San Francisco when the bubonic plague struck the city. In 1906 COGIC leader Rev. C.P. Jones sent C.H. Mason, D.J. Young, and J.A. Jeter to Los Angeles to explore the unusual and supernatural occurrences in the West in Los Angeles. It was while there attending the Azusa Street Revival that Charles Harrison Mason received the Baptism in the Holy Ghost with the biblical sign of speaking in tongues. In his book *Avant vs. Mason*, McBride provides further insight into Mason's Pentecostal experience from Mason's own account included in a deposition one year after the group returned. In it Mason provides a poignant statement to the court of his desire to receive all that God had for him. He states that while sitting with his legs crossed on Azusa Street, that he gave up to God, believing He would baptize him with the Holy Ghost.

> *After a while my very soul began to cry to God just like a pump without a sucker, and after a while you catch the water and the man is strong, even physically, so, after a while my desire seemed to become intense within me, and every breath seemed to become heavier as I looked to God. I sat there a while and I heard a sound just like the sound of wind, a great wind. I heard the sound like in the Pentecost. I heard it just as real. I sat there, some on my left, some on my right, and I gave up to God, not resisting him; I determined not to resist him, and after a while I went through a crucifixion, and after I had gone through that I was completely empty, my mind was sweet, at rest; my flesh was sweet, at rest.*
>
> *I sat there a while giving up to God. The anthem of Heaven seemed to rise then; I felt myself rising out of my seat, without any effort. I thought at first it was imagination; then I saw it wasn't imagination. Well when I was drawn to my feet there came a light in the*

> *room above the brightness of the light of God. When I opened my mouth to say "Glory to God," a flame touched my tongue and my English left me, and I said "Glory" and then my hands was moved by the power of the Spirit of God. He had complete control of me. Now when this was over I was filled with the presence of God. I didn't move a foot; I sat there just as I am sitting now; I knew everything going on; the people even talking in the room. I was looking at them just as I am looking at you. God didn't knock me out. I saw others that were knocked out.*[52]

The right hand of fellowship was withdrawn over a disagreement with Jones and other leaders who did not believe in speaking in tongues. The initial reluctance of Black churches may have been more practical than spiritual—the carrying on of the Pentecostals embarrassed those who attended mainline churches. Butler suggests "The improving literature of the day tied...religious uprightness to racial uplift, but it promoted a particular type of religiosity. Many of those who touted bourgeois were appalled at certain types of African American Christian practices, such as shouting and dancing...The emotionalism of former slaves' religious practices did not fall in line with the bourgeois notion of respectability."[53] Mason knew that his encounter with God through the Baptism in the Holy Ghost was real and this Baptism enlarged his vision to take the Gospel of Jesus Christ and Pentecost throughout

---

[52]McBride, Calvin S., *Walking in a New Spirituality,* 2007: iUniverse, Lincoln, NE, 67

[53]Butler, Anthea, *Women in the Church Of God In Christ: Making a Sanctified World,* 2007: The University of South Carolina Press, Chapel Hill, 14

the Southland, around the country and to the world. Bishop S.M. Crouch said of the COGIC Founder "He was not a local man but a universal man; he was for the world." [54] Although segregation and Jim Crow laws ruled the day, it was not unusual for Mason to minister the love of Jesus to anyone regardless of race, gender or ethnicity. In his book about Mason, *He Made Millions Happy*, long time COGIC evangelist Elder James Logan Delk wrote "He made an impression on me I can never forget. I hope the reader, especially the Colored race, will realize the significance of a white man writing about a colored man."[55] Through revivals, outdoor meetings, prayer services along railroad lines and cotton field gatherings Mason and others like him formed their own fellowships. Respect for Mason as a man of unusual faith grew causing scattered holiness churches, especially those led by Blacks, to gather under the COGIC umbrella. Mississippi's "Do Right" church with sanctified churches in places like Texas merged with the COGIC.

The COGIC reorganized as a Holiness-Pentecostal organization in 1907 after Mason called for all like believers to meet him at the Saints Home Church in September 1907. The meeting was led by Elder R.E. Hart, Elder Eddie R. Driver and Elder D.J. Young. They left the meeting with plans to convene the first Holy Convocation

---

[54]Cornelius, Lucille The International Outlook, The Official Organ of the Church Of God In Christ Home & Foreign Mission Department, *Minutes of Mission Day, November 11, 1965 at the 58th Annual Holy Convocation of the Church Of God In Christ in Memphis, TN, Bishop S.M. Crouch Presiding.* 7

[55]Williams-Goodson, Glenda *Biographical Profiles of Early Church Of God In Christ Leaders* in Louis F. Morgan's article *"The Flame Still Burns,"* Charisma Magazine, Volume 33, Number 4, November 2007, 58

in Memphis, Tennessee in November 1907. All who were saved, sanctified and baptized with the Holy Ghost (who came to be called saints) now had freedom to worship without restraint as the Spirit led. The first Holy Convocation and National Meetings were held at Saints Home Church Of God In Christ located at 392 Wellington Street in Memphis, Tennessee at which time 10 congregations attended.[56] The children of Church Of God In Christ church planters were exposed to stories like these, of men and women determined to win souls regardless of the price. These early converts braved social injustice, were ostracized from kith and kin and took life threatening risks to carry the Gospel while forced to ride in cattle cars during traveling circuits. As they preached, not a new gospel but a reawakening to gifts promised by God as recorded in the Acts of the Apostles, the generosity of individual saints expressed true *koinonia*. In the Jim Crow South saints like Elder Joseph Williams and Gladys Williams were offered churches to sleep in if on rare occasions the pastor or one of the member's house was overcrowded. Bonding occurred as those who were saved and filled however disdained by family members, were welcomed into the new family of the sanctified.

Like many Black churches the COGIC congregation was predominantly female led by males and relied on a number of women for the support and success of the church during its formative years. The fact that Mason's propensity in allowing females to hold important positions was sometimes problematic but Mason insisted on parity in spite of the gender of those rendering service. For example, a plea was made for delegates to prepare to present an offering to Eulia Sparks, Railroad Secretary

---

[56] Ibid, 78

and Editor of the Whole Truth, the church's official news organ:

> This young woman's worth to this body of people cannot be estimated—for years she has stood beside Elder Mason and shouldered the burden, assisting in caring and providing for the welfare of the Church in general...To your credit and for your help she has been the provider of means of our reduced rates to Memphis for these years...bring along a special offering for Sister Sparks.[57]

Female pioneers such as Sparks boasted that they served in every capacity of COGIC ministry from janitorial work to preaching and ministering with the exception of ordained elder. Best states that the rejection of females for ordination from the beginning of the Church...may be rooted in [Mason's] earlier affiliation in the Baptist Church which enforced the same policy regarding female ministers.[58] Adrienne Israel explains that in addition to their prominence in spiritual matters among many of the West African societies, women wielded authority over specific areas of life--farming, marketing, trading, or household and family affairs—set apart as their domain. To institutionalize their power they formed solidarity groups from which they gained a strong psychological sense of self-esteem. Some West African societies ensured women political power that transcended their domain by

---

[57] Year Book of the Church Of God In Christ for the Year 1926, Elder C.H. Mason General Overseer, Compiled by Lillian Brooks Coffey, 4748 Forrestville Avenue, Chicago, Illinois, Re-copy of Original Print with excerpts by Elder Jerry R. Ramsey, III

[58] Best, Felton O. *Breaking the Gender Barrier: African American Women and Leadership in Black Holiness-Pentecostal Churches 1890-Present*, 155

EARLY COGIC LEADERS LEFT LEGACY OF MISSIONS SUPPORT

Bishop Charles H. Mason
Church Of God In Christ Founder

Bishop O. T. Jones, Sr.
Second Senior Bishop

Department of Women Overseer and National Mothers
1911 – 1975

Mother Lizzie Robinson
Overseer of Women
1911 – 1945

Mother Lillian Coffey
2nd National Mother
1945 – 1964

Mother Annie Bailey
3rd National Mother
1964 – 1975

developing what anthropologists have called a 'dual-sex' system. Women's councils not only governed women's affairs but their representatives also voiced women's interests at each level of government from the village to the king's court. Although the dual-sex system gave prominence to women in community affairs, they remained, as a group, subservient to husbands.[59] Viewing Mason through early 20th century sensibilities, Butler makes the case that the COGIC Women's Department became a space whereby Mason's fundamental belief in equality successfully modeled the dual-sex system found within the former slave communities and laid a strategic foundation for inclusiveness. In the fictive COGIC family Bishop Mason was referred to as "Dad Mason" while top female leaders were called "Mother" (whether in the States where they oversaw the work of women or on the national level).[60] Mendiola adds that Mason's dual-sexed structure for female spiritual development and leadership caused the hierarchy to move from a working relationship to a status relationship.

Mason's core strength to identify strong female leaders the church needed to collaborate with in spreading the gospel of holy living through sanctification and the power of the Holy Ghost caused him to immediately begin his search for an Overseer of Women's Work. The name Lillian Brooks was floated but Brooks herself felt that only a few years out of her teens at the time, she was too young. Four years after the reorganization of the

---

[59]Clemmons, Bishop Ithiel, Essay by Adrienne Israel, Mothers Roberson and Coffey – Pioneers of Women's Work: 1911-1964, in *Bishop C.H. Mason and the Roots of the Church Of God In Christ,* 1996:Pneuma Life Publishing, Bakersfield, CA, 106-107
[60]Mendiola, Kelly Willis Ph.D., Approved Dissertation, *The Hand of a Woman: Four Holiness-Pentecostal Evangelists and American Culture, 1840-1930* 2002: University of Texas at Austin, 100

COGIC Bishop Mason met Lizzie Woods when he conducted a revival in Arkansas.

She was born Elizabeth Isabelle Smith and along with her parents Mose Smith and Elizabeth Jackson was a slave.[61] After the Civil War she heard someone calling Liz, Liz, Liz. Though profoundly impacted she did not understand that it was the voice of God. She went on to become prominent as an entrepreneur selling subscriptions to *Hope Magazine*, a religious woman's quarterly designed to teach women how to read. Later Joanna Moore, the founder of *Hope*, urged the American Baptist missionary society to send Woods to school for two years after which she became matron of the Baptist school in Dermott, Arkansas. Woods proved to be an outstanding organizer of women and now became a community leader.

COGIC historian Theda Bara Wells in her book *Time to Remember* sheds light on Robinson's activities as a result of her Pentecostal experience. After her leaders discovered she had received the Baptism of the Holy Ghost, Woods was fired from the position of Dean of Women from the Baptist Academy. Lillian Brooks urged Woods to attend the Pine Bluff, Arkansas Convocation and in 1911 she attended the National Convocation in Memphis, Tennessee. She was appointed Overseer of Women's Work in 1911. Finding that the work among the women lacked organization, Woods used the organizational skills gained through her entrepreneurial activities with *Hope* to create a system for women's ministry. Wells states Woods was the *right* woman at the *right* time and Mason made the *right* move in appointing her.

---

[61]Butler, 13

> Mrs. Lizzie Woods, since receiving the baptism of the Holy Ghost was prepared more than ever to teach the unadulterated Word of God. Bishop Mason, through his keen spiritual insight, saw that she was an organizer and was able to inspire and direct. Her job was to organize and create such a work as would be beneficial to the development of the church. Bible Band was first, then when she found women that meet together just for prayer she combined the two into the Prayer and Bible Band.[62]

By establishing the Women's Department shortly after the COGIC's reorganization Mason aligned himself with the teaching of the Apostle Paul in Galatians 3:27-29, indelibly stamping his approval of women in ministry. While he did not embroil himself in the controversial subject of women in pastoral leadership, his contract with the women, beginning with the Overseer of Women (National Mother) position, facilitated a new paradigm for the transformation of their role as the church rapidly spread throughout the United States and around the globe in a healthy, Christ edifying manner. Well advanced in years Robinson organized the women in areas she felt were under the Department's sphere. In Chapter 5 of her dissertation, Kelly Mendiola states "With women in foreign fields as missionaries, women planting churches as evangelists and missionaries to non-COGIC areas, a magazine, *Lifted Banner*, and Prayer and Bible Band Topics, Mother Robinson's Women's Department was systematized and organized as she had set out to do.[63] Woods paid a high price for her efforts. Wells reports Robinson was later imprisoned, beaten and rotten eggs were thrown at her for her stand in the Holiness-

---

[62]Wells, Theda B., *Time to Remember: 100 Year Anniversary Celebration 1907-2007,* Church Of God In Christ, 16-17
[63] Mendiola, 100

Pentecostal doctrine. Despite dangers and struggles, she forged ahead using her organizational skills to venture into child evangelism and foreign missions.

Inherent in the thinking of COGIC pioneer women was the fact that not only did the church have responsibility of redeeming the soul but it must also use its influence to redeem the social order. The COGIC Home Missions movement continued to spread the gospel of Jesus Christ and the power of Pentecost through its teaching in church revivals, the streets, prisons, and hospitals. The message they carried into the community and throughout the United States was that Christ offered deliverance from poverty, crime, family deterioration and despair. This teaching had tremendous impact throughout communities around the country. Evangelist Carrie Cayson tells of her colorful life before becoming sanctified and how the teaching of Pentecost resulting in her being baptized in the Holy Ghost transformed her. Born in 1885 Cayson says, "I lived by my wits. I was a gambler. A way out sinner that seldom lost a fight with the help of my trusty switch blade knife. On April 7th, 1917 I came to Cleveland with a young man I met in Shreveport. I recall one Saturday night being in a black jack game. I lost all of my money to one man. I went home and returned shortly with my gun. I promptly relieved this poor man of my money…It was while I was rooming with a good Baptist lady from my home town that I attended a revival at…the Church Of God In Christ, Elder Mack E. Jonas, Pastor [and] I went to the altar." Early COGIC settings offered a strong teaching ministry through a variety of venues beginning with the Cradle Roll of the Sunshine Band for ages up to twelve, to Purity Class for teens, and Young People Willing Workers for older teens and young adults. But it was the Prayer and Bible Band that women were trained in practical ways how to live and enjoy the abundance of a joyous and sanctified life.

After being filled with the Holy Ghost Cayson followed the Prayer and Bible Band with a teachable spirit. She was taught by older missionaries on how to live saved and later became a missionary. She then joined the mothers as they went from house to house visiting the sick, cooking their meals, cleaning their homes, washing their clothes and *then* praying. This zeal caused Cayson to declare "we were never tired when there was work to be done for the Lord. Yes, the Lord has been good to me. He enabled me to distribute clothing among the needy in Ohio, in the South and even in British Honduras.[64]"

The Holy Ghost transformed Cayson from a life of wickedness into a leading soldier in the growing army of Home Missionaries, a vital link in the spread of Pentecost throughout the South and North. Yet other missionaries wished to serve beyond America's borders. They found an answer to their call in COGICs Women's Department and its home and foreign missions auxiliary. In the 21st century the need for clarification whether the Missions Department operates solely under the umbrella of the General Church or the Department of Women periodically causes tensions to flare. One camp feels foreign missions should operate under the Department of Missions while home missions remain under the Department of Women. This in part reflects the concern that females will not receive their due as the incubators and birthing of the Home and Foreign Missions. The COGIC website states that the Missions Department officially began fourteen years after

---

[64]Cayson, Carrie, *A Testimony for Jesus,* 4, 6, 9

its reorganization as a Holiness-Pentecostal Church when Robinson recruited Elder Searcy to work in Missions.[65] Again, Wells writes "Mother traveled far and wide. She met Elder Searcy in Portland, Oregon and urged him to come to the Convocation in Memphis. His interest was missions. Thus he became the Secretary Treasurer of the Home and Foreign Mission. However he did not remain." According to the Official Manual of the Church Of God In Christ—On December 2, 1926, at Memphis, Tennessee, the Council of Elders of the Church Of God In Christ, during the Day's Session, organized a Missionary Band, later called the Home and Foreign Mission Board, to work on a broad, unselfish, Christlike and International Plan. The purpose of the Organization shall be for the winning of lost souls to Christ, and to establish the work of Grace in the hearts of believers; to encourage a holy life and the Baptism of the Holy Ghost and Fire among all the Nations of the earth. This Board shall meet yearly at the National Convocation at Memphis, Tennessee, or at the demand of the Executive Officer. The meeting is essential so that the Workers at Home and abroad may give needful advice and information on Home and Foreign Mission Work. The Groups are called—Mission Bands; Collection and Distribution of Materials; Home Missionaries; General Missionaries; and Foreign Missionaries.[66]

Mattie McCaulley was the first female to answer the call to foreign missions. She left Oklahoma in February 1926 for a journey that would take her to Panama where she met and worshipped with AG members then on to her

---

[65]Wells,16-17
[66]Patterson, Bishop J.O., Rev .German R. Ross, Mrs. Julia Mason Atkins, *History and Formative Years of the Church Of God In Christ with Excerpts from the Life and Works of its Founder Bishop C.H. Mason* 1969: Church of God in Christ Publishing House Memphis, 68

assignment in Trinidad. Arriving there one month after leaving the United States she saw "souls saved and the sick healed then established a little [Church Of God In Christ with] Prayer and Bible Band, Sunshine Band and Sunday School." All around the country COGIC women left the comforts of home to board ships that would take them to Sierra Leone, Liberia and Haiti where they lived lives of deprivation while sharing their new found faith. Some went untrained while most (e.g., Beatrice Lott and Pearl Page Brown) received medical missionary training prior to migrating from America. Earlynn Byas McDowell, granddaughter of Bishop C.H. Mason states that as late as 1960 "Mother Coffey sent my sister, Barbara Lavonne Byas, to Toronto, Ontario, Canada and paid for her missions training before she was sent to Tijuana, Mexico then Cuba."[67]

While Lizzie Robinson laid the foundation for the systemization of the Department of Women it was Lillian Brooks Coffey who would use her influence to move the Department from its 19th century leanings into the 20th century causing one pioneer to recall "thanking God for Mother Coffey freeing us!" On her way to becoming the Second National Mother of the Church she served Mason and his wife as their nanny, accompanied him along with older sisters on his circuit, and sang and read the Bible for him during evangelistic crusades.[68] Coffey was briefly

---

[67]Interview by author with Earlynn Byas McDowell. McDowell states that Barbara slept in facilities in shanty towns in Mexico while ministering to hundreds of children and adults. Along with Clydell Tillman Mason (no relation) she ministered to the poor in Jamaica. In 1961 she received training by International Missionary Francina Wiggins when she returned to the U.S. States and the two led street preaching and revival services. Barbara and International Missionary June Blackwell conducted tract ministries.
[68]Goodson, Glenda *Bishop Mason and Those Sanctified Women!*, First Printing 2002, Second Printing 2003: HCM Publishing, Dallas, 19

married to Samuel Coffey and the couple had two daughters, Laverne and Delores. The marriage did not last due to what she called her "single-minded devotion to the Lord and the church" along with a brutal travel schedule as she built the women's ministry. Unusually gifted in administrative ability she became a uniformed volunteer for the U.S.O program in the Chicago area and along with Dr. Mary McLeod Bethune, was active in the National Council of Negro Women, receiving much acclaim as a civic leader.

Most international missionaries initially went out "by faith" with little financial support or expectations of receiving consistent income. A story by Pearl Page Brown as she travelled by ship to Haiti illustrates how God honored their willingness to sacrifice. "Mother Coffey and the Women's Convention gave me a one-way ship ticket and $100 and promised to pay the rent for the orphanage in Haiti. [I boarded the] *S.S. Evangeline* to Haiti. [That] was all I had for supplies and to do everything I needed to do when I got there. The Holy Ghost told me to go upon the top deck although we [Blacks] were not to go there. I was hesitant but I obeyed. I thought I would be told to go below but [there were no protestant ministers on board] and the steward asked me to minister Easter Sunday. I told them I was on my way to Haiti to minister and she asked me if I would conduct Easter services."[69] Brown ministered to the group and through God's intervention that Easter Sunday her white "congregation" collected over $200 to assist her in her work. Lillian Brooks Coffey succeeded Mother Robinson

---

[69]Note of Thanks to Mother Mattie McGlothen in *Sewing Circle Artistic Fingers 43rd Women's International Convention*, p.1-2 and Interview by author with Pearl Page Brown in San Jose, CA September 2010

as the International Supervisor of the Department of Women.

Elizabeth White

CHAPTER FOUR

*History of Evangelism and Missions in the
Church Of God In Christ*

Blacks strove to find wholeness as oppressive laws continued to marginalize their lives and community. One opportunity which began in the 19th century was the relocation of Blacks to their homeland in Africa. Some Blacks landed on Africa's shores from outlawed slave ships while others escaped oppression by colonization efforts made by white political leaders, slave holders, clergy and Blacks themselves. The Baptist tradition, out of which many pioneer COGIC leaders sprang, had a long history of foreign missions involvement with Blacks like Rev. Lott Carey establishing the first Baptist church in Liberia in the mid 19th century.

Believers departing from the Azusa Street Revival left California taking the fire and teaching of Pentecost around the country and the world. Florence Crawford, a minister and member of the Azusa Street leadership team, worked closely with Apostle W.J. Seymour in ministry and print publications. In December 1906 she journeyed to Oregon at the invitation of an independent church where she told about the wonderful Pentecostal experience and reported back that many seekers were saved and filled with the Holy Ghost. After the successful revival she returned to Los Angeles but felt the Spirit calling her back to Oregon. One of the pastors requested that she take over his church on Southwest Second and Main Streets and the Apostolic Faith Church of Portland, Oregon was born in 1908 under her leadership.[70] One of the basic tenets of the church was to spread the gospel to the world through evangelism and missions efforts. This may have been the church where Elder Searcy, who historian David Daniels believes was White, received his training and later played a key role in the establishment of the COGIC Missions Department. Individual Pentecostals impacted the world including African Americans who quickly spread the message across the globe. Bishop C.H. Mason was known to ordain and send out anyone Spirit filled no matter the color. An unsubstantiated report tells of Mason signing papers sending two white female missionaries to Brazil as early as 1914. At his 1961 home going celebration, Ida Baker stated that with the permission of Bishop Mason her mother, Lizzie Robinson, started the Home and Foreign Missions (H&FM) at her home at 2864 North 28th Avenue in Omaha, Nebraska. Despite these ventures into global missions there was no official Home and Foreign Missions Department of the COGIC until 1925.

Upon Mother Robinson's invitation to the Memphis Holy

---

[70] The Apostolic Faith Mission of Portland, Oregon, *The Apostolic Faith History, Doctrine and Purpose,* Pediment Publishing 2005: Canada, 21

Convocation, the House of Prayer International Home and Foreign Mission Board (of Portland, Oregon) under the leadership of Elder Searcy, became affiliated with the COGIC. Mrs. Mattie McCaulley was the first international missionary to be sent out by the COGIC (see Chapter 9). Searcy's group remained with the church until June 1926. When the House of Prayer withdrew the small balance remaining in its treasury was given to Bishop Mason. He was to take disposition of it in the cause of Foreign Missions.[71] Mother Robinson, keen to continue spreading the gospel and helping those in need, recommended Elder C.G. Brown to Bishop Mason who appointed him Executive Secretary of Home and Foreign Missions. Under his leadership the Department would move forward around the world. Without diminishing how God worked through the five revival movements identified by Ogbu Kalu occurring throughout the continent of Africa which were precursors to modern day African Pentecostalism it is documented that Elizabeth White, formerly of the Assemblies of God, planted the first *Church Of God In Christ* mission at Wissikeh, Liberia, West Africa, a country about the size of the State of Ohio. Though the name Wissikeh means nests of witches, the Lord used Mother White to bring the light of His love to the area making the Wissekeh Mission the "Birthplace of the Church Of God In Christ in Africa."[72] A mural of Mother White, exhibited in a church near Wissekeh, displays the devotion and reverence the Liberians have for the first missionary of the COGIC faith. The work needed to be further set in order and the Elder's Council made recommendation of the following as members of

---

[71] Moody, Carlis L., *Church Of God In Christ Department of Missions History and Organization*, 1996: Memphis, Tennessee, 3

[72] Goodson, 40

SOME COGIC MISSIONS OFFICIALS THROUGH 1970

Bishop S.M. Crouch
Appointed Missions President 1937

Bishop O.M. Kelly *Vice President*

Bishop S. R. Martin
Succeeded Bishop Crouch

Bishop A.B. McEwen
Bishop of Foreign Fields

Mrs. Ida Baker
Treasurer

Mrs. Elsie Mason
Executive Secretary

Bishop F.D. Washington
Field Secretary

Bishop H.W. Goldsberry
Mission Director Ghana

Bishop R.L. Fidler
Field Secretary Editor Int'l Outlook

the first Missions Board on 12/2/1926: Elders J.R. Anderson of Milwaukee (President), V.M. Barker (Vice President), Charles Pleas of Kansas City, MO, (Recording Secretary) C. Range of Chester, PA (Corresponding Secretary) and Mother L.M. Cox of Trenton, NJ (Representative). In 1937 the Board reorganized and Bishop Samuel Crouch was appointed president of the Department of Home and Foreign Mission of the COGIC. Crouch was saved at the age of twelve when he heard the unmistakable voice of God telling him "I have need of thee." Already active in the work of missions, Crouch set out on a worldwide tour to review, inspect, refurbish and rebuild COGIC foreign holdings. As a result, he visited 48 countries building orphanages, schools and churches in Africa, Mexico, South America, the Philippines, Japan, China, Korea, Bermuda and Honduras. In California, he maintained a home where missionaries lived rent free[73].

Bishop Crouch was later joined by Bishop Richard L. Fidler of Racine, Wis., who brought together the work of Cuba and much of the Spanish-speaking people of the Americas under the COGIC umbrella. Under Bishop Fidler *Mission Outlook* became the Department's official paper. As word of COGIC spread around the globe, with emphasis on the fact that a Black man led the organization, more churches wished to affiliate including those outside the United States. In 1939, Overseer A. B. McEwen was appointed Bishop of the Foreign Fields. He later succeeded in having Elder Joseph St. Juste, a native Haitian minister, appointed overseer with some 96 churches affiliated with the COGIC. After the death of Overseer St. Juste, Bishop Esau Courtney was appointed.

---

[73]Williams-Goodson, *Biographical Profiles of Early Church Of God In Christ Leaders,* 54

He was succeeded by Haitian national Elder Lopez Dautruche who was consecrated Bishop of Haiti in 1947. Upon the elevation of Bishop Crouch to Third Assistant Presiding Bishop, Bishop S. R. Martin of Seaside, CA, was appointed president of the H&FM and led it until 1973 when he was appointed Bishop of California N. W.

As a result of the labor of pioneer missionaries souls were won and mission stations around the world continued to grow. In 1945 Bishop C. Pleas was appointed Bishop of Liberia. In 1948 he traveled to the country arriving in Monrovia in September and formed acquaintances with government officials, among them His Excellency President Tubman, leader of the Republic of Liberia. There was no church edifice or other group in Monrovia, therefore Bishop Pleas and Elder Valentine Brown, a native minister of the Church, procured a sight on top of a hill located along Broadway Street and in four weeks, the walls were completed and the building was ready for roofing. Bishop Pleas held the first COGIC Holy Convocation in Africa. In the summer of 1949, Elder O. T. Jones, Jr. of Philadelphia was sent to Monrovia. That same year Mrs. Francina Wiggins was appointed to Liberia to assist Mother White at Wissikeh Station. Mother Wiggins was later transferred to Monalu Station and was instrumental in building a church, a school and a mission complex.

Elder Charles Kennedy and his wife Mary Beth traveled to Liberia in 1956 to serve at Tugbaken with Mother Martha Barber. After one year at Tugbaken a group of native Liberians asked Elder Kennedy to visit the hinterland with the possibility of reopening Wissikeh, established by Mother Elizabeth White. The Kennedy's found the work in decline and went to work rebuilding.

In 1973, the Department was placed under the supervision of an interim committee to include Bishop F. D. Washington, Chairman, Bishop J. A. Blake, and Bishop C. L. Anderson. Under this committee, Bishop R. L. Fidler became the Executive Secretary. In November, 1975 at the National Holy Convocation in Memphis, TN., with the consent of the General Board, Elder Carlis Moody, Sr. of Evanston, Illinois, was appointed by Bishop J. O. Patterson, Sr., as President of the Department of Home and Foreign Missions. Elder Moody immediately reorganized the Mission Department and a new Missions Board was selected with Elder Carlis Lee Moody, Sr., President; Elder J. W. Denny, Executive Secretary, Mrs. D. M. Patterson, Treasurer, Mr. Oknewa Onwuckewa, Finance Sec., Elder Benjamin Crouch, Chairman of Finance Committee and Elder W. W. Covington, Vice-Chairman of Finance Committee.

One of Elder Moody's first tasks was to visit Haiti and reregister all of the COGIC properties there. Since his appointment Bishop Moody has labored untiringly for the cause of missions. He has visited the work in Haiti, Canada, Jamaica, Mexico, Belize, Nassau, Germany, Dominican Republic, Puerto Rico, Virgin Islands, Liberia, Ghana, Nigeria, Panama, England, India, Sri Lanka, Kenya, Columbia, Trinidad, Malawi, Brazil, South Africa and Barbados. A visionary Bishop Moody has added Youth On A Mission (YOAM); Student Aid – a ministry of support to foreign students' Touch a Life – child support ministry; Nurses Aid Ministry; Sister Church Support Ministry – a church in the USA giving support to a church on the mission field and the bi-monthly Voice *of Missions* magazine.[74]

---

[74]Moody, Carlis L., *Church Of God In Christ Department of Missions History and Organization*, 1996: Memphis, Tennessee, 4-6

Beatrice Lott

CHAPTER FIVE

THE DIVINE CALL WAS GREAT

International missionaries usually describe their call as coming directly from God. Whatever the danger or obstacle, COGIC pioneering international missionaries willingly signed up to engage in a great adventure to do mighty works in God's name and for His glory. And just as the young led the exodus from the South to the North beginning in the 1920s[75], younger members, female for the most part, of the COGIC would heed the divine call to international missions.

> *We went to Africa, my friends*
> *We met wonders rare*
> *There were vistas opened without end*
> *The future was laid bare.*

---

[75] In 1890 boll weevils destroyed cotton crops which sustained Southern blacks; entire Black communities moved to Northern cities and by the 1920s 450,000 had migrated in search of jobs, better schools and less legal racism. Young adults usually left first, obtained employment and housing then the remainder of the family followed.

Paris of course is in style,
And Berlin, London and Rome
Can show you things worthwhile,
But none as were shown.

To hear the helpless cheer a crown,
Or praise same rusty thing
Those dark ages handed down
Was most astonishing.

But the things that made our hearts rejoice
Were those that God approved,
We know that we to Africa went
And were by the Spirit moved.[76]

This poem is attributed to Mrs. W.C. Ragland and Miss Beatrice Lott, early missionaries to Liberia, West Africa. Although the women referenced the continent the poem embodies the heartfelt sentiment of each COGIC woman who served the Lord on any continent He called them.

In studying past events one must keep in mind that God is the initiator of history and when viewing missions history (or any history) the writer has to consider what God allowed to happen on the earth through the lens of politics, sociology and technology. Tom Brokaw called the World War II generation The Greatest Generation and COGIC members were a part of that generation serving around the globe. From 1941-1945 they wrote letters to the Whole Truth from "Somewhere in France, Somewhere in the Pacific, New Guinea, and the Philippines. They fought on the front lines and liberated concentration

---

[76]Williams Bishop R.F and Elder U.E. Miller *Facts about the Temple*, Mason Temple, Memphis, Tennessee

camps. It is not farfetched to think that Lott and Ragland's reference to living in post World War II Berlin could have been a possibility as Blacks in the military and those working in Germany were not uncommon. One soldier serving in Tinian wrote to the young people back home that they could stand because, "although sin is thick around me...the Holy Ghost is helping me and...I am young too."[77]

In 1945 Black virtuoso Rudolph Dunbar conducted Tchaikovsky's Pathétique for the Berlin Philharmonic Orchestra for 2,000 Berliners and 500 allied troops. Later, a young Nettie Jones Dillard lived in post war Germany with her military husband and witnessed firsthand the devastating effects of the war as well as opportunities open to enterprising young Blacks.[78] Reports during this time were made by COGIC preachers that they established COGIC fellowships in Germany despite attempts by racists to hinder them from having fellowship services on American Army bases. It was only through strong protests by the Blacks and sympathetic Whites they were able to conduct Pentecostal services subsequent to and during WWII. While stopping in Berlin the women could have chosen to locate these fellowships and settle or live in Berlin outside the mainline Pentecostal umbrella yet they would obey God's guidance and go where He led them. World War II ended the Great Depression but the decade also saw the birth of the nuclear era and the beginning of the Cold

---

[77] Whole Truth, *COGIC Boys During the War 1941-45*, 20
[78] In a 2009 interview in Seattle by the author, 84 year old COGIC Prayer Warrior Mother Nettie Jones Dillard recalled many invaluable works of art such as Dresden's were sold door to door by German survivors for as little as nickels and quarters and paintings by the masters that had not been stolen by the Nazis as little as $25.00. Many enterprising soldiers took advantage of the poverty to help the Germans.

War. In London declarations were made by the Pan African Congress for those ruled by colonialism to unite and reject any power that would seek to diminish their rights (Americans Paul Robeson and Adam Clayton Powell were involved in this movement).[79] They were aware of world events and independent, bright young women like Ragland and Lott were ready to embrace everything life had to offer. Many parts of Europe welcomed people of color and in Paris Blacks, encouraged to join those already in residence, would have found a small but active disasporic community. In choosing to follow a path less glamorous they opted to service as other COGIC women had labored before them.

Beginning with Mattie McCaulley and Elizabeth White, the field of missions and education was an area open to women's development. That Ragland and Lott chose to live in the "open vistas" of Africa offer a glimpse into their understanding that the life of the missionary, far away from familiar culture and economy, was worthwhile. Their heart rejoiced because their God approved of them bringing the light of His love and power into dark traditions of superstition. Their future was laid bare to untold possibilities of designing strategies to provide for physical, psychological, and emotional needs necessary for kingdom building. The driving force for early pioneers was indeed their love for God, obedience to what they understood Him to want them to accomplish and their love for humanity. Single women and married couples answered the call and accomplished outstanding feats. These women made hard, practical decisions to live under the providence of

---

[79]Saheed A. Adejumobi, "The Pan-African Congress," in *Organizing Black America: An Encyclopedia of Black Associations*, Nina Mjagkij, ed. (New York: Garland Publishing, Inc., 2001).

God's will and their poem does not portend emotionalism. They needed an anointing to do the hard work of foreign missions and emotionalism does not produce anointing. Although God called them they sought advice from older men and women of the faith. Seasoned leaders did not wish those who would serve the church as foreign missionaries to act as if some new thing has occurred heretofore unknown through Scripture and create contention on the mission field. In fact, Dorothy Webster (Exume) volunteered for one year serving Church of God in Christ National Supervisor Lillian Brooks Coffey after receiving her call to Haiti.[80] The older women also wished to ensure that the younger women were committed. In this instance the twenty-five year old Webster arrived in Haiti with the blessing of Mother Coffey and the power of her office firmly behind her. Both interviewees and their families explained that God's call to missions' service was so great that they found themselves compelled to respond positively. It was their obedience to their call that they found their sacrifice accompanied by inexplicable joy of the Spirit.

A few of the church's first missionaries journeying to the foreign field independently and without official backing were not dissuaded from obeying God's call. Though the callings to foreign service for some are lost, the following passages document the calls of some missionaries to serve. Supervisor Lee Van Zandt of Brazil is not included in this current work, however, her calling demonstrates that God's directives in working for the people sometimes begins in early childhood.

---

[80]Telephone Interview by author with Marlil Provost of Norcross, GA, daughter of Haitian pioneer Dorothy Webster Exume, October 2010

LELIA T. JANUARY — *A DIVINE CALL THRUSTS HER INTO AFRICA*

Mother Lelia January was a Holy Ghost filled member of the COGIC originally from Kansas City. When she first sensed the divine call to Africa, she informed her pastor, Bishop Mason, of her plans. Bishop Mason granted her the opportunity to leave but did not grant her the full status of a foreign missionary because, according to him, she did not seem fully prepared for such a major mission abroad. Despite the difficulty, January was able to raise funds on her own to travel to her Liberian destination.

Nyema writes that on the first Wednesday in March 1938, a Spirit-filled Mother and Evangelist Lelia T. January arrived in Monrovia, Liberia, West Africa on board a passenger ship. Mother January's mission was to come and minister to the lost souls in Africa (particularly Liberia).[81]

BEATRICE LOTT — *THE HOLY GHOST SAID GO TO AFRICA*

As Beatrice Lott began what would be three days of speaking in tongues, untold numbers of people came to see her. When the interpretation of the tongues came the Spirit said "Go to Africa" and her tongue was loosed. In the following account Lott shared her remarkable call.

During a revival service [held at Dallas' First Pentecostal Pages Temple COGIC] called "The Time of Refreshing," I was caught away in the Spirit for three days and nights and could

---

[81]Nyema, The Right Reverend Amos K. Sr., *Brief History, Progress Report and Needs of the Church Of God In Christ of Liberia to Presiding Bishop G.E. Patterson*, October 2001

only speak in unknown tongues. The Lord readily gave the interpretation: "You've been called to Africa now. Go! Go! Go!" This anointing was so great and so real that fear came upon all who witnessed it."[82]

Lott's caretaker, Dr. Lisa Peeples recalls Lott sharing the plans immediately following the call to missions. "Her pastor, [the overseer of the Texas COGIC], Bishop E.M. Page saw that she was called to Africa and the cry went out to the saints all over the state to help send her on her journey. Many of the saints came and brought everything she needed and put it on the stage. One of the saints said 'girl look at my knees, I've been picking cotton to send you to Africa'. They brought a sewing machine, her bed. They could see the move of the Holy Spirit upon her. The saints brought money. She needed to do nursing training. I have her papers where she took her exams.[83] It seems that during that time the Department was very organized and very powerful. The saints in Texas shipped the things to New York. When they were leaving off the dock in NY there was a gathering of saints. They were singing "If Jesus Goes With Me I'll Go Anywhere." They sent her away like that."

WILLIE C. RAGLAND – *SHE IS THE NEXT MISSIONARY TO AFRICA*

In order for any woman or man to enter foreign service they had to present compelling reasons they were fit, committed and qualified to represent the church. It is not recorded what Mrs. Ragland said to convince Mother

---

[82] Personal and Telephone Interviews by author September 2009 through November 2010 with Dr. Lisa Peeples, Caretaker for Beatrice Lott
[83] Courses taken at the Chicago School of Nursing, 100 East Ohio Street, Chicago, IL were taught by RNs. Lott completed 18 classes. Each of actual tests shows one test with a grade of 80 and another 87 with the scores for the remaining 16 classes ranging from 90-100.

Robinson and leaders of her calling. However, Mother Lizzie Robinson strongly urged the saints to stand with Mother Ragland in her call to Africa, sending out a letter through the Whole Truth newspaper in 1931. In 1934 she was sent to help Mother Elizabeth White.

DOROTHY WEBSTER EXUME — *SHE DREAMED OF HAITI*

Between the ages of 8 and 12, Dorothy Webster heard messages about African missions at Liberty Hill Baptist Church and said, "When I grow up I want to go and help them." Many years later as the desire to do missions grew, she mentioned this desire to Mother Beatrice Lott, Missionary to Liberia. Mother Lott initially sought a missionary for Liberia.

Webster was a praying young woman and after praying about missions she had a dream. The Lord told her that Mother Elizabeth Bracey, a Haitian mission supporter, was the key to interpreting the dream. The COGIC was organized in Haiti in 1929. At that time there were over 10,000 COGIC members in Haiti. After collaboration and negotiation between Mother Coffey, Mother Lott and Overseer St. Juste of Haiti, Dorothy would soon be assigned. Not all understood these early missionaries desire to leave the United States and advice was forthcoming regularly. Dr. Juanita Faulkner, the niece of Bishop O.T. Jones, Sr. remembers her mother's words to Webster "If I were your mother I would not let you go to Haiti" to which she replied "but it is a calling." Undaunted and with the blessings of International Supervisor Lillian Brooks Coffey and approval of Bishop C. H. Mason, Missionary Exumé entered the French-speaking Republic of Haiti in July 2, 1947 as a missionary accompanied by Mother Coffey and Bishop A B McEwen.

PEARL PAGE BROWN — *THE HOLY GHOST SENT ME*

According to Mother Pearl Page Brown the Holy Ghost compelled her into foreign missions work. *"In 1959…the Holy Ghost sent me to Belize, British Honduras to minister and He brought me home the day before a hurricane destroyed portions of Belize…I went on my own in the power of the Holy Ghost.*

Brown recounts that after she arrived home the Holy Ghost had another assignment, waking her from her sleep and instructing her to go to Haiti quickly. She contacted Mother McGlothen who advised her not to go on her own but let the church send her. Mother McGlothen and Bishop S.M. Crouch recommended her to Mother Lillian Coffey. *"The Lord blessed me to secure a passport in one day. Mother Coffey gave me a one-way ticket to Haiti and Bishop Crouch gave me God's blessed assurance that the Lord would supply all my needs according to His riches in Glory…I didn't know much then but to be obedient to the Holy Ghost."*

After her return she was recommended to serve in Liberia by Mother McGlothen and Bishop S.R. Martin.

NAOMI LUNDY — *THIS MAN NEEDS ALL THE HELP HE CAN GET*

When the Lord began to deal with Naomi Lundy about entering foreign service she was willing to obey but felt she needed clarity on how He wished her to proceed. The presence of the Lord pressing upon a deep and burning desire to serve and Lundy felt she needed urgent direction. She went on a total fast[84] and on the seventh day of the fast her mother told her she had to eat. She obeyed but not before the Lord said to her that there is a person that needs your help and she would have to be very consecrated.

The Lord gave me a vision of a harvest field. A little short man was standing in the field holding a sickle but I could only see his head. I asked the Lord the meaning of the vision of Africa. He answered "this man needs all the help he can get."

After the vision she counseled with her pastor who prayed with her. During the COGIC Holy Convocations the saints came together in a time of worship and to take care of business. At the time the Missions Department and Women's Department worked closely with missionaries desiring to enter international services and at the next Holy Convocation Lundy met with Mother Lillian Coffey. She was encouraged by Mother Coffey who informed her if she was one to go she would see to it. She also told Lundy that she would have to prepare herself causing Lundy to enroll in the Chicago School of Nursing and successfully completed a one year course in practical nursing.

MARY BETH KENNEDY AND CHARLES KENNEDY – *COME TO AFRICA AND HELP US*

Mother Kennedy always had missions on her heart. From the time she was a little girl she declared she would be a foreign missionary. Her initial missions work began in

---

[84] A total fast is one in which the individual forgoes all water and food for the duration of the consecration. Many of the early saints participated in total fasts oftentimes entering church for three day and three night shut ins. Other testified in fasting for up to seven days in this manner.

Puerto Rico. She and her White husband, Charles "Chuck" Kennedy migrated there when she was told their children would be more readily accepted. She taught school and learned Spanish. In the interdenominational church they attended there were missionaries who served the poor of the country. Working with doctors from the town she learned medicine and became a licensed midwife. She received the call while living in Puerto Rico when she had a vision of a man in Africa asking her to come.

"And as I prayed one day, well I was getting closer going back to my roots, but this particular day my daughter was sick. I stayed home with her rather than take her out to church. But I was having my own private devotions and as I prayed there was a man standing on the continent of Africa. I saw that shape of Africa and the man stood there and said come over and help us. I said that can't be real but yet I knew that God had spoken. I knew the Lord had called and I didn't want to change, I didn't want to move, I didn't want to go somewhere else. I didn't know what Africa would be like. I'd never been there. I finally said yes. I told Chuck."

Elder Kennedy, a graduate of Massachusetts Institute of Technology, was an aeronautical engineer, where after graduating he was employed as an instructor. After teaching a while he went West during the war and worked on dive bomber airplanes in an attempt to discover what caused the wings to fall off. However, as he studied spiritual matters it occurred to him that it was wrong for him to do things that would kill people. As a matter of conscience he left that lucrative field and began working with the peace movement for different groups before settling in with the Quakers of Philadelphia. When his wife informed him of her vision of a man standing in Africa asking them to come, he led them in prayer after which he agreed the vision was of the Lord. It was Elder Kennedy who initially followed the men to Wissikeh to examine the mission before relocating his wife and children there.

LEE VAN ZANDT — *CALLED AS A CHILD*

Beginning at the age of three or four Lee Van Zandt was visited with dreams. In them she was dressed in white and speaking to people who were not like her. Upon awakening she would ask her mother "Where is Jamaica?" or "Where is Africa?" As she grew into young adulthood the dreams increased in frequency. In one dream the Lord called her to preach in foreign lands. When she told her mother, the response was to go back and tell the Lord that she could not preach because girls did not do that. She got on her knees and obeyed her mother. Her father, an assistant pastor in the COGIC, also informed her that God did not call women to preach. As her father worked on his job as a plumber, he said that one day the Lord asked him, "Who are you to say whom I could call?"

Willie C. Ragland

CHAPTER SIX

HERE AM I, SEND. . .A WOMAN?

Female leadership success should come as no surprise to those acquainted with Christian service. Both the Old Testament and New Testament offer role models: the wisdom of the prophetess Huldah (2 Kings 22:14), the strategic planning of the matriarch Rachel (Ruth 4:11), the boldness of the prophetess and judge Deborah (Judges 4:4), and the intellectual prowess of the daughters of Zelophehad (Numbers 26:33, 27:1-4) along with those noted in the New Testament including the faithfulness of the temple attendant Anna (Luke 2:36), the organizational skills of Martha the disciple of Jesus (Luke 10:38), the anointing of Mary the mother of Jesus (Luke 2), and the trustworthiness of the *diakonos* Phoebe (Romans 16:1) among others. The story of Priscilla found in Acts 18 reveals a married woman who God used to interact with the nations of Rome, Greece and Asia Minor. Some commentators suggest that since Priscilla's name is almost always listed first, she was the more prominent member of the power couple. Whether this is true or not her leadership seemed to be normative in that no explanation of her role was provided in the Lukan account. The talents and gifts of other women, both single and married, would be used in God's sovereign plan throughout the ages.

One of the most fascinating power figures of the Middle Ages was The Abbess Hildegard of Bingen, a former member of nobility who experienced her first vision before she was five years old.[85] Abbesses were women of power and the strong independent Hildegard, became the founder and CEO of the Rupertsberg Convent and has been favorably compared to the great philosopher, Peter Abelard.[86] Those who study female leadership development view her use of the monastery to define herself culturally in a role other than wife or mother. Additionally, this 10th century visionary's insight into the politics of the monastery was noteworthy causing Archbishop Henry of Mainz to intervene on her behalf. Hildegard's understanding of rulership, fealty laws and homage, enabled her to use her influence to "guard the goods and privileges of the [Rupertsberg] house" and served as a precursor to religious women's successful spiritual leadership today. Like women before and after her Hildegard understood her divine vocation and, determined to succeed, laid strategic plans to carry out her calling.

Because of their commitment to God Priscilla or Hildegard may be viewed as emblematic of women

---

[85] Johnson, Penelope *Equal in Monastic Profession*, The University of Chicago Press, Chicago and London
[86] Amt, Emilie *Women's Lives in Medieval Europe*, Routledge, New York/London: 1993, 233

zealous in performing whatever deed required of them. Deeply committed women have stepped up to the call of God in every age. And in the 20th century, who better understood cross cultural matrices than American Black women whose powerful DNA was forged by slavery and later the racist legal legacy of Jim Crow law?

Prior to becoming the famous COGIC college educator, visionary Arenia Mallory chose working with COGIC missionaries rather than performing on stage or as the concert pianist for which she was trained. She traveled with a ministry couple meeting other ministers and missionaries on the evangelistic circuit and while in Kansas City, Missouri she was asked "What are your plans for your life's career?" The eighteen year old Arenia, the child of Mr. Edward and Mrs. Mazy Brooks Mallory, firmly turned her back on a life of privilege by responding, "I want to become a missionary in Africa. I have a desire to help my people."[87] Mallory left her mother's home with $100 and the caveat that the saints would eventually abandon her. (Later her mother would become an ardent supporter.)

During relocation to Mississippi at the request of Bishop Mason, Mallory was shocked but quickly adjusted to cross cultural mores particular to the South. For example, during her trip to Mississippi she found that coloreds were required to travel in separate cars. Upon her arrival she discovered it dangerous for Negro men to defend her honor when white men, who gathered daily at the station, made crude sexual insults. By the year 1926 she was

---

[87]Simmons, Dovie Marie and Olive L. Martin, *Down Under the Sun: The Story of Arenia Conelia Mallory,* 1983: Riverside Press, Memphis, TN, 6

firmly entrenched in the ethos and culture of the COGIC and set out to make Saints Industrial and Literary Academy one of the South's premier facilities of higher education. Opportunities would later allow her to realize her dream of helping her people by educating African students through the Friends of Liberian Youth organization she established for that purpose.

Did stories of the church's dynamic global vision to carry out the Great Commission, already established in Africa by the work of Elizabeth White, inspire her? What did it mean for any Black Pentecostal woman to "go into all the world?" That female role models provided organizational leadership was well proven through the work of Lizzie Robinson and the first tier of female leadership serving in the new roles of State Mother. These women, traveling companions to Robinson, learned how successful entrepreneurial networking systems provided discipline in organizing their spheres of influence among women's ministries. The sanctified women used these lessons as they migrated North as powerful tools in spreading the message of sanctification from its rural beginning to the urban settings of Detroit, Chicago and other primary destinations for Blacks.

Women labored for souls and the Holy Ghost performed miracles in tenement houses, storefront churches and on street corners. Legendary in COGIC circles, intercessor Elizabeth Dabney prayed for three years for change to come to the "wicked" neighborhood she and her husband found themselves in. Evangelist twins Leatha and Reatha Herndon were reported to have "prayed out" upwards to one hundred churches then requested men to lead the congregations. Annie Pennington Bailey, destined to become the third International Supervisor of Women of the COGIC, was one of those who preached on street corners. It was through her street preaching that Haitian national Joseph Paulceus was saved and filled with the Holy Ghost. Paulceus returned to Haiti and established the first COGIC there in 1929. The church began at 165 Rue des Fronts Forts, Port-au-Prince.[88]

With their service as overseers in missions stations female international missionaries more closely followed the lessons of Galatians 5. Establishing the Church Of God In Christ in 1929 in the world's second largest continent, whose 800 million human inhabitants account for around one seventh of the earth's population they viewed themselves as neither male nor female but equal ambassadors of the kingdom.

Pentecost is growing in a number of African countries. Kalu says that though the Roman Catholic Church remains the premier Christian body in Africa, Pentecostals represent over 100 million on the continent. In 2000 the largest percentages of those self identifying Pentecostals were: Zimbabwe (20%), Tanzania (20%), Malawi (20%), Kenya (14%), Nigeria (11%), Ghana (10%), Zambia (10%), Democratic Republic of the Congo (8%), South Africa (8%), and Uganda (4%).[89] In addition to the apostolic work done by charismatic Africans the embryonic work performed by COGIC female missionaries can be attributed to the growing Pentecostal witness on the continent (as well as the organization's strong presence in approximately 60 countries). Female

---

[88]Noble, Mae *Christianity's African Roots: A Curriculum Emphasizing Aspects of The African Heritage of Christianity,* first published in 1980, 170
[89]Kalu, Ogbu, *African Pentecostalism: An Introduction,* Oxford University Press, New York: 2008, 5

overseers carried a heavy load yet provided leadership in every area of the foreign missions work. Because they persevered and refused to give up through hardship, they were respected in their roles. And according to COGIC Bishop Amos Nyema, it is one of the oldest and strongest denominations in the Republic of Liberia, West Africa.[90]

At a time when few Americo-Liberians lived in the country (by 1916 there were only 12,000 to 15,000 Americo-Liberians)[91] it was Elizabeth White who volunteered to return. It is safe to assume she had no children and may have entered service as a single woman. White was said to have been married briefly but her marriage was annulled and her only known relative was a brother. It has been suggested that living in nonwestern countries more suited single women like White since men would be forced to uproot their families. Prior to her COGIC affiliation she entered foreign missions work on the continent in the 1920s and set about to evangelize and build under the auspices of the Assembly of God (AG). Stories are told that because of her fair complexion the AG thought she was a White woman. It seems that the color line washed away at the Azusa Street revival was resurrected. When they found she was Colored their relations cooled. Whatever the true story, after three years of working with the Assemblies of God at Cape Palmas, Liberia White served with the United Pentecostal Church in Liberia prior to her affiliation as a member of the COGIC.

---

[90]Nyema
[91]anglicanhistory.org/africa/lb/missions1928, *Handbook on the Missions of the Episcopal Church*, Liberia, New York: The National Council of the Protestant Episcopal Church, 1928.

White was sent back to Africa by COGICs Mission Board circa 1929-30. In Monrovia White met Americo-Liberians steeped in the traditions of the mainline churches, who had carried on mission work since the 19th century. Those entering Liberia by the 1930s found a country with a population of about 2 ½ million people. Its Constitution was patterned after that of the United States. After the civil laws came the tribal laws with each tribe having a paramount chief or king who controlled the entire tribe. She would have found the country's topography a dense tropical rain forest, full of trees yielding valuable lumber or dyestuffs, and also home to all kinds of dangerous animals. Despite the difficulty White, considered the dean of COGIC African missionaries male or female, ventured into the hinterlands of Liberia to establish the Wissekeh (Maryland County) mission and worked with native Liberians from the Kru, Vai or Grebbo who were resistant to outside influences. The villages were far apart and there were no roads. She walked through the bushes for 10, 15, 20, 25 or 30 miles on paths so narrow that individuals were unable to walk two abreast. Upon her arrival she met with the Nyambo and Tobou tribes in Bilbo, Manolu and Wrouke. Interviewees stated that in those days secret societies were formidable with witchcraft in control and sacrifices made to idol gods. White, armed with the knowledge that God was faithful, was undeterred. It was the work of White and other women like her that convinced many of their disciples that the love and power of God would lift them spiritually, educationally and economically.

Missionaries interviewed emphasized they were not interested in becoming new colonialists or patronizing African Liberians. Neither did they seek personal recognition or power for themselves. They were there to lift standards, both naturally and spiritually. To understand the extent of their achievement one has to recognize that female missionaries had to make their election and calling sure in order to gain the confidence of those who would be served, remain firm in their belief and move forward from village to village without any intimidation whatsoever. They had no dash to give, only Jesus' amazing love propelled them into areas restricted by their gender. In the American fifties and sixties as youth began their exodus from rural life into cities mothers cautioned their children if they were ever in trouble find an inviting home and then ask for the lady of the house to get results. Working with the women to get results proved true in the dual sex system of West African society. Females, like women everywhere, desired that their children become upwardly mobile and the keen insight by the missionaries in dealing with the women was the first step in meetings with village elders to champion their cause. They also had the support of Christians in the area. Mother White appointed Rev. William K. Brown pastor of the church at Manolu and although his previous attempt at establishing a school was unsuccessful, her authorization for him to open a school and serve as teacher until arrangement could be made for a permanent one was a good move. Rev. Brown appealed to the chiefs and leaders who gave the school eighteen young men for the Manolu Mission School. After further negotiating with tribal leaders early missionaries like White were able to mine minerals, fruits, palm oil, and cane. A major source of revenue was harvesting rubber trees and COGIC missionaries planted these to support their work. Beatrice Lott, with a vision to help the African Liberians to become self-sufficient, procured 40 acres of land and planted rubber trees to sell to Firestone. (Unlike Haiti, which was ignored by the United States beginning with Jefferson, Liberia has been important to America strategically and has been visited by high profile leaders since it became a republic. President and Mrs. Franklin D. Roosevelt visited Liberia in 1943 to discuss among other issues the commitment of Liberia continuing to supply rubber to the U.S. for the war effort.[92] On a visit in 1957 Vice President Richard Nixon was given the title honorary paramount chief and robed by Paramount Chief Akoi Tellewoyan of the Boday and Wubormai Chiefdoms.)

Out of sheer necessity, women working overseas have always been more "liberated" than those remaining in the States. While the Home and Foreign Missions Board dictated policy, COGIC leaders allowed great freedom to international missionaries like White to serve in a flexible autonomy. Women for whom ordination was unthinkable found that as representatives of the headquarters they could use their gifts and talents to evangelize, build schools and orphanages, plant churches and train men to lead those churches. White's work among the natives at the Bonniken Mission Station resulted in the establishment of a small congregation of new believers with whom she served as overseer. White understood her authority as overseer to establish more churches and build the work of the COGIC. Bishop Abraham Brown recalls first meeting White at Bialbo near Tugbaken when he was a nineteen year old preacher from the United Pentecostal Church conducting evangelistic services. After he made the altar call she was moved by his sincerity and anointing. When he closed the service she approached him about working with her group near Monolu, a town outside the city of Cape Palmas. Saved at age twelve, he previously worked

---

[92] www.africanwithin.com/tour/liberia/relations.htm

there with his uncle Rev. William K. Brown accompanying him from house to house holding services and prayer.

> [Mother White] brought me to Manolu. I was not at Manolu before because there were no schools. At Biabo I was holding a service and made an altar call. This is where she saw me and knew that I was coming from Manolu for which she sent me back to Manolu to help my uncle who had started a school and a church work over there. I was young. I think I was about 19 years old and [in the service] she got moved and wondered where I come from because she knew a man name Brown from Manolu. I told her that was my uncle and she said your uncle is there struggling looking for a teacher…to help and building up a house for teachers. If you agree to go with your uncle and help him out then I will send a teacher there. That's how she brought me out from Biabo to Manolu.[93]

Men like Brown were important to the work for a number of reasons—to persuade village kinship networks to embrace the gospel, work for less pay, they resisted certain diseases and could work as interpreters. In the 1930s Brown learned to speak English while working for Americo-Liberians and the energetic young minister's ability to speak indigenous languages caused him to become White's interpreter. She preached and he interpreted then conducted the altar services in dialect. As she led her team on the field the work continued to grow until it was necessary to send another Missionary. Mother Robinson recommended Mrs. W. C. Ragland of Columbus, Georgia to the Mission Board to serve as her assistant. At the close of the Holy Convocation in 1931, Mrs. Ragland was appointed. In the first part of the year of 1932, she sailed to Liberia. There the two women

---

[93]Brown interview

negotiated with native Liberians for material, haggled over pricing and then supervised the erection of a stucco church building, the first in Africa. The strengths forged by having to think quickly and work effectively caused the leaders to excel but sometimes the dreams came with a high price. Missionaries worked grueling schedules with days beginning as early as 4am. In instances too numerous for the interviewees to recall they returned from neighboring villages or caring for the sick long after midnight. And though obedience to their calling gave them satisfaction, one largely ignored area in the life of the international missionary concerns the stress of diminished physical functioning caused by lack of proper rest, illness, and the loneliness of missing family lives or as Bonanno says even being able to unexpectedly bump into an old friend. After spending four years in the severe heat, Missionary White returned home for a much-needed rest. A COGIC emissary was sent from the United States to accompany her back home. (This was not unheard of and would be repeated. Fronz Exume reports that twice his mother had to be brought back to the United States and hospitalized due to exhaustion. The last occurrence was around 1968 with him and brother Amilcar cared for by Dr. Willa Battle while Dr. Cora Berry took care of their sister Marlil.)

Missionary Ragland remained in Africa carrying on the work until Missionary White returned in 1935. While on furlough White and other missionaries spent some time being reacquainted with friends from COGIC and other faith communities, visiting churches, and sharing with congregants how God was moving in foreign fields. In addition to raising awareness of foreign missions work, these visits also served as fund raising tools for the mission stations. Other fundraising was done through mailing pledge letters. Maxine Haynes Kyle, daughter of Bishop F.L. Haynes, who briefly served as the third COGIC Bishop of Texas (prior to its 1954 division into four jurisdictions), recalls in White's frequent visits to Texas she visited churches around the State. She also shared stories at their home. "Out of respect my dad would allow Mother White to say the Lord's blessing before we ate. Afterwards we would hear stories of the work she was doing in Africa."

Nyema lists the following missionaries who served Liberia after White's departure and successfully impacted generations: Mae Ragland, Beatrice Lott, Francina Wiggins, Martha Barber, Lelia January, O.T. Jones, Jr., Charles and Betty Kennedy, June Blackwell, Naomi R. Lundy, Pearl Page Brown, and Marva Cromartie.

The work of Lelia January is emblematic of COGIC foreign missionaries. Bishop Nyema recalls Mother January's dedication to serve Monrovia, a town reminiscent of the American Old West where ranchers came to gather supplies, purchase goods, pick up mail and get the latest gossip from back East. By the 1930s the structure of the COGIC mandated that missionaries were not released to enter foreign service if they were not prepared by having medical training or had completed other requirements yet Mother Lelia January traveled to the continent with fire in her heart to win lost souls. According to Nyema upon Mother January's arrival in Monrovia, Mother Rosetta E. Harding took her to the home of Mother Barclay. The Methodist presence in Liberian began in 1833 when Missionary Society of the Methodist Episcopal Church began sending black and white missionaries. During the mid-1850s the mission board ceased sending white missionaries.[94] Mother January affiliated with the First African Methodist Church of Monrovia upon her arrival since there was no COGIC at the time.

> In 1939 Mother January began to conduct crusades and prayer meetings around Monrovia. In 1940 she invited the Saints to a meeting to inform them about her decision to go back to the States to inform Bishop Mason about what the Lord was doing in Liberia through her ministry. Because she was not an accredited missionary, she did not have the authority to establish a church in Liberia on her own.[95]

Due to her arrival in Liberia as an independent missionary, Brother John K. Reeves and others suggested since Mother White was fully appointed and accredited by the COGIC, that she be called from the hinterland of Wissekeh to start a church. After composing a letter, January gathered the saints in Maryland County to inform them and it was there she brought her last message, "The Everlasting Existence of the Faith," before she died surrounded by the saints. The church was turned over to Elizabeth White in October 1940 and following a series of meetings directed the saints to form a COGIC. By this time the number of individuals claiming membership was three hundred, and they gave their allegiance to the COGIC by affixing their signatures to a proclamation sent to Bishop Mason. Thus the first COGIC was formed in Montserrado County. Among those signing were Mother Rosetta E. Harding, Father

---

[94] Park, Eunjin, *"White" Americans in "Black" Africa: Black and White American Methodist Missionaries in Liberia, 1820-1875*, Studies in African American History and Culture, Graham Russell Hodges, General Editor, 2001: Routledge, 31

[95] Nyema

Valentine Brown, Father Thomas Cassell, Sis. Annie Howard, Sis. Harris and Mother Esther Gray.[96]

Religious support, social support and spiritual connection proved invaluable helping missionaries in their resiliency to persevere amid hardships. The majority of people clustered around the coast but COGIC missionaries forged inland into the tropical rain forest. Beatrice Lott told of clearing the jungle and stopping to look at her bloodied hands. Schools and churches had to be built so she wiped the sweat and blood on her garment then continued the work. Missionaries shared management strategies to accomplish some amazing accomplishments. Through interaction with one another, a shared sense of belonging, commitment to promoting the love of God and their church's Bible based doctrine they built what would become three missions' stations in Maryland County (Wissekeh, Manolu and Tugbaken) with boarding schools in Liberia and schools and orphanages in Haiti. Despite sometimes experiencing inner disillusionment caused by cultural identity transitions or, in the beginning, just a lack of stable financial support, under the direction of the missionaries a series of meetings were held and the number of churches grew to fifty including those established in the Ivory Coast.

Prior to adding pictures of President John F. Kennedy and Dr. Martin Luther King, Jr. three things individuals around the U.S. could count on seeing in the homes of most saints were a Bible, a picture of Bishop C.H. Mason with handiworks of God in the foreground (Mason had an uncanny ability to interpret, for example, trees shaped like a hand or animal giving spiritual meaning) and the Whole Truth newspaper the latter of which would be

---

[96] ibid

used by pioneer missionaries to get the message of missions into the brotherhood. In fact, one of the primary reasons the names and service of international missionaries became rapidly familiar throughout the brotherhood was that reports of foreign missionary activities in the field came through newspaper articles and souvenir books. Through letters printed in the newspaper missionaries reminded the saints of the part they needed to play in building the kingdom of God. What better media than through the eagerly awaited Whole Truth newspaper, which served as the official organ of the COGIC? The newspaper was so important to the life of the saints that it was almost reverenced in and of itself with testimonies of healing being wrought through placing the newspaper on the afflicted one's body resulting in the individual being healed.

These media kept saints abreast of the activities of her international missionaries and served as an additional means for fundraising. In 1946 a story of the work of the Calvary Temple School established in Belize, Central America and the students who gained literacy through the church's efforts inspired readers. Later in 1957 they updated the saints on the work.

Whole Truth – February 1957, Number 2 Volume XXXII

BELIZE, B.H.

Blessed be the God and Father of our Lord Jesus Christ, who hath blessed us with all spiritual blessing in heavenly places in Christ. Eph. 1:3

We have just closed a one week campaign in the Stann Creek Town under our Dist. Supt. Eld. Laing, Missionary H. Taylor, Ministers G. Domingo, H.Cattouse and Bro. Lloyd Miguel. We are now establishing a work in the capital of this district. We held our services in the open air, and each night we expounded the word of God to hundreds of folk gathered to listen, and by the indication of upraised hands, and personal contact, we found out that they are really hungry for the full gospel which this church has for everybody who can and will believe. They want us to stay in their midst, and thus constrained us to secure a building which by prayer and fasting we hope will be a lighthouse in their town.

Among the many churches in this town there are none like this great Church Of God In Christ. The people are godly proud that our Founder is still alive, and that he is a Negro, also that our brothers and sisters in America care for us. We are hereby asking you dear saints in America to help us. We need clothing, books of all kinds, Bibles, musical instruments and finance. We are confident that many of you saints have things lying around that could be of much service to us in Stann Creek, more than you would think they would. Therefore, I am asking your help for we are determined to carry out our Lord's command and commission unto the uttermost parts of the earth. Will you heed the Macedonian cry, come over and help us? Please send all donations for the Stan Creek work to Br. Hond., directed to Eld. Melbourne Laing, Dist. Supt.

Stann Creek, c/o Calvary Temple, Regent St. West, Belize B.H.

May God bless you all for your open hearts for us.

Eld. M. Laing, Dist. Supt.
Sis. H. Taylor, Dist. Miss.
Min. H. Cattouse, Reporter

Whole Truth, December 1955

GOLD COAST, B.W. AFRICA

CHURCH OF GOD IN CHRIST

BISHOP C.H. MASON, SENIOR BISHOP & CHIEF APOSTLE, LADY J.T. EPTON, FOREIGN MISSIONARY, PRIVATE MAIL BAG, KUMASA,
GOLD COAST, B.W. AFRICA

OPEN LETTER

To the Officials Staff of Home and Foreign Mission Board & to our beloved Bishops, State Overseers, State Mothers, Pastors and Congregations of the Church Of God In Christ.

I send you greetings in the dear sweet name of Jesus.

Beloved I am making this appeal on behalf of our missions here in dark, dark Africa. I need your prayers and financial support, millions are worshippers of idol gods here, tens of thousands are suffering from malnutrition, leprosy, sleeping sickness, T.B, Guinea worm, blindness, madness. I need your help to enable me to carry on this great Kingdom work, our few preachers are very very poor and members are poor and in destitute conditions. It is very difficult for any foreign missionary to stay at her or his post of duty in the foreign fields of their callings, without financial support from the home churches. My living conditions are very bad. I am suffering from insect and mosquito bites, dysentery. I walk miles in the dark bush in the muddy water roads to serve our missions. I pray for so many sick and afflicted people until I feel very very weak in my body, yet the people still cry for me to pray for their deliverance from diseases.

I am very sorry to say that I have only received $50 from the home churches through Bishop CROUCH since my return to Africa in December 1954. When I returned from Africa in 1953, I was unable to tour the states to raise funds for the work in Africa due to my ill health. Our senior elder Mr. Kofi Asaie has given the church three story cement building, there remains a mortgage of $2,600 of which we have to pay. The first floor will be used to train our girls from the dark bush missions, domestic science, child care and home nursing. The second will be used to make sure missionaries and workers.

They needed help and the church's infrastructure, local congregations and individuals came to their aid. Images are defining and today if one thinks of pioneer female missionaries at all, youth does not come to mind. In souvenir books the faces of international missionaries, frozen in time, stare back with solemnity or ever so sternly. Who were these women and what was their motivation? They were ministers of the Lord who started young and were eagerly looking to fulfill all potentialities in the purpose for which they were chosen. They were ordinary women who liked to "fix up", do their hair and enjoy life. (Towards the end of her life Beatrice Lott, saying that woman will do anything to be beautiful, refused to let her hair grow gray and requested even on her sick bed that her caretaker rinse her hair with Ms. Clairol Sable Brown, give her a full facial and keep clear nail polish on her nails!) It made sense for energetic and idealistic youth to enter foreign service and the age of the average COGIC missionary in the 1930s and 1940s was in the mid 20s Lott was in her late twenties or early thirties when she arrived on African soil; Exume obeyed her call to go to Haiti in her twenties. Believing in the imminent return of Christ, the women were willing to give their lives to the cause of evangelizing and during the wait for the end-time, conduct practical exercises, build schools to educate their new communities.

Little is known of the personal lives of many of the early pioneer missionaries but by the 1930s, 1940s and throughout the scope of this project members of many congregations were found to have changed from low income to the middle class. Educator Dorothy Webster

(Exume) taught high school French classes prior to entering the mission's field. Mary Beth Kennedy and her husband Charles were both college trained and left what could have been a life of comfort to travel initially to Tugbaken to assist Mother Martha Barber at that Mission then re-establish the Wissikeh Mission. All were anointed by God to work for the people. Given the legacy of prohibitive academic opportunities for Blacks the youthful, vibrant and bright COGIC woman using her hard won education in the segregated 1930 and 1940s was admirable at the least. When Black schools fought against inferior financial support (Southern Black schools received $15 for educational funding compared to $80 white schools took for granted) families and friends felt the choice these women made was unthinkable. In 1939, Beatrice Lott joined the missionaries and a work was established at Tugbakeh. Lott died in 1996. At her funeral the late Bishop Robert Chapman, Ohio Jurisdictional Prelate, remarked that after reading in the Whole Truth that a young woman with so much promise "would give her life to Africa we talked about it everywhere!"

Early Sunday School literature began listing overseers in 1929 and later state mothers in the Continental United States. By 1948 Mrs. D.J. Young, who took over the publishing of the Sunday School literature after the death of her husband, began listing overseers of foreign works but no foreign workers were shown.[97] Though females had served in foreign fields since the 1920s when

---

[97]D.J. Young Foundation Archives, Dr. Ladrian Brown, Founder/Executive Director, *The Sunday School Quarterly Vol. 31 No. 4. 1948 4th Quarter and The Sunday School Quarterly Vol. 32 No. 4. 1949 4th Quarter* D. J. Young Publishing Co. listed "State Overseers" Elder Patrick, J. J., Pembroke, East Hamilton Bermuda (Bermuda Islands); Bishop Morten, C. L., 1026 Mercer St. Windsor, Ontario Canada (Dominion of Canada); Elder Hunt, R. H., General P.O. (sic) Nassau, Bahamas (Bahamas Islands)

Elizabeth White volunteered to return to Africa, from 1952 through 1955, only the following six females were shown to be serving outside the United States.[98] (Names are spelled as shown in the quarterlies.)

Mother Elizabeth White. Bethel Home Box 6,
Cape Pulma Lyberia West Coast Africa
Martha Barbara Bethel Home Box 6, Cape Pulma Lyberia
   West Coast Africa
Beatrice Lott Bethel Home Box 6, Cape Pulma Lyberia
   West Coast Africa
Willie Raggsland 927 Lawyers Lane, Columbus, GA
Mary St. Juste 165 Rheu Port-Au-Prince, Haïti
Kittie Fazier Bahamas Island
Willie Holt Hawaiin Islands
Dorothy Webster 2250 E 73rd St Cleveland, OH (Haiti)

The list did not include Mother Francena Wiggins, however, her missions work at the Manolu Mission Station from 1949 to 1964 is noteworthy. Wiggins was sent to Liberia to assist Mother White at the Wissikeh Station. She was then assigned to Manolu where she built a church, a school and a mission complex. There she met twenty-two year old Abraham Brown who previously worked with Mother White. He was energetic, saved and filled with the Holy Ghost and could help with the many young people at Manolu and White gave him his first appointment in the COGIC. He was initially reluctant to accept the position of assisting his uncle in opening a school at Manolu thinking she did not mean it as he only had a fourth grade education.

---

[98]ibid

> I was in kindergarten at 15 years [old]...we don't go by age. She said...if you go I will open a school out there. I said if you mean it. She said you stubborn, you bonehead don't talk to me. [I said] I'm only 4th grade and I can't teach anything. She said yeah you can teach ABC. So she took me from there and appointed me.[99]

The school grew and Mother White hired a native Liberian as a teacher. Brown helped to build the teacher's a house and fixed up a little camp where the children would come until a better school was constructed. When the teacher broke the moral code defining appropriate sexual behavior (within marriage) mixed cultural signals upon his reporting the teacher's sexual advances to Mother White caused confusion. In his village those who do wrong would be dealt with in a way that they could save face. They let the elders know of the infarction with a warning to watch for the thief or other miscreant behavior.

> He liked to run around with people's wives. And the girls that I had when I was coming to prayer he wanted to love on them. So I told Mother White. In my country if anything is wrong in the community...you would watch out. You keep it and you don't tell them. But with Mother White when you tell her she would call the person and say you foolish, you bonehead this is what you be doing down here? And she said this one told me. She called your name! The wicked people they don't like that and they can do you harm. So I went to Mother White and I told her now I'm running a revival trying to get these young people saved. I said you have more people to work with than me on the mission but this man is not saved. And the attitude he have...She said you bonehead, you got the Holy Ghost but the book you don't know. Work with this man. Be patient. So after

---

[99] Brown interview

the close of the school year I left.[100]

Hurt and disillusioned he avoided the mission from 1940 to 1946. Drifting from his close relationship with the Lord in his words he was ready to "sow into his weakness, an angry dog ready to fight." His military training left him with proficient ability in boxing to do so and one night he had an altercation with an Americo-Liberian. "At first I wouldn't listen to those who cautioned me that as a poor boy from the rural I would be put in jail for fighting the American Liberian." That night the Lord spoke to him in his sleep. "He told me that I was getting to be too much and needed to go and look for the missionary." He packed up returned home telling his mother what the Lord had said. Since the mission was 25 miles away he waited a year while working on his family's farm prior his return. It was then he fully accepted his calling into the ministry. The Lord then gave him another dream commanding that he return to Manolu. Someone needed his help. Upon his arrival he went to pay his respect and to greet Mother White. He learned that Mother Wiggins wanted to preach to Manolu but did not have an interpreter. Now the twenty-two year old's assignment was to help Mother Wiggins and the two had great success. In addition to interpreting he was a handyman and performed carpentry and landscaping. Additional duties were to keep students in line.

Prayer was key to the success of each mission's church growth, Sunday School classes, schools and building programs. In each station prayer began as early as 4:30 or

---

[100]ibid

5:00 with the missionaries leading the workers and children in prayer until the breaking of day after which they bathed and then sent the children to school.

Whenever there were particular needs, special prayer walks around the villages or prayer services would be called. Another praying man, Home and Foreign Missions President Bishop Samuel Crouch, arrived shortly after Mother Wiggins' assignment to Manolu. He heard someone in the prayer room and listened as they blessed God shouting Hallelujah and Glory to God. After a while he woke Mother Wiggins who informed him that it was only a young preacher and mission worker in his customary morning prayer. She delightedly informed him that Brown disturbed the place every day beginning early mornings and if it had not been for his hard work and keeping the children in line she would be at a disadvantage. Bishop Crouch called him into the house, prayed for Bro. Abraham, and assured him he was on the right track. He vowed to send someone to license and ordain him. In Haiti, Fronz Exume remembers that each Saturday his entire family too relied on the power of prayer, regularly spending Saturday mornings in fasting and praying at the orphanage.

The predominantly Black COGIC was unique to the foreign mission field. Historically sending organization were white, then Black with white affiliations. The sending agencies provided training and other support for schools and orphanages for their missionaries. Given the originality of the work (schools were built and students learned to read as paths toward upward mobility but the thrust was to learn of Christ and His power over sin and shame) coming through the Black Holiness-Pentecostal COGIC, there were few models these first pioneers could look to. They sailed into

Africa or flew into Haiti under divine direction understanding that they faced cultural dissonance, danger and loss of First World amenities. Not everyone was cut out for foreign missions work and missionaries suffered for their cause. They faced a standard of living well below that of their home country, drums served as the chief means of communication and, early dual-sex systems notwithstanding, by the time COGIC entered Liberia the culture dictated that women have little voice in government, the community or the home.

Their accomplishments are all the more impressive considering further challenges of limited resources, hard and long working hours in addition to activities of hostile voodoo priests or witch doctors. Yet they demonstrated the resiliency and flexibility needed to cope with any circumstance. Bonanno defines resilience to loss as "the ability of adults in otherwise normal circumstances who are exposed to an isolated and potentially highly disruptive event...to maintain relatively stable, healthy levels of psychological and physical functioning.[101]" For Beatrice Lott, their call strengthened them in the field as they built the moral lives of the sons and daughters they indoctrinated and caused them to creatively re-invent themselves when, upon their return to the United States, they faced the dichotomy of gender bias with less official influence in policy or decision making within the church. Soon after their return the contributions of these women were forgotten. While it was noted that few attended the funeral of the great trailblazer Elizabeth White, interviewees were not dissuaded that they made the right

---

[101]Bonnano, George A. and Anthony D. Mancini, *Predictors and Parameters of Resilience to Loss: Toward an Individual Difference Model,* Journal of Personality, 2004, 20

decision in answering their call. While none of the women interviewed felt they were due extraordinary praise for only doing what God called them to, they subsumed underlying tensions due to issues such as the neglect of retirement considerations as further reasons to pray. This locus of control was forged through a personal spiritual connection with God and a love relationship with Jesus. In what could have been demoralizing circumstances He gave them gifts of decision, perseverance, humor and creativity causing them to navigate successfully through what sometimes seemed like biblical wilderness wanderings. For Beatrice Lott the entirety of their work was a love task. The COGIC supported its missionaries but as the work grew the small stipend was not enough. Emblematic of this spiritual construct was their optimistic response to unfulfilled expectations in not receiving basics, e.g., money to pay teachers or themselves. Their sense of purpose caused them to look toward God's provision and continuing to serve, their status, acquired at a distance, rose in Stateside circles.

Some left promising careers, others like the beautiful hazel eyed Beatrice Lott with two serious contenders for her hand forsook suitors who in the early 20th century could have offered upward mobility and notoriety within the church, to enter a vastly different culture. Great physical and spiritual battles accompanied their entrance into service which could have caused stress to be so disheartening they could have given up. In fact, some admitted that thoughts came to reject their calling yet they bravely entered jungles, with bush was so thick the men used machetes to cut through, as they ventured 30 miles into the interior to land they would transform into great missions' towns. Upon their arrival they slept in mud huts prior to construction of permanent living quarters. Bishop Abraham Brown recalls that by 1950 the church was welcomed by the majority as they transformed the society through providing educational opportunities, vocational training, medical aid and the gospel. Yet in the early stages of the Pentecostals' missions work braved hostility from many in the villages.

By the time World War II began work at missions stations were going well. As the forces of combat surged around the continent of Africa, mandatory evacuation by the U.S. government caused all Americans to leave including missionary service workers. Lott, Barber and six native Liberian children left Liberia on the 19th day of May on board the *M.V. Susan* and were at sea seventeen days. They faced real dangers on the journey home as the Germans were famous for torpedoing boats and sinking ships. No telegrams could get through and a spurious tale was passed on to Lott's mother that her ship had been attacked and her body was at the bottom of the ocean. Despite sea sickness and possible enemy attacks, Lott and the others survived both the dangerous passage and equally dangerous tongues to arrive safely in New York. The plans for the students from the hinterland of Cape Palmas included advanced education in the United States and return to serve Liberia. Lott provides insight into their aspirations for the children she and Barber adopted and for the hope of Liberia in a 1952 interview:

> In Liberia the older people do not so easily turn to Christianity as their children. With me I have two girls: Lillian Coffey Lott (Qualla) and Esther Ragland Lott (Yedde), the latter having been with us since the age of four days. Her mother died in childbirth. These girls belong to the Grebo tribe and speak the Grebo dialect. They have learned the English language well in the five years they have been in training. They are also becoming quickly adapted to the American ways of living. These girls are very

industrious as well as ambitious. They plan to become nurses for whom there is a great demand in Liberia. They are also studying the piano and are making splendid progress.[102]

The work of the missionaries was not done at their return to the United States. They busily engaged in ministering and their messages inspired women like Dorothy Webster, a teacher in the public schools of Cleveland, Ohio who felt the Lord's call to go to the Mission Field. Missionary Lott wished Webster to accompany her to Liberia with her but Webster was led to the Republic of Haiti for her field of ministry after having a God given dream interpreted. The works of these founding mothers are the roots from which many contemporary mission activities continue to grow. Women like Webster did not necessarily view herself as trailblazers but understood that her call was to use her gifts in obedient service. Wishing her older mentor success she declined the invitation to Africa and after a time she performed tremendous achievements in Haiti. Founding schools was an important aspect of missionary strategy and the young teacher would excel in establishing at least ten Haitian schools including those in Carrfour, Bel'air, Cantoff and Gonaives and assisted the Battles in establishing a school in Boutilliers. She'd send money to these schools for feeding programs so that the children could eat at least one hot meal per day. Webster-Exume also planted approximately twenty churches throughout the island with the help of Haitian national ministers.

---

[102] From *An Interview with Miss Beatrice Lott, Returned Missionary to Cape Palmas, Liberia, Africa,* 35th Annual Ohio State Convocation Church Of God In Christ, August 5 through 14, 1952, Elder U.E. Miller, State Overseer, Mrs. Lola Young, State Supervisor

After the war the missionaries were released to travel and Lott immediately returned to Liberia taking Miss Barber with her. Black Pentecostals like Lott connected with the citizens of the host country because, in her words, "there's a different feeling [in Africa]. It's something about the land and the people." She would remain for an additional ten years. Decades later, former students fondly recall the ministry of the missionaries and shared exactly how they presented the plan of salvation and the power of Pentecost. In tribal governments nothing was done without the permission of the tribal or paramount chief and elders. Motivated to go to any length to present the love of the Great Creator, who could save them from their sins and fill them His great power, missionaries cut through the bush of Africa's tropical forests to evangelize remote villages. Guided by the Holy Ghost first and foremost they invited them to experience a personal encounter with God through Jesus Christ. Additionally, the possibility of literacy attracted them with paramount chiefs and elders initially sending only their boys to the missions. Alexander Gbayee left his father's farm and entered the Tugbaken mission in 1948.

> I came to the Tugbaken mission after the missionary's visited our village. They came to our house and showed my father that you could look at a paper and get a message with news. My father told me to go to the school to get a message from the paper.[103]

Successes with Gbayee's father and other village elders caused an uptick in the church's mission's efforts. They introduced the power to live free from continual sin through receiving the Baptism of the Holy Ghost

---

[103]Interview by author with Alexander Toley Gbayee, currently the Liberian Consul to the United States (Chicago and the Midwest)

empowering them to experience lives of sanctification, holiness and righteousness. The Liberian mission town continued to grow and through reports to the H&FM along with letters sent in to the Whole Truth newspaper a headquarters review was required. These visits bolstered the standing of the missionaries in the eyes of the larger denominational missions' community and encouraged the mission workers. By the time Bishop Charles Pleas arrived in Monrovia the church had grown to such an extent that the saints wished to construct a building. Pleas led the saints in starting the building project and under his direction most of the project was completed. In 1949 Elder O.T. Jones Jr., arrived in Monrovia and while there preached, lectured and counseled various religious and educational groups, all of which were not COGIC. As a liaison to Mother Lott and Mother Barber particularly, and associate minister Jones completed the church building on the Crown Hill, Broad Street site started by Bishop Pleas. The name of the new church was Holy Temple Church Of God In Christ.

Early COGIC foreign missions demographics include few husband and wife teams. Later, Missionary Paulette Griffin and her husband Elder Shelton Griffin would serve in Sierra Leone; however, in the late 1950s events caused Mary Beth Kennedy and Charles Kennedy to become the first COGIC husband and wife team to serve outside the United States. An intercultural couple from Pennsylvania, they relocated to Puerto Rico after the birth of their first child with the belief the environment would prove friendlier. After their call to Africa, the couple agreed to sell almost everything they owned and give the remainder away to move back to the U.S. mainland. At that time foreign missionaries, their stations and addresses were listed at the end of Sunday School books.

The only foreign missionary Kennedy had seen was the Haitian pioneer Dorothy Webster. She found Mother Martha Barber's name on the list and wrote to the Tugbaken Mission Station in Liberia asking if Barber could use the couple's help. Receiving Barber's invitation to come Kennedy's went to work preparing to leave. Her MIT trained husband entered the college classroom to work and save money for the trip. The COGIC sending agency was the Home and Foreign Missions Board which fell under the auspices of Mother Coffey and the Women's Department. Candidates wishing to serve in foreign countries applied to the Board and if they were considered to have potential were interviewed during Holy Convocation. It was decided that Mary Kennedy would attend the 1956 Holy Convocation where she met with National Mother Lillian Coffey and others to explain reasons her family would remove themselves from a life of comfort to one of deprivation.

> When you're twenty something you know everything anyhow. I said Mother Barber invited us. It's her mission and we can go. I don't even know why we have to go and talk with these people. I didn't understand anything about Boards and the Board is eventually in charge of an organization. But I didn't realize that. I went before the Board but I wasn't nearly the way I should have been. Like humble. And sweet. And charming. Not any of those things. It was more of the attitude of a chip on the shoulder, humph, what do you all want? Why are you all bothering me? I want to go serve God overseas. Why don't you just say yes? *You're* not going. *I'm* going, so what's all this about? That was my attitude. It was not at all a proper attitude. But I didn't realize. Nobody had ever taught me. At any rate they approved it. Mother

Coffey was not particularly happy about my attitude but they approved it.[104]

With the Board's approval they would join Mother Barber at Tugbaken, but had several hurdles to overcome. First, she naively thought that the church would fully fund their travel to Liberia. At the meeting she discovered mission's dollars were stretched thin and only meager funds would be allocated for travel to Liberia. (They were given a transportation grant of $300.00. See Appendix 1:5 for 1956 Home and Foreign Mission Financial Statement.) Undaunted, the determined couple and their two children (the others were born in Africa) moved in with her mother and saved their money to enter service.

A cause for concern for women like Dorothy Exume in Haiti or Betty Kennedy on her way to Africa was the issue of children accompanying their parents to the mission field. While missionary children experienced an education that could not be found in American schoolbooks there was the issue of deprivation. In an interview by the author Beatrice Lott stated when drums signaled that ships were near not only were the children excited but her expectations were high as the cargo might bring food or other necessities. In many instances she returned empty handed. Other issues faced by workers or their offspring were more embarrassing than detrimental. In Haiti, Amilcar Exume remembers when funds would not arrive in time tuitions were not paid or utility bills became past due. While his family served in Haiti their cars or vans were forever breaking down near his junior high school and to his teen horror it was common for his friends at Union

---

[104]Interview by author with Mary Beth Kennedy, Tugbaken and Wissikeh pioneer September 2009

School, who never seemed to have that problem, to see them pushing. When the vehicle worked there was a strong possibility of running out of gas in the stifling heat as he accompanied his mother to the market. Other instance caused annoyance. They were dismayed when the water pipes gave out and rain water collected on the roof and drained into the reservoir behind the house. The Exume boys would have to pump it into holding barrels. However, it was when illness struck the children that the faith of the missionaries was severely tested. In Haiti, malaria was a particularly dreaded disease.

> My sister had malaria and almost died. She must have been about eight. Basically we didn't have any kind of health insurance and we couldn't afford the Haitian hospital. The Battles [of Minnesota] came through. They took my sister to a Haitian hospital. By American standards it wasn't...service people from the States would not have gone. They didn't diagnose her with malaria. My brother got malaria also and there was no money to take him to the hospital. As it turned out my uncle who used to work for the World Cup organization came by and he suspected that my brother had malaria. He was also a health aid kind of person and he gave him some shots and my brother got better. There was a kid that lived on our property–there was a house right behind our house–he got malaria too and he got better. They finally treated my sister.[105]

It may have been due to these kinds of reports that by the time the Kennedys Mission Station was approved the church requested that they allow their "precious little children", ages six and four, to stay in the United States, possibly boarding and continuing their education at the

---

[105]Interview by author with Amilcar Exume, oldest son of Dorothy Webster Exume

Saints Industrial and Literary School in Lexington. The Kennedys responded that when God called them into Africa He knew that they had children. They took the risk and refused to leave them behind. (In Africa all four of Chuck and Betty Kennedy's children had near death experiences.)

Despite following a strict budget when the time arrived to purchase the family's tickets the Kennedys' discovered there was money for only one adult fare and the ship that would transport them to Liberia would not reduce the children's fare.

> I checked and we had enough money for one person to go. That was all. I said if we skimp here and skimp there we might finally get enough for two people. But that was still Elder Kennedy's and my fare and we had two children and what was supposed to happen about that? So the Lord just gave me and I wrote to the owner, the CEO of the *Farrell* Steamship Line. I said the Lord has called us to go to Africa and that we both were highly qualified and that we could get good jobs here in the States. But we felt that there was a tremendous need over in Africa and we were willing to sacrifice that and go to Africa. But we did not have the money for four people. If they would let us just be in the same stateroom, the children could sleep in there with us. And we would give them food from our plate. And just let them go free.[106]

They arrived at the New York Harbor with four full fare tickets for the entire family provided by the owner with the children having their own stateroom. In her book, *A Visit to Wissikeh* Mary Kennedy describes that on the 19 to 20 day voyage none of them became seasick. Ships did not go to Cape Palmas so they safely completed the first

---

[106] ibid

leg of their journey when they arrived in Monrovia. Next they flew four hours from Monrovia to Harper, the capital of Maryland County and its largest city. The Kennedy's did not know what to expect culturally with Elder Kennedy, with limited exposure to the continent only from old Tarzan movies, having particular concern because of his color. They served at the Tugbaken Mission for one year. Unlike neighboring Congo where some Congolese experienced cruelty when Belgians cut off their hands or even slaughtered them, Liberia rightfully boasts that the country has always been free. However, Liberians suffered lack of development as there was no outside financing, like that in the Congo, to build infrastructure with comprehensive road systems. Hardwood seats placed in the back of trucks served as transportation over muddy paths. Filled with great anticipation and building excitement, the Kennedy's hired a truck to take them to Cape Palmas. As they approached the Tugbaken Mission the weight of their belongings caused the bridge to collapse and the front of the truck crashed through and fell over the bridge. At the sound of the crash the children from the mission campus were first to arrive at the accident scene. Notes Mother Kennedy, "They came pouring out of the houses and down the hill to meet us...so happy to see us. And Elder Kennedy said that his fears of Africa evaporated at that point. He wasn't afraid anymore, ever."[107]

The family settled in with the conscientious Mother Barber, worked a year at Tugbaken and became acquainted with their environment. Hostility between Americo-Liberians and native Liberians began in Liberia's national infancy based on land, commerce, superior

---

[107]ibid

attitudes by the Americans, and "light" vs. "dark" complexions among other issues. The Kennedy's had to learn and make adjustments to the Liberian culture and on the mission. For example, the couple never expected racism practiced by the Americo-Liberians against the African Liberians.

> We were so surprised when we first got to Africa because Elder Kennedy got in trouble...about it [with some who] cow towed to the Americo-Liberians. A lot of people did because they were the wealthy class. They were the ones who ran the government. The other people were definitely second, maybe third or fourth class citizens. It was very noticeable and Chuck was shocked. Knowing full well the "black" thing in America and being against that and then to go over there.
>
> Of course I was shocked too because you just don't treat people like that. For instance let's say "Carol" is Americo-Liberian and "Charley" is straight African Liberian. Carol comes in the front door and Charlie goes to the back door. Carol sits down in the living room and Charley, if you let him, sits out on the porch. I couldn't believe it when I first went there and Chuck couldn't either.[108]

Avoiding these kind of humiliating and self-image battering occurrences was crucial to the success of missionaries like the Kennedys. The fact that they were two different colors as well as they were on the mission serving a universal God who loved all peoples and cultures was a factor in teaching their children true equality. The late Charles Jr. and his siblings saw people as *individuals* with good and bad characteristics.

---

[108] ibid

The Tugbaken Overseer was very strict with fierce determination to win souls for the Lord and the Kennedy's learned much which helped them later in their own mission work. Mother Barber had a saying, *Duty Bound*, which captured her understanding of the role she played as Mission Overseer. Whether dispensing medicine, teaching school, or serving in the church she declared it was her duty as a Christian to work within her calling to Africa. For the women with children this duty and their resolve sometimes weakened when they weighed their adult decision to sacrifice for the kingdom with how the children fared. Knowing that deliverance rested with the sovereign God the unbearable became bearable and what they accomplished through duty served as further proof of the love of God to those they set out to win.

After a year at Tugbaken a delegation of men led by Bro. Jeremiah and Daniel Tobe walked 15 miles from the interior to Tugbaken. They requested that Elder Kennedy accompany them to Wissikeh, to explore the Mission Station established by Mother White now fallen into disrepair. The couple had never heard of Wissikeh but with the men insisting they needed missionaries in the interior Elder Kennedy agreed to take the journey. After inspecting the station he returned and declared that they could serve the Lord to a great extent there. They prepared to relocate to Wissikeh and hired a guide. Transportation in Liberia was by walking, dugout canoe, truck or hammock. Traveling by hammock looked as if an individual did nothing but Mother Kennedy had already found it to be rough. It would be hard but she rationalized that she was in her twenties, in reasonably good health, did not need anyone to carry her and opted to walk. With the guide leading them, surprisingly the family was not overwhelmed while stumbling up mountains and sliding down their sides as they went further into the forest to get to Wissikeh. With no real bridges they crossed rivers balancing on slippery tree trunks. If that was not enough they suffered cutting from the tall razor grass growing which hid snakes living throughout the jungle.

The bias of nature is toward wilderness and now arriving at Wissekeh Mother Kennedy agreed that the jungle takes back what belongs to it. Viewing trees growing inside the cement block frame, the buildings destroyed by termites (termite mounds were taller than adult males), everything made of wood erased and only four walls standing, the couple resolved to resurrect the work of the COGIC at Wissikeh. Since there was not even a residence for the missionaries they stayed in a mud hut while repairs were made. At Wissikeh God trained the Kennedys to be what Bower calls a true missionary team, that is, as parallel workers they expressed mutual support even though assignments may have been functionally unrelated. In the true missionary team both the husband and wife involved in creating a nurturing home environment and ideally both are enabled to find fulfillment in the stewardship of their abilities and gifts.[109]

As they worked Father Kennedy made repairs while Mother Kennedy gathered the children, initially holding classes under a nearby tree. Team work

---

[109]Bowers, Joyce EMQ, October 1985, pp. 356-359 and *Roles of Married Women Missionaries: A Case Study*, International Bulletin of Missionary Research January 1984. Bowers, a former educational missionary to Liberia with her husband identifies four role patterns and states that all are valid for the married missionary: (1) Homemaker, (2) Background Supporter, (3) Teamworker, and (4) Parallel Worker.

intact those they served were attracted to their teaching in weekly Bible studies, preaching multiple services, and offering practical solutions to problems. God opened doors and by October 1957 Paramount Chief Bannie allocated 200 acres to the missionaries as noted in his letter to Chief Hinneh of Wissikeh Town.

Riding on a hammock, Mother Barber visited the Kennedys at Wissikeh and found her mentees doing well. Their schedule was demanding but Mother Kennedy indicated that prayer and fasting regimens were key to their success. One occasion is illustrative of the Kennedy's living up to the names the Africans gave to them: Dote (he stands alone) and Kuoro (she who conquers). Elder Kennedy and the students cultivated the land and planted vegetables only to have nearby cattle destroy it. When village leaders did not respond to requests to keep the cows off the mission farm they took action.

> Wissikeh had more cows than anywhere around because cows were a measure of wealth there and people from down around Harper or other towns would bring their cows back into the jungle where they would eat and they would not have to take care of them. However, the cows from the town came in broke down our fences and ate all the vegetables and all his crop. Elder Kennedy was very, very annoyed about it. He rebuilt it and told the townspeople to keep the cows out of the garden because they were responsible for taking care of the cows. So it happened again. No matter what anybody else did if he knew it was right he was going to do it. Father Kennedy believed in peace and did not believe in fighting or war.
>
> The third time it happened, he said…we are going on a fast…and will go into the town of Wissikeh and fast until they said they would do something about the cows.

The entourage entering the village was a sight to see. The entire mission including Elder Kennedy, Mother Kennedy and their children, some of the missions children and the young people. The group stopped in the middle of the town and stayed there.

> So the people came and begged us to move. They didn't care if we were there in the daytime but then when night came and we didn't go home...they are afraid of the dark over there, they are afraid that there are evil spirits in the dark. And of course that's when a lot of the devilment does go on. It is evil spirits but it's also in human bodies. They begged us to go home. We didn't. He said as soon as you do something about those cows. They said we'll talk about it tomorrow and he said we won't go home. He was very stubborn. So I'm going to do what my husband did. I just stayed there with him. The children were going to do what we both did and they stayed too. So we all stayed there, all the mission children, we stayed there all night.

The following day village elders came and requested that they leave but did not agree to confine the cows. They again refused to leave and continued their fast which placed Mother Kennedy in a vulnerable position because of a lingering heart condition. As the sun burned hot she grew weaker and villagers, fearing she would die, sent for senior missionary Mother Barber.

> Mother Barber walked all the way from Tugbaken which is about 15 miles but she walked all the way to get there. They said she's the older missionary and she'll make them go. But she couldn't. Nobody could make Chuck do anything. He said I'll go when they do right. So she talked to them. Eventually they did say they would build a fence. And they did repair the fence. It was broken down again. But she did walk. She showed a lot of dedication on her part.

Eight miles away at Manolu Naomi Lundy experienced the same demanding schedule. Many of the newly won souls were students drawn to the missionaries teaching and eager to learn. Lundy's day began around 4:30 and a bell rang around 5:30 a.m. for morning prayers. Breakfast was next followed by another prayer by the students prior to classroom instructions taught by a missionary or native Liberian teacher. Church services followed, children completed homework by lantern light and the last patient seen after the medical clinic closed at 12am. Sometimes in the midst of their schedule they made their way to a nearby creek as Jabbeh says they had no running water and washed their clothing in the creek.

During the defined period the women entering foreign service had to rapidly adjust to cultures not having basic assistance for the poor and other infrastructures common in Western society. But they were resourceful. Rice farms were plentiful and the Mission Station also planted pumpkin. They bought meat from the hunter and burned wood to cook palm butter, soup and other dishes.

Students needed to learn new technology to move their forward in the world outside the village. Outside help was sought though sometimes the outside world brought heartache. Some struggles are just human struggles and the missionaries were sometimes hurt. President John F. Kennedy called to nation and its youth to serve the world by offering technological, educational and humanitarian assistance to poor countries. He chose Sergeant Shriver to head one of these, the U.S. Peace Corps, and agency workers fanned out across the globe in places like Liberia. One of Mother Lott's adopted daughters, Lillian, fell in love with a Peace Corps volunteer who had come to the Mission Town as a teacher. From the start Mother Lott held reservations. However, Lillian was fascinated and fell in love with the educated, learned and sophisticated man. They married and had a daughter though Lillian had difficulty in child bearing. The Peace Corps teacher abruptly decided to relocate to Angola without informing anyone. While there Lillian once again became pregnant and the mother and child died. Lott did not receive any news of this until a month after the body was sent to Los Angeles for burial, again without informing anyone. They suffered hardships and heartache but what they accomplished! Many souls were won to Christ!

Hiebert defines culture as a system of beliefs and practices that are built upon implicit assumptions that people make about themselves, about the world around them, and about ultimate realities. Despite the missionaries having an affinity with their African brothers and sisters in terms of shared ancestry there was much to learn cross culturally. They had to study and understand the host country's customs in order to convey biblical truths to the new believers. Missionaries interviewed stated emphatically that they were not there to become "spiritual police" looking for and rejecting indigenous customs as pagan. Drum beating, used in their churches back home, were considered heathen in some circles! Yet they taught that deeply rooted customs or besetting sins of having multiple wives in Liberia or visiting voodoo priests in Haiti were unbiblical and prohibitive for Christians. Having won over powerful leaders and having their support, upon accepting Christ as Savior, some children and adults became pariahs in their villages and were often treated cruelly. For example, when the missionaries provided American clothing tribe members forcibly appropriated them from students. Therefore, the basic policy was instituted that children boarding at missions stations were not allowed to go out of the mission to visit relatives for a number of months. Arriving parents or other relatives talked to them at the compound gate. Additionally, keeping the children close severed them from practicing old customs and further enculturated them into new ways of living and viewing life.

After the gospel message, education was paramount. The mission schools taught the children to speak, read and write English, sometimes in unusual ways. With little or nonexistent funding for government mandated materials and books the missionaries were compelled to innovate while waiting for help from the States. The ten year old Gaybee had never seen a car, the missionaries were without lights or electricity, the students studied by lanterns yet God blessed them with creativity. (Gbayee was saved through Mother Lott's witness to him one night.)

> Martha Barber was the teacher at the school. The majority of the people in the class didn't speak English. When we went to the school we used an interpreter - one was Peter Nimeley and the other was Gaspar Hney. We didn't have books. She created books from magazines and the drawings that she made. We used those books until someone sent some books from Chicago.
>
> When we got the books we were so happy we marched around the village for almost two days carrying the books on our heads. That's how we learned English.[110]

The leader-activists understood the need to impact those who looked up to them and trained older mission students to assist. While in high school Benjamin Jabbeh worked closely with the Kennedy's as head boy and they overcame

---

[110] Gbayee interview

the language barrier by removing him from cutting the mission compound's grass and working as their translator.

The children eagerly learned and auditorium assemblies to show off their new knowledge held precious memories for interviewees. They began these programs with prayer and Scriptures after singing the Liberian National Anthem, "*All Hail, Liberia, Hail.*" The word of the success of the mission schools spread across the area and Jabbeh reports that the Superintendent along with the principal of the Plebo High School ventured far into the forest to visit the Wissikeh School. Mother Mary Kennedy tells the story of a 29 year old man in the 5th grade, never having the opportunity to receive an education, proudly reading the Scripture at one of the school programs. Vocational guidance was given in the areas of sewing, cooking, bookkeeping and practical nursing. At the time Liberia was home to at least sixteen tribal groups with the language of commerce predominantly English. Students were taught the basics as well as English for this purpose but without widespread translations reading English enabled them to study the Bible for themselves. Curriculum at Wissikeh also included learning German, Latin, Spanish, French, Hebrew and B'Lo.

Missionaries ensured students were equipped to become productive citizens in their countries. For advanced education they sponsored a number of them in America with many beginning study at COCICs Saints Industrial and Literary School. Others graduated from American colleges and entered teaching, nursing or other professions. After five years at Tugbaken Martha Barber sponsored Alexander Gbayee's immigration to the U.S. where he attended Wheaton Academy, completed an undergraduate degree in Anthropology at Wheaton College, a Master's Degree in Education at the Loyola University in Chicago and taught school after graduation before becoming a principal for Londale Elementary School. Later this son of the Tugbakeh Mission taught college before serving his country as Liberian Consul General for Chicago and the Midwest.

Outside the United States the work of the women was regulated but not tightly controlled. This arena provided them opportunity to ascend beyond their ascribed role in the gender based American society. These servants performed the ordinances of the church, evangelized and were the primary overseers. With notable exceptions of Elder Sullivan (early missionary to Sierra Leone), Bishop A.B. McEwen, Bishop Esau Courtney, Bishop Richard Fidler, Elder O.T. Jones, Jr., Elder Charles E. Blake, Evangelist Archie Buchanan, Father Charles Kennedy, Bishop Samuel Crouch, and Bishop Carlis Moody few COGIC ministers ventured past Monrovia or Port au Prince in the early days of missions. This may have been because COGIC men, many married with children at a young age, would have to figure out a way to sustain their families. Nevertheless, those raw foreign fields were tough and Bishop Carlis Moody remembers walking seven miles through dense bush to visit the Wissekeh Mission when the group was unable to use the roads. Yet the women availed themselves to taking charge of the work.

Early missionaries received basic missionary medical training prior to joining the foreign service. Pearl Page Brown attended Biola School of Missionary Medicine. There she received instruction on how to pull teeth, treat tropical diseases, public health, sanitation, laboratory science, pharmacology, and therapy. Medical clinics were stocked with gallon cans of Vaseline, penicillin tablets and injections, sterile gauze, adhesive tape, iodine, camphor phenique, snake bite kits, castor oil, turpentine, Phenobarbital, nose drops, sulphaquidine for dysentery, chloraquinne tablets and injections for malaria and first aid kits. Jabbeh was later trained to work in the medical clinic and took blood pressure. On a typical day they treated ulcerated and infected legs (penicillin and sulfa powder), victims of leprosy were referred to nearby leper colonies, yaws (a disfiguring and crippling disease) or a child brought unconscious after witch doctors could not resuscitate her.[111]

The COGIC Haiti was established in 1929 after Joseph Paulceus, an early 1920s convert of street evangelist (later International Supervisor) Annie Pennington Bailey, returned to his country.[112] (For information on establishment of COGIC in Haiti see Chapter 11.) Bishop Joseph St. Juste was appointed as the first Overseer of Haiti's COGIC by Bishop A.B. McEwen, who had complete oversight of all foreign field work for the denomination. The Church in Haiti grew rapidly. Bishop Louis Sauveur St. Juste succeeded his father to the bishopric. He was followed after ten years of service by Bishop Esau Courtney, who served three years. Bishop Lopez Dautruche was appointed to the bishopric in 1974.[113]

Dorothy Webster (Exume) was the first American administrative missionary to the country. She was also the first assigned female African American missionary to

---

[111] Kennedy, Mother Mary Beth, *A Visit to Wissikeh*, 5/28/58, 1, 7-12
[112] Goodson, 28
[113] Noble, 170-171

Haiti and Haiti's first female Pentecostal missionary.[114] It was Exume who persuaded Bishop Mason to purchase land in the country and founded the COGIC school and orphanage in Haiti in the 1940s, adding much to the work. Day to day activities were strenuous but rewarding and the scope of her work went beyond the role of a social service worker or administrator. Realizing that she would do well to live permanently among the community she did so and began caring for the poor. Exume rescued orphans from off the streets as well as from cold hospital rooms. Her official day started at 6:00 a.m. and ended at almost midnight, seven days a week. Early mornings she ensured that the orphanage's children were fed and completed morning devotions long before daylight then checked on the school and orphanage operations. As the dawn broke individuals from the community gathered at the front gate for food and medical distribution. Her youngest son Fronz explains

> We were involved in missions work from the time we were able to talk and walk. We moved to a house in the Belmont area where it was typical for the house to have a gate and a wall. There are times when the people who congregated at the gate were so numerous that mom shifted the policy and they had to line up. The Haitians arrived at the house as early as I can remember to request help. Mom would spend time at the gate to receive them or [Almicar, the oldest, Marlil or I] would go to the gate and bring back word who was out there and tell her what they needed. Mom would send them food, soap, money for medication, nutritional supplements. There are times when the people would come to the porch."[115]

---

[114]Ibid, 171
[115]Fronz Exume interview

Next, Exume and her driver Michelle Dijuste dropped her children off at school before going into town to purchase what was needed. Amilcar Exume observed his mother exercising faith in their daily ritual to the post office. More often than not, a check would await her with a note saying the sender was thinking about her. While the children waited, sometimes completing homework in the customs office Exume "spent hours at customs...to get the clothes and other things people sent to Haiti. Barrels of stuff. She would go to one official and negotiate and she'd get shuttled to another one. They got tired of her and gave her the barrels." As a mother Exume further wished to have her children grounded in their American culture while appreciating the diversity of their adopted home. Fluent in Creole, Fronz relates "Mom refused to speak to us in Creole. She refused to respond in Creole. She did not want us to lose our fluency in English." She made sure that during Christmas they visited American families like the Turnbulls where they ate turkey and mango pie. She ensured her children were balanced. There was no television to keep them occupied so they jumped rope, played marbles or *cayes*, a rock game, with their friends. Their mother somehow found funds to purchase bicycles and loaded with lunch sacks containing butter or peanut butter sandwiches, the children went exploring. She also wanted them to understand they were to respect all persons including those they observed were in need of basic sustenance. The Exume children studied American curriculum at Union School, an American private school grades 1-12, learning alongside children whose parents worked at the U.S. Embassy, the children of corporate executives and some Haitians.

> Union school is still open. We were taught French as a second language. The books, grading, grade promotion was based on the American system. When a student leaves there their transition to an American school will be seamless. We learned alongside these children after which we would be involved with street children. I'd play with little buddies in the street in the neighborhood living in one room shanties and on the same day played with children living in multimillion dollar mansions without drawing a distinction. Mom had us grounded in a good way.[116]

While missionaries oversaw the church and schools, when personal refreshing was needed they attended local or denominational churches. In Haiti Bel 'air was a thriving church where they worshipped in English. A Church Of God In Christ, Bel 'Air, was established in Haiti by Mother Annie Bailey's protégé, Joseph Paulceus sometime around 1929-1930. This may have been the church Exume would have attended until it was destroyed by Hurricane Flora in October 1962.

International missionaries synthesized their main role identity as mother with their mission's related work. (Pearl Page Brown states that her daughter Eleanor traveled over 20,000 miles with her as she shared the gospel.) Dorothy Exume returned to the United States for the birth of each of her children but soon after returned to Haiti to care for her other children, the orphanage students. Exume's daughter, Marlil Provost explains being taken to the country during her mother's Haitian mission work:

> I was born in Los Angeles but my mother took me to Haiti before I was a year old. My time there was in and

---

[116] ibid

out but I stayed there until 6th grade. There is documentation where [Mother] established churches there and turned them over to men. She was instrumental in the House of Refuge which is now a major work. It was at that time funded by Dr. Walter Battle of Minneapolis and his wife Dr. Willa Battle. She founded the Mason School and others. Ebony did an article on her in the 1950s.[117]

How does a young person find God or why would individuals look for hope in some of the world's most impoverished areas? Experiential knowledge gained by offspring of international missionaries would impact them for a lifetime. For foreign missionaries and their children life was about serving God and everything was measured in terms of how God's children were served. To those served the missionaries were the face of Jesus. They were not only sharing food or medicine but the kindness of God. Exume's children remembered that she gave what she had and if vegetables from the market or cans of herring were not available, she fished in her pocket book and found coins. They learned and listened to the challenges of the work and frequently accompanied Exume to the home of Bishop St. Juste. Though paralyzed from a car accident, the administrator used his keen intellect to cultivate a cadre of young men emphasizing holiness first and education. Fronz Exume says he appreciates the fact that his mother felt that, although they were young, they were *persons* with the ability to do God's work and noted they were always an integral part of whatever goal his mother sought to accomplish. There was time for play of course but the suffering he observed as a child was immediate and not theoretical. Even at a

---

[117]Provost interview

young age he was intrinsically aware that his mother modeled what it meant to speak directly to suffering by providing sustenance. More importantly women like Exume pointed individuals to the way out that came from what he termed transformative possibility. "When she [gave] people food she blessed it. She would encourage and affirm them to find God in their life."

The missionaries used funds economically, not always building entirely new facilities but added to existing structures. Schools were usually named for Stateside pastors and others who sponsored the facilities. Mother Exume brought Bishop Mason to Haiti where he reviewed the work of the *C.H. Mason School* (he was scheduled to return in 1960 but did not, perhaps due to illness). Another educational facility, the *Odessa Newman School*, was named for a Texas Northeast Jurisdictional Supervisor who continued foreign missions support of her predecessor, the educator Jurisdictional Supervisor Emma F. Barron[118] who assisted in sustaining the Haitian work through annual visits and consistent funding.

Other COGIC schools included the *Roy and Mae Winbush School*, and the *Ella Deans School*. Pastor Emanuel John, born in Port au Prince, was a student as Mason Elementary. Those going to foreign fields planting churches overall mirrored the church structure of U.S. headquarters adding bonding and consistency across the

---

[118] Like Mother Cora Berry and Mother L.O. Hale in California, Barron is legendary in Texas circles as one its premier educators. One of the first female graduates of Prairie View A&M College (Class of 1915), she was the first assistant principal of COGICs Page Normal School located on 300 acres in Hearne, Texas which closed after burning down in 1927. She not only funded missions but also paid for students to travel to America and underwrote their education.

globe. It also helped that newly won converts sent representatives back and forth to America each year for holy convocation. Children adopted by the missionaries gained insight in the working of COGIC U.S.A. policies and shared this knowledge upon their return. John's mother Missionary Emilia Liberius John served as District Missionary of the Thomassin District and worked closely with Mother Exume. With sisters such as Missionary John and Missionary Ann Stewart much was accomplished in the church through Department of Women's teaching. Others were supported through monthly funding. According to Bernice Abrams, caretaker for Mother Emma Crouch, long before her appointment as International Supervisor she sent thousands of dollars to Mother Webster Exume's orphanage and girls she adopted. Mother Crouch kept detailed journals of her life. In 1970 she writes in her diary of a visit to Haiti (stopping to encourage the work in Jamaica) where she worked at the orphanage, visited churches and provided funds and training.

Innovative thinking was critical and a hallmark of those working in mission fields. When funds were not available to purchase undies, Exume found a way to fashion panties for the girls using flour and grain sacks sometimes donated by President John F. Kennedy's U.S. Agency for International Development. The large sacks were delivered to the orphanage by U.S. Marines or a call would come from the U.S. Embassy for a pick up. Fronz remembers his mother toiling often through the night pedaling the sewing machine to make the panties. Each sack featured an emblem of an American flag and two hands shaking. "When they washed them and hung them on the line you would see a portion of the emblem [from the flour or feed company] on the panties! In terms of missions work and values she was indispensable."

Missionaries found it made sense that citizens of host countries serve as officials at their schools. In Haiti some outstanding educators included Leon Tamphile, Luce Derates and principal Sylvia Dessource.

> "[COGIC] had an all girls orphanage and a school. At that time our school went from grade one to grade six. The principal and all the teachers were Haitian and we learned mathematics, reading, writing and French. Every school in Haiti required uniforms and ours were green shirts or blouses for the girls and our pants were khaki.[119]

Exume and other Black Americans did not bring a lot of money into the country of Haiti. They brought faith in a God of endless possibilities even in the midst of suffering and pushed education as a means of escaping poverty. Through sharing herself totally and identifying with the suffering of Haiti—whether the need was for food, medicine or education—Exume gave herself so freely that she impacted a generation. Exume served as priest, missionary and pastor, however, some took umbrage when Haitians and others referred to her as the Mother Theresa of her day. She demonstrated that living a life of sacrifice brought temporal and eternal rewards and hope caused the Haitians to look up. Haitians loved America

---

[119]Interview by author with Pastor Emanuel John, former C.H. Mason Elementary School student in Haiti. He would leave Mason after 6th grade to attend Lycee Alexander Petion Public School and after graduation enrolled in Freres Salien College where he majored in Business but affirms that fundamental to his success was the teaching received at Mason. He currently pastors Lake Station, Indiana's Christ Temple COGIC and oversees two Haitian churches, Carrefour-feuille and La Tournelle.

and their American guests. After a group of missionaries and leaders from America visited their church and no interpreter was available then eight year old John knelt before God and promised if He would teach him English he would give the gift back to him. His mother purchased books written in English as well as a French to English dictionary. By ten or eleven years old he was fluent in the English language and became one of the official interpreters for incoming COGIC officials.[120] Later Exume's children would also interpret for visiting preachers.

During his tenure as Bishop of Haiti, Bishop Esau Courtney was known for his love and enthusiasm for the country. Former members recall that he never arrived empty handed, preparing weeks and months in advance gathering items from anyone who would donate. Webster-Exume welcomed the groups he led there, including his family, and the medical supplies, clothing, food and other needed items the teams helped her to distribute to poor Christian and non-Christians. His fervor caused some to liken his work to a personal mission. Initially traveling to the country twice a year his visits became so frequent that he finally built a residence

---

[120] COGIC had a keen interest in nearby Haiti with many officials traveling back and forth from the U.S. John interpreted for a Who's Who among COGIC Leadership: Bishop Esau Courtney accompanied by Bishop Guidry of New Jersey, Bishop F.D. and Mother Ernestine Washington, Bishop Carlis Moody, Mother Louise Cryer, Mother Mary Melvin (she provided funds to build a cultural center where young women learn history, sewing, and cooking as well as other arts), Mother Mary Walton, Sis Lucille Bazemore, Mother Mary Gullick, Elder Havious Green, Bishop J.S. Bailey, Mother Annie Bailey, Pastor Robert Brown, Bishop Melvin Clark, Superintendent James Lee, Supt. Bobbie Moore, Bishop Barnett Thorogood, Bishop J.W. Denny, Mother Odessa Newman.

there, hiring a houseboy to oversee it during his absence. He was a favorite with the children. After his meeting with the pastors, he held Bible Bowls for students rewarding the child with the correct answer pennies, a dime or quarter from a large bag of coins he collected just for those occasions. Humor added to bonding and commitment with Stateside officials, sometimes in the middle of cultural confusion. John tells the story of garbled translations on one of Bishop Esau Courtney's visits.

> "One thing I remember well about him when I was first learning how to communicate in English. He sponsored a little girl, Fifi, for school. He came one day and didn't see her and asked, 'where's my gal?' No one else spoke English so they turned to me because they wished to know what he was saying. I said I don't know what gal is. I finally said, the bishop wants a gol! A gol is a poking stick. If you have a mango tree you use the gol to knock the mangoes down. Wishing to please the bishop the people took off running and they came in with the sticks. He asked, John what did you tell the people? When I came to understand I realized what it was."[121]

Other cross cultural encounters, though humorous years later, were potentially dangerous. The year 1961 was pivotal in the life of the Civil Rights movement with nonviolent youth in the forefront. Following the direction of James Farmer and the Congress of Racial Equality they risked their lives as Freedom Riders journeying into the brutality of the Bull Connors South. America, at war with itself, was ridiculed by Communist Russia and other countries for demanding freedom in the world while allowing mobs sanctioned by local law enforcement to beat its citizens. After especially brutal attacks by Ku

---

[121] John Interview

Klux Klan inspired mobs in Alabama and Mississippi seemed to stall the student movement Diane Nash, a student at Fisk University, rallied fellow students to move forward. Benjamin Jabbeh entered a country taut with unresolved racial tensions. He arrived in New Orleans August 28, 1961 on his way to Saints College in Lexington, Mississippi. Although he had been advised on prejudice and racism he did not understand that Blacks were not intended to enter restaurants through the front door or eat with whites.

> Prior to coming to the United States, my cousin Lillian Lott who lived in the U.S. with Mother Lott had graduated and returned back to Liberia with Mother Lott to teach on the mission at Tugbaken. She said when I go to the U.S. to order hamburger and Coke. Once I arrived in New Orleans, I found a restaurant and noticed a sign on the front door "White Only." In the back there was a sign for "Negroes." I did not go to the back door but decided to go through the front door with my Liberian cap on my head. When the white customers saw the Black man come in and recognized the African cap, they told me I could eat there. The white girl asked me what I wanted to eat and I ordered a hamburger and Coke.[122]

Added to the fact that he had miscued a cultural taboo in the volatile 1960s there was no one there to meet him to take him to the campus. Fortunately, he found a taxi that charged him $12.00 for the trip to Lexington.

The activities of the Black Pentecostal missionaries demonstrated the compassion of Christ toward the Jew and the Gentile, the male and the female, the bond and

---

[122]Interview by Marva Nyema with Benjamin Jabbeh January 2010. Jabbeh went on to become the National Director for the Kennedy's Community of Caring nonprofit organization in Liberia.

the free. Yet these actions were tempered by their duty to teach their brothers and sisters the responsibilities required as new technology entered their way of living. Mission overseers understood when individuals are poor or destitute like the subsistence farmers encountered in African Liberian villages, they can easily fall into a trap of entitlement. Using the motto *"Help yourself first, and somebody will help you,"* these leader-activists left an indelible mark on the countries they served both within the church and without. Muslim Mandingo traders were very sophisticated in commerce having long monopolized trade among those living in the interior. Now missions students, who worked mainly as farmers, with increasing numbers migrated from villages. The missionaries taught the value of being paid money for hard work done outside the farm. One former Liberian student recalled that after arising at 4:30 or 5:00 in the morning to wash then pray, they had their breakfast, attended morning church, then completed their "contract work" before going to school. The contract work entailed gathering rocks or hauling sand in five gallon containers. After school they cut wood, the boys dug sand at the creek with the girls carrying the buckets on their heads. For this they were paid two cents per day and purchased hair grease or bought combs. Some of their wages were given in the Bishop Mason, Esther, Ruth or Deborah Sunday School classes. None of the children minded the hard work or sharing their money; they were just happy to live on the campus.

> For us it was a wonderful thing earlier. We didn't have schools up there. Monrovia is not like Chicago or NY but the opportunity or facilities for churches were there. The government didn't build any school in our particular area. The missionaries being there was a blessing. We were

> learning English and learning how to read and write. As far as work is concerned we were doing just like the villages. We had a rice farm. Then we had bananas for the students on the mission because the missionaries didn't have that much money to buy anything. There was no electricity and all we used was kerosene lighting.
>
> I left the Tugbakeh mission and went to another mission at a Baptist for high school in Monrovia. When I came back Mother Lott had electricity with generator.
>
> The major progress of the missionary was soul service. They built a church house. Most of the time we were doing memory work when we couldn't read things like The Lord is my Shepherd. The major concern of the missionaries was the church so we went to church. For the missionaries it was an opportunity to share the word and do God's work. We went from village to village carrying the gospel. Sometimes in the Christmas season we went from several of the villages. Some days we may go to this village to preach. That is what they were doing.
>
> We played soccer. We had several other of the games we played at home like wrestling. We had running. Missionary Barber taught us how to play baseball.[123]

Because they released themselves to obey their assignment completely, the missionaries overcame any apprehensions they may have had about traveling deep into the jungles amidst poisonous snakes, leopards or other wild animals. Sam Boley recalls that prior to Robert B. Letourna leading a government project and built a fifty or sixty mile road, four young men at a time took shifts carrying the women in hammocks from village to village as they spread the gospel, carried medicine deep into the jungle or visited other Mission Stations. He explained that the missionaries

---

[123] Sam Boley interview

"gave us our beginning…and all of them were wonderful."

The teaching did not stop at basic education but encompassed the spectrum of their lives.

1. **The importance of record keeping.** They taught them to keep meticulous records of what the Lord accomplished through the Mission Towns. Mother Lott even kept ledgers showing every individual from the village who paid for their child's uniform themselves.

2. **Practical wisdom.** The missionaries also taught practical lessons that many former students live by today: *"do not let the sun go down upon you when you have done something wrong"* or *"never be too proud that you cannot reconcile your mistake."*

3. **Purity was stressed.** One way they helped ensure students received the lessons they offered in living an empowered life through Jesus Christ was by stressing to them to avoid fornication. And since healthy physical attraction causes the same emotions in every culture, at Wissikeh Elder Kennedy was faithful in getting up in the middle of the night to guarantee that the boys were safely in their beds and not in the girls' rooms. Nah said that during all the years she lived at the mission only one girl became pregnant.

4. **They demonstrated sacrifice.** Many times the missionaries paid the student contract workers and others before paying themselves but sometimes there was no money at all.

5. **Christ's love meets every need.** After establishing an orphanage, African Liberian women brought their

children to the Mission Station and left them because they could not care for them. Others, whose mothers had died, were also brought to live on the campus.

Young women serving on foreign fields originated from Ohio, Illinois, Georgia, Texas, Pennsylvania and around the country. Though progress was slowly being made in upward mobility some entering foreign service witnessed the harsh existence of blacks while living in the South or heard of atrocities perpetuated against Blacks during annual furloughs. In the North, some experienced a different kind of inequality when men, skilled in trades, were prohibited from union membership. America, a nation of laws, would slowly though sometimes violently cure inequities through legislation. Until that was done, brave young men and women on the home front were willing to risk their lives for a better tomorrow in America through sitting in or bus boycotts. As a result they were attacked, beaten and jammed in jail cells without beds or sufficient water. The missionaries in Africa, Haiti and other locales also sacrificed for the cause of Christ but tread carefully meeting opposition, sometimes formidable, with faith. Having the mind to make a difference where God planted them they too transformed societies. When women encountered by the missionaries sought better living and educational opportunities for their children the missionaries offered free (or subsidized) public education in schools they established and nurtured them in orphanages they built all the while relying on God to sustain their efforts.

Indigenous women who sent their children to the missions' schools—both boys and girls—supported the women and shared what they had: encouragement, cola nuts, palm butter or monkey meat and other offerings given to show their appreciation.

From many conversations with her mother Marlil Provost reports that Exume had no initial plans to open a Haitian girl's orphanage. After discovering that Sis. Doris Burks had a place for girls but was unable to feed them, out of necessity she went to work gathering whatever government documents and private funding she could to assist the women and children. Later the COGIC would take over but the home, still in operation, is a testament to Mother Exume's labor of love. Exume rescued children, one or two at a time, she found in the abandoned baby rooms at the Haitian hospital lying on cold floors, suffering from parasites and other major health issues. Others had living mothers who pretended to be aunts or cousins when placing their children in their care.

> There was a doctor on a monthly basis for the orphanage and other doctors helped. She was the director of that orphanage until the mid 70s when she left the orphanage in the hands of Lucille Hayward who was originally from California. Later, Bishop Dar'trouche…came in and asked Sis. Hayward for the certificates so the church could take over the orphanage. From that point until now it has been completely in the hands of the church. [Mother] had concerns for the older girls as they graduated from high school. A lot of those girls stayed in Haiti with impoverished lives [but] she provided trade schooling for some [and] many were able to go to college…becoming nurses and other professionals. That was the first group.[124]

Mother Coffey and Mother Elsie Mason were ardent supporters and personally donated medicine and funds

---

[124]Provost interview

for schools and orphanages. They may have assisted Exume in completing the Brook Camphene Housing Project a development in which she was intricately involved from planning, purchasing materials, and selecting individuals to be housed. Bishops assisted financially and traveled there to perform manual labor. They were led by God on how to carry out each detail in their lives of teaching those who looked to them for instruction. One area in which single missionaries could have proved vulnerable was their ability to instruct non-Christian women on the principles of Christian marriage and motherhood. They exemplified femininity but their words could have rang hollow as they were neither wives nor mothers. One missionary stated that when asking God how to relate to married women the voice of the Lord told her to "just teach the Word." And at these facilities fathers, mother and children of the host countries were taught, counseled and the Word of God was explained by the American "Mothers." Although a history of prejudice by Americo-Liberians persisted well into the sixties, most newly arriving COGIC missionaries viewed the aborigines not as heathen but recognized them as children of a universal Father.[125] Seeing the missionary's working together while treating them with dignity, students gladly labored for their food and helped any way they could. Some students were chosen to take care of the missionaries while others served as cooks. Beatrice Nah, a budding thirteen year old, recalls living at Tugbaken.

> My auntie carried me to the school at the mission in 1957. The people used to carry their boys and girls there. I went to school for awhile then I learned to

---

[125]Kennedy, Betty Lee, *A Letter from Liberia*, Whole Truth Magazine, April 1957

cook, clean and wash for Mother Lott. People had different missions. Mother White was the first missionary at Wissekeh. Mother Ragland was the first one at Tugbaken, and Mother Wiggins was in Monolu. Mother Barber and Mother Lott came to Tugbaken. When Mother Lott came, Mother Lundy was [in Manolu]. I saw Mother June Blackwell when she was in Manolu and Mother Lundy. Mother Blackwell died by accident after she returned from Africa. After Mother Lott went back, Mother Paul. Brother Abraham was in charge when they left. [126]

At Tugbaken Beatrice Lott cared for orphans, fed and clothed them and taught them about Christ. Some native African or Haitian children were adopted. In Exume's case many of the adoptions were not always conventional. Finding a baby or small children abandoned on the street or lying in a cold hospital room she brought them to the orphanage.

> There were occasions where children would be abandoned and mom would take them into the orphanage. She placed her name on their birth documents or would say 'put my name there' and the girls would have our family name. There were times when some of the girls from the orphanage would come and live with us in Haiti or the U.S. All the girls were pretty much adoptees and mom thought of all them as her daughters. Even after they left the orphanage mom continued relations with the women.[127]

Some native Liberians felt that if a child's mother died giving birth the child was evil and no one wanted the child in their homes. The child would be abandoned and given nothing to eat until it died. Ester Boley was one

---

[126] Interview by author with Beatrice Nah, former Tugbakeh Missions student currently of Rochester, Minnesota October 2010.

[127] Interview by author with Fronz Exume, youngest son of Dorothy Exume

such child when Mother Lott found her and adopted her as her own. The belief persisted and when Mother Lott returned from furlough she found Ester abused. She hid because she did not wish Mother Lott to see her body covered with sores. When she came out Mother Lott embraced her and vowed never to leave her again. She officially adopted her, brought her to America and sent her to private schools.

Francina Wiggins

CHAPTER SEVEN

Signs and Wonders Followed Them

Some women working in evangelism and ministry have experienced difficulty in finding a free course to operate in the fullness of their calling. While facing doubt in their ability to work in this area they also fought to overcome prejudices in order to obey their God given calling. Yet those who persevered in their assignment were rewarded with the satisfaction of knowing that God was pleased with their lives. Kelly Willis Mendiola notes an interesting dream 1880s writer Anna Shipton tells causing her to understand that women as well as men were called by God. Shipton stands in an open house next to a river and her persona in the dream asks "Why does a man's hand (that is, physical strength) cast with greater power and distance than a woman's?" Shipton describes feebly throwing bread onto the waters to have it wash back to shore. But then a miracle happens: "As I spoke, life came into the scattered morsels, as if it had suddenly been transformed, and it made its way unassisted by the waters into the midst of the broad river." Shipton then presents the bizarre central image of the dream: "I saw a woman who walked on the water, sometimes feeding birds, and sometimes working with a spade: she looked neither to the right nor to the left; she was not watching for results like me, but always at her work. A little while and I saw her *beneath* the water, and then waves, transparent even in the darkness, flowed over her head; but she still kept faithfully at her work, never raising her head, but delving patiently in making deeper channels for the river. I saw that it was not sand she threw out, but heavy clay and loam." The women fervently believed that, when He wished, God could make their contributions count for something. The central image of the dream, the woman patiently and untiringly working above and beneath the water, is symbolic of...unnumbered and unnamed women...who went about the work of comforting, inspiring and challenging those around them through the language of evangelical religion. [128]

By the early 20th century the work of religious women in the United States was still relegated to teaching while preaching fell under the male's domain. Those called into the presbytery as international missionaries of the COGIC did not necessarily attempt to change the culture. However, they responded to their call and overcame gender challenges in mighty fine ways indeed with signs and wonders accompanying their preaching. In Africa and other countries before native pastors were trained these pioneers demonstrated skills God equipped them with to do the work of ministry. Understanding that they were individually empowered by God to plan and carry out the work, they performed miracles of salvation, healing, and deliverance. In the midst of evangelizing they developed entire mission towns. In Haiti and Africa

---

[128]Mendiola, 1-2

they were involved in entrepreneurial activities, acting as general contractors or negotiating prices for rice sold from their farms. They united couples in Christian marriage, buried the dead and conducted the sacraments of the church. Beatrice Nah remembers missionaries journeying from town to town preaching the gospel as well as the fellowship of the missionaries when they walked the eight miles from Manolu to Tugbaken or fifteen miles to Wissikeh. She recalls that church services were very nice and "the missionaries used to preach and then they had some pastors." Music served as an entrance of revealed religion and a convenient way to teach the native Africans. "Most of the time before Mother Lott preached on Sundays we sang songs taught from the hymnbook. A favorite was *Jesus Keep Me Near the Cross.* When people would die Mother Lott would do the funeral. She married people too. This was before she trained the men to become pastors. She trained Gasper Hinah to be pastor.[129]

The Great Commission is about kingdom disciple making and as God continued to work through them new disciples were gained. While stories are told of solid foundations being laid for spiritual growth, some individuals imposed their views and opinions with the result of seeming to make disciples for themselves. Speaking to the danger of making western culture the message an Indian evangelist said "Do not bring us the gospel as a potted plant. Bring us the seed of the gospel and plant it in *our* [italics added] soil."[130] Missionaries

---

[129] Beatrice Nah interview
[130] Hiebert, Paul G. *Cultural Differences and the Communication of the Gospel.* www.uscwm.org/uploads/pdf/psp/hiebert_cultural.pdf

interviewed understood this tendency and were in constant in prayer for God to show them the way to lead. COGIC missionaries like Lundy were careful not to impose Western interpretations of the gospel on the Liberians but said they stuck to teaching *God's truth*. On weekends teams traveled further into the jungle teaching and preaching and individual tribe members accepted Jesus Christ as Lord and Savior. Lundy says in one village "the Lord said teach them what Moses gave – the *Ten Commandments*. The Spirit of the Lord came in that place and they danced!" Gbayee spoke of powerful preaching by the missionaries and Liberian national preachers where "we witnessed rich, rich, rich experiences. We would sing in our dialects then either Mother Barber or Mother Lott preached. Old men who talked the dialect would assist them in ministering. Once, when Mother Barber preached about *a Short Hand Writing on the Wall* the Spirit came and fell on us and it took [us up] almost a week or so. Missionary Lott preached about the children of Israel coming across the River Jordan and the Spirit lasted for weeks. "Once Robert Kuma, a native preacher, stayed out in the woods for three days. When he came and preached it looked like the whole area shook when the Holy Spirit came in." The Holy Ghost was also performing signs and wonders in Haiti with several accounts of Haitians who only spoke and understood Creole, praising the Lord or prophesying in the English language.

International missionaries including Webster-Exume demonstrated that God was faithful in shoring up their emotional and physical courage while working in impoverished countries. Despite suffering they were committed. When Beatrice Lott broke her arm she allowed it to mend then quickly made up for lost time. She also suffered from amoebic dysentery and to the day of her death only drank bottled water. Mary Beth Kennedy saw each of her four children at the point of death. God was faithful in healing them all and they left a legacy of trusting God.

Following Webster in Haiti were Missionary Anna Jewell McKenzie and the diminutive Pearl Page Brown the latter going on to visit twenty-seven countries, ministering in most as well as the U.S., and the Honduras. She served at Missions Stations at Manolu, Liberia for three years and in Haiti. At times the Christian foreign service worker did not realize the extent that the multidimensional aspects of obeying their call would come to include facing unknown encounters. A report of the Baptist minister who had fallen into the Cavalla River and was eaten by crocodiles could have deterred them from purpose. However, they were constantly online with God and when facing obstacles like crossing dangerous, crocodile infested rivers, the Lord always brought them to victory. The refrain of all international missionaries interviewed was that their tours brought a source of joy, peace, strength, spiritual rest and inspiration despite the danger. Pearl Page Brown took the gospel to the jails, hospitals, market places and to the Firestone Rubber Plantation. She remembers crossing the Cavalla in a leaking boat in order to spread the gospel with the Lord protecting them from dangers unseen.

> We were so close to death this beautiful sunny afternoon. We hired the truck on the French [West Ivory Coast] side to drive us to the nearest town to [get to the Cavalla River]. This was a big help because, when we finally reached the town we only had to walk one hour to the Cavalla River to wait for a canoe to carry us back to Liberia. God was with us: men, women, girls and boys

were delivered miraculously, the power of the Holy Ghost was poured out upon believers as we laid hands upon them. There was no beautiful Church Building, in fact there was no church at all, but glory hallelujah God was there with His Mighty Miracle working power to deliver these precious souls, under a brush arbor.

We can truly say that the Angel of the Lord encampeth round about them that fear Him, and delivereth them. This is exactly what happened to us. The driver of the truck could not understand why his truck would not go further, we were about fifty feet over a river on a poorly constructed bridge and the right side of the floor of the bridge had broken, the front right and rear wheels of the truck had slipped off the edge, and God sent His angels to stand in front of the truck to hold it back and would not let it go any further. If the truck had moved another inch it would have meant death to all seventeen of us. God spared our lives, the men jacked the truck up and rebuilt that side of the bridge and we were blessed to return to Liberia with a glorious report of victory.[131]

Other perils were imposed by the elements and wild animals. Once as a man walked through the jungle with gun cocked, he felt something pulling his leg and a 16 foot python had him. He killed the snake and made his way to the Mission Station where Mother Lott placed medicine and bandages on what was left of his leg. The natives ate the snake meat after removing the man's leg and a baby deer from it. Mother Lott kept the skin, using it as an illustration during furloughs. Texas Superintendent James E. Hornsby remembered the saints switching off lights during Texas Holy Convocations to watch the

---

[131] Page, Pearl *Africa Missions in Action International, Church Of God In Christ*, 22

35mm reels on which the snakeskin was shown. She left the snakeskin with Dr. Mallory, a strong mission's supporter.

Spiritual constructs formed from their relationship with God and His power assisted those serving in Africa or Haiti when encountering behavior attributed to demonic domains. When questioned regarding the tremendous healing and deliverance found in 21st Africa Uganda Prelate Bishop Bobby Henderson (COGIC Vice President of International Department of Missions) states that once Africans, long associated and familiar with the supernatural, understand that God's power is the greatest power in the universe and it is He that loves them and longs to set them free they receive His deliverance from all manner of sickness and disease. When confronted by demonic activity caused by control by witch doctors and other behavior from unbelievers these female pioneers did not back down but stood in the authority of Jesus Christ and dealt with it. Amilcar Exume remembers "the church way of looking at things was that they would not dispute them but told them that Jesus' power was greater than all that. Haitian worldview was magical…superstitious… [and] considered that spirits were all around. Hearing voodoo drums I remember having nightmares when I was young. If you walk to your front door and you saw some dirt in a pile in America you would be upset because someone put dirt in your yard. In Haiti it may have been a spiritual hex… [but] you would plead the blood of Jesus and you didn't worry about hexes." In Liberia missionaries dealt with incidents ranging from annoyance when tribal chiefs did nothing about cows breaking into missions gardens where students and teachers planted cassava, oranges, butter pears (Americans call them avocado), guava, greens, sweet potatoes, corn, cucumbers, pineapples, bananas and plantains to overcoming fear of those being threatened by witch doctors.

Abraham Brown's conversion is an example of God's power setting the captive free from sin and superstition. The Assemblies of God arrived in Liberia some time before the COGIC missionaries and that Pentecostal group birthed the mission's work of Rev. William Brown, Elizabeth White, Bishop Abraham Brown and others. (Abraham Brown would serve the COGIC as interpreter, carpenter, Mission Town overseer, Dean at Saints College and become a bishop in the Church Of God In Christ.) Brown accepted salvation after hearing a message about the love and power of Jesus Christ from relatives who had been saved and healed through the AG ministry. He remembers that as a child his family offered sacrifice to idol gods, represented by teeth and hands, on hills and creeks. His cousin attended the AG mission school, got saved, came back to the village and preached the Ten Commandments. Brown's brother had cancer and the witch doctors, after placing potions around his neck and instructing him not to take a bath or wear cloth for a year, could not heal him. Then his brother was saved and healed through the ministry of the AG missionaries. The miraculous healing convinced villagers that the power of God was great and curious but skeptical boys like Abraham Brown wanted to learn more.

> We worshipped idols and [now I said] they got on my nerves saying the idol can't talk, can't see or do anything. Now [they said] it's wrong to commit adultery, to steal. The [idols] my daddy got in his house, they say it's not God. But my older brother got healed of the bone sickness, got saved and filled with the Holy Ghost. It was some power! One night when we went to church [the

> preacher] he said to me if you lift your hand and confess that you believe in Jesus Christ as a Savior born of God then He saves and you are a saved man. The things you used to do then you don't do them no more. And give yourself to the Lord and you pray until the Baptism of the Holy Ghost come upon you. And the Holy Ghost will give you strength anytime you want to commit sin.
>
> I was young but I listened very keenly. One night we went to the church that was in a house. No church at that time. We worshipped in people's houses. When the power of the Lord hit me and I started speaking in tongues my mother took me out and poured water on me. She got so mad. She thought it was an evil spirit that would get on me because foam was coming out of my mouth. It seemed like the more she poured cold water on me the higher I got. So she struggled with me all night until the Spirit went down. That was 1934.[132]

COGIC missionaries fanned out encountering resistance from family members and witchcraft practitioners firmly standing on the truth of God's word. They did not deny that the enemy had power. They told the Liberians that the power God was mightier than anything witch doctors could do. Peeples recalls a witch doctor's attack on Beatrice Lott and those at Tugbaken by killing a goat and having indigenous members drink the blood while it was warm. "On another occasion the witch doctor came to the mission, threw a little girl up who would spin in the air, showing his authority over the missionary's power. Then he would roll her like a ball on the ground as if he were saying, "I have power."[133] Lott and others withstood them and many Liberians were delivered from witchcraft and idol worship.

---

[132] Abraham Brown interview
[133] Peeples interview

Although she lived in Africa for many years Mother Kennedy did not realize the severity of the practice of witchcraft and cannibalism until she returned to the United States. In addition to teaching children in grades 1-12 she routinely taught young men or women about taking temperatures and other facets of nursing that she had learned while living in Puerto Rico. One young man, a childhood friend of her son, was especially apt and opened his own clinic.

> God was faithful and some of the students were very good [in nursing] and continued to do the work after we returned back to the States. One of the things that tears my heart out, it's just so sad for me, is one of my little Sunday School boys was eaten. He was a grown man but he was eaten. He had his own little clinic. It was just a mud house but it was his own little clinic with shelves he'd made. He was so proud when he showed it to me and I was so proud of him. And a year or two later when I heard he was dead and had been killed and sacrificed in witchcraft I couldn't believe it. Witchcraft is very, very strong. I think about the time when Charles used to travel with the young man who was sacrificed way back beyond where we were. He and his friend would go and preach. Charles, Jr. was about 10 or 11.[134]

Voodoo, associated with wickedness and the demonic, was one of the dominant religions in Haiti brought from Africa. Frightened by the inhumane and cruel treatment during their bondage, it is said that a voodoo priest informed Haitians that he would make them invisible from the white man, enabling them to escape slavery. In the early 70s even throughout the 80s it was difficult to live in Haiti and not know something about it. Rather than becoming subject to the disturbed effects of those

---

[134] Kennedy interview

cowered by or controlled by demonic influences, it was vitally necessary that international missionaries demonstrate confidence by utilizing the power and authority of God to master every adverse activity. Souls were at stake.

A frequent visitor to Dr. Juanita Faulkner's childhood home, Dorothy Webster's melodious voice captured and held them spellbound with stories of helping the Haitians overcome obstacles. "Her words just flowed. [She] had a standoff with a witch doctor who came into the church. She had to show [all of them] that God was all powerful. When she got through praying and looked around he was he was gone!"[135] Faulkner describes a scene when one of Dr. Exume's adopted daughters Ramone St. Juste, who had been Spirit filled at the Holy Trinity Church of God on Christ shortly after her arrival in America and safely ensconced far away from her village "eyes got big [with fear] when the talk turned to voodoo."

Indeed in Christ there was neither male nor female and He used whomever He chose to pull souls out of darkness into the light of His love. Page-Brown explains that one had to be solid in her belief while serving the Haitian people.

> In Haiti and Africa, there were human blood sacrifices. They did not want us there. The voodoo leader [in Haiti] came to my home chanting voodoo and spitting fire. The Holy Ghost sent me to the door and I threw the door open and drew my pistol, (the Bible) and I lifted it. The Lord changed my English to French. [The voodoo priest chanted] "um may yea, um may yea" meaning I'm gone.

---

[135] Interview by author with Dr. Juanita Faulkner of Philadelphia. Faulkner and John Singleton financially supported teachers at Haiti's C.H. Mason School as well as provided missions support to African missions.

> The Lord ran him away from the orphanage. God taught me how to deal with voodoo spirits.[136]

Despite the danger, the Lord gave them victories. Charles Kennedy, Jr., tells of a time when he was used by God to preach to a witch doctor who gave his life to Christ after hearing him. The man was an accomplished witch man and very proficient in all that he did. He had three wives. He had killed numerous individuals and predicted the future to others.

> Alfred, John and I would go on a Sunday to carry the gospel to a little bit more remote part of Liberia. As a result the father or uncle of two of the boys ended up accepting Christ and he became the pastor of the church several years later. After he was saved he testified he said the children came out and preached to me when he should have been preaching to them. That was after he got saved.[137]

The former witch doctor became a very powerful force for Jesus Christ in that community after God totally delivered him. He also knew country medicine and if an individual was snake bitten he knew how to get the poison out.

The women forged ahead careful to define cultural boundaries yet proclaimed that their religion was based on a faith relationship with Christ resulting in more kingdom victories. The practice of local **African women** selling their girls was interrupted after the entrance of the missionaries, who pled the blood of Jesus until the Spirit broke the custom throughout the villages surrounding

---

[136] Pearl Page Brown interview

[137] Interview by author with Elder Charles Kennedy, Jr. son of Wissikeh missionaries Charles, Sr. and Mary Kennedy September 2009

them. For those already sold the missionaries took money and purchased them from the witch doctors and slavery, brought the girls into the missions, and taught them the ways of the Lord. Other miracles were more spectacular. The women demonstrated their sense of purpose by dedicating themselves to a regimen of fasting and praying. High expectations that God could perform any miracle grew out of this spiritual discipline. Foreign workers also reported that the social and spiritual support of positive relationships were vital to accomplishing the job they were sent to do. Naomi Lundy, Overseer of Manolu from 1962-1966, experienced a heightened sense of achievement during her tenure in Africa after witnessing the Lord work the miracle of raising an African Liberian from the dead. Missionaries had close fellowship with other Pentecostals, Baptists, whites and blacks. A group of seven Black and White missionaries crossed the Cavalla River accompanying Bro. Abraham Brown to the French side of the area when they were called to pray for a man who died three days prior to their arrival.

> The young man was lying on the floor stiff. God is a miracle worker! We prayed. They said that boy had been lying in a dark room for three days. We had to join hands and surrounded him for hours of prayer. When one got finished the other prayed. When one finished the other one prayed. After a while we saw the young man's chest start going. After a while he lifted one of his arms. I never did a lot of dancing on my feet or shouting but when I saw that I danced! Afterwards, someone gave him to drink and the first thing he said was that he wished to go to church and worship the God of the missionaries.[138]

---

[138]Interview by author with Naomi Lundy in Philadelphia September 2009

On other occasions the missionaries joined the native Liberians in cutting through the bush with machetes to evangelize in neighboring villages.

Despite hard work and daily sacrifice they were rewarded as they served "these least of these." Giving to the church and sending the children to missions caused tensions in the villages and darker forces attacked the work. The Lord was faithful to each of the international missionaries who trusted him while working in the field and after they returned. Armed with the Holy Ghost power they continued their work even when witchcraft workers attempted to use their power. The women worked closely together and Pearl Page Brown, moved to action when she heard of an attack by witch doctors against a fellow missionary, traveled to the mission armed with the power of God. She shared how God defeated the power of the enemy after a prolonged period of fasting and prayer.

> She was a lovely person. She encountered bad witchcraft at Monulu Mission. I was a witness to it. I went there and fasted with her three days and three nights. I went from Tugbake (at Mother Lott and Martha Barber station, the Kennedy's were at Wissekeh).[139]

Mother Naomi Lundy entered foreign service at Cape Palmas in 1962 and worked as a nurse, taught the Word of God as well as vocations in Monulu, Liberia through 1966. In the 1965 Holy Convocation she shared that she experienced many trials as she brought the message of Christ relying on the saints to deliver her from unseen and dark forces.

---

[139] Pearl Page Brown interview

Bro. Amos Nyema took care of the boy's dorm and I took care of the girl's dorm. One of the bishops had built the missionary house and the girls had a place. I had dining room with a kitchen and an office. I was there three years at Monolu. Sis. June Blackwell was there when I first came but she was going home. Mother Wiggins – I met in Memphis–Mother Coffey was the one that actually got me going. I think about her often. We used to have beautiful services when I came home in 1966. I went in 1962. I got a little apartment here on the 12th floor. An efficiency. God was moving by His Spirit.[140]

---

[140] ibid

Martha Barber

CHAPTER EIGHT

The Macedonia Call – A Network of Helps

From the time of Mother Mattie McCaulley's work in Trinidad and Mother Elizabeth White's in Liberia, Church Of God In Christ members have been fascinated with the work of foreign missions. As early as the mid twenties, reports were made that in developing COGICs foreign work Bishop A.B. McEwen, Bishop of the Foreign Diocese (Africa, Bahama Isles, Bermuda, Canada, Haiti, West India, British, West Indies) traveled extensively using his own funds to carry the gospel. Documents evidencing extrinsic factors in the church's support of global missions reach back to the 1925 Holy Convocation when the saints raised at least $140.21 for foreign missions with Bishop Mason turning over $20.10 of it to Elder Alfred Cunningham, Overseer of the Churches Of God In Christ in British, West Indies.[141]

---

[141]Coffey, Lillian Brooks, *Year Book of the Church Of God In Christ for the Year 1926*, 53

The Whole Truth newspaper was vital to the dissemination of information concerning all aspects of the work. In it erring pastors were publicly reprimanded or received back into the brotherhood, news was shared of individuals healed and delivered in meetings and revivals, and the developing department and auxiliary ministries noted. In a 1931 article Mother Lizzie Robinson urged overseers, pastors and State Mothers to assist Mrs. Willie Curtis Ragland in making her way to Africa. Below is the transcription of a typewritten letter found in the correspondence of Beatrice Lott (brackets are corrections of typographical errors only) requesting support of Whole Truth readers. The letter encapsulates the entire missions of those going out to non-Western countries for the cause of Christ's kingdom.

Box 45
Cape Palmas, Liberia
West Coast Africa
By Beatrice S. Lott

To the Saints scattered abroad and the Lord's people everywhere:

Grace and peace be multiplied unto you through the knowledge of God and of Jesus our Lord.

What a beautiful night this is. The moon is shining through my window and across my desk, as I write this letter to you. It seems as if though it is trying to speak. If I could understand the language of the moon, I believe it is "declaring the glory of God, and the firmament sheweth His handywork. Day after day uttereth speech, and night unto night sheweth knowledge. There is no speech nor language where their voice is not heard. God has set a tabernacle for the sun. "How great Thou art."

This is Monday night, which is known as Women's night, in the church, here at Tugbake. The church is practically women. They spent the day cleaning the mission ground.

Our early morning, six weeks, Bible School came to a close last Friday, with wonderful success. It was well attended. We were up 5 a.m., with the "Prayer Warriors" in charge, and at 6:30 a.m. our classes were in session. "Back to the Bible" was our slogan. God has provided unusual strength for me, both natural and spiritual, since yielding to His divine. Through the medium of our Bible School hearts have been deeply touched. Those with indifferent attitudes have been changed. "The entrance of His Word giveth [light]". "What truths in the gospel are to be found, Christ saved us all from ruin, [Hallelujah]!

We are yet striving towards our goal, for the electric Dynamo for Tugbake. We thank those of you who are reading the Whole Truth and have been touched by our request, but we [haven't] accomplished our aim, as yet. Please write us and let us know that you are praying for us and standing by us, in this mighty warfare. "We have just begun to fight."

Hundreds of experts from many countries, and [various] walks of life have, and are visiting this small Republic. They are making large contributions, giving scholarships to hundreds of Liberian students, improving the country. Most missions are making rapid strides.

A few weeks ago the Queen of England was guest to Liberia. Many other Presidents and diplomats have visited here. On Feb. 2nd Russia's Soviet Spaceman arrived here and he received an arousing welcome. On Feb. 11th a United States Medical Team, known as the Operation Brother's arrived here, with several tons of medical supplies on board.

The Team is headed by Dr. Hingson a Western Reserve professor of Anesthesiology, who led an earlier medical mission around the world. This idea was started by the Baptists, but there were others who felt that the Baptists alone could not solve the world's ill, hence the Team should develop on a brotherly basis, resulting in Operation Brother's. There are Jews, Protestants and Catholics, comprising the Team.

All of these and many others are making tremendous contributions. While our missions, (The Churches of God in Christ) have in time past been in the remote section of Cape Palmas, the road which has been constructed, has cut through a part of our mission-property, thus putting our mission in the front.

The organized programs of our National Home And Foreign Mission President, Bishop Samuel Crouch, and our National Supervisor of Women's Department, Mother Lillian B. Coffey and their Staffs, along with other most worthy individuals have made it possible for your missionaries to do a more effective work here. Although we have not attained as yet, but we are not ashamed of our work now. "We must work the work of Him that sent us while it is day, the night cometh when no man can work."

This week, Lillian and little Rosalind are vacationing with Sister June Blackwell, at Monolu Mission. On the fourth Friday we are looking forward to our having Fellowship Meeting of Missionaries and Workers.

Our young people are begging for pen-pals, in our home churches. Please write them, it would encourage them to continue in the church. A few names listed below.

Mary Davis, Susan Johnson, Ruth Hinley, Beatrice Nebo, Mariah Wah, Will B. Poklo, Jacob Kkede & Willie Wilson.

Write in care of your missionary, at the above address.

Your humble servant,

In regions beyond,

Beatrice S. Lott

The results of distributing information through the technology available to them proved successful. For the response of the Women's Department sending $1,000 for the Dynamo and Lott's letter of appreciation see Appendix 2:3 and 2:4.

International missionaries dealt with the poverty of soul and body. And for the mass poverty they encountered they needed money. To this end missionaries raised money while on annual furlough, churches held rallies, individual sent small sums and the headquarters provided small monthly stipends. Returning to the United States, they raised funds by exposing their work touring Lutheran, Baptist, Church Of God In Christ and other churches with an interest in missions. Most brought back photos and reels of their work on the continent and traveled from church to church sharing the great things God was doing in Africa and Haiti, the two dominant COGIC missionary destinations.[142] When her adopted daughters were old enough Beatrice Lott and the two girls dressed in African Liberian attire, sang in their dialect and shared what God had done. Dr. Juanita Faulkner shared that "Bishop (then Elder) Esau Courtney had Mother Lott come to Holy Trinity in Trenton, NJ. She would bring a lesson and it would be about Africa. She spoke lovingly of her mission. A couple of times she wore African dress and a turban. Both Mother Barber and Mother Lott would make an appeal and we would

---

[142]During this period some COGIC women labored overseas with other organizations. Noted COGIC faith healer Vera Boykin, who turned 102 in 2011, answered a government sponsored ad for teachers and worked for years in Ethiopia. She adopted and brought back Ethiopian girls who were educated and currently live in the U.S. To find a partial list of more COGIC sent international missionaries and their stations see Chapter 9.

help take care of the school. She lived on almost nothing."[143]

Hiebert suggests that for global Christians who have learned to live deeply in a culture as Dorothy Exume and her family did, there is always a tension in the inability to adjust to one culture, either their own or the adopted. Fronz Exume somewhat agrees with the assumption while also believing missions parents are able to successfully integrate both worlds. He remembers his excitement returning to the United States during the summers, connecting with friends and relatives and raising funds for the work in Haiti.

> I wouldn't trade my life for the world. I was excited to go to Haiti and excited to go the U.S....reconnecting with friends. Coming back to the U.S. meant vacationing, getting with family, eating cold cereal and watching TV. There was no set pattern—we pretty much traveled every year. We had summers in U.S. and school year in Haiti or vice versa. For example, mom was in New York with [Bishop] Ithiel Clemmons and we were there for the school year. Then mom was at ITC [studying at Mason Theological Seminary] and we were in Atlanta [until 1972]. We weren't baggage with mom. When we came here we also had a job to do and helped mom's work. We'd sing and read Creole. Sometimes churches would invite mom to speak and they would want to hear about Haiti. Mom would ask us to sing a song in Creole so the people could hear the words. It would have a different dimension. In 1975 we came back permanently.[144]

The inspiring stories and strong visual presentations generated excitement and made significant impact for greater support for foreign missions. Bishop Courtney

---

[143] Faulkner interview
[144] Fronz Exume interview

moved beyond financing missions and became a frequent visitor to Africa and Haiti. Despite limited direct contact with South Africa because of travel restrictions between the United States and that country, by 1963 the South African Church Of God In Christ had grown to 124 ministers in Transvall, 45 in Bechaunaland, 54 in Cape Province, 36 in Natal, Zululand and Swaziland, 33 in Rhodesia, and 13 in Johannesburg Township. Bishop Courtney traveled to Botswana where he preached to thousands and in South Africa he shared the Good News with 20,000 souls. He and his wife also adopted Esther, a Haitian orphan.

In the South, international missionaries also raised funds and gathered clean clothing to send back to their missions. Maxine Haynes Kyle never forgot Mother Elizabeth White's visits with her parents, Bishop and Mrs. F.L. Haynes. "She told us wonderful stories and we felt we should help. We would can fruit and vegetables to send to Haiti and Africa. Cousin Bea (Beatrice Lott) would come and stay with us too and she would collect money, food and clothing. Neaul (General Board Member Bishop J. Neaul Haynes) planted okra and he was proud of that okra going to the foreign field."[145] Faulkner found herself "crying whenever Mother White came [from Africa] because she had no bed to sleep in. She was an old woman then. I knew it was important for me to save my pennies."[146] Members from all walks of life answered the call to assist. Soul winner, church founder and State Supervisor (Eastern and Western New York) Mother

---

[145]Interview by author with Maxine Haynes Kyle, daughter of Bishop F.L. Haynes, Third Bishop of the State of Texas, prior to its division in 1954.

[146]Here Faulkner refers to a practice whereby on Sundays after the general offering was collected small children passed baskets, sometimes decorated, with signs that said "Pennies for Missions."

Maydie Payton distributed clothing and sent money to support foreign missions work around the globe. Pastor Joseph R. Williams his wife Mrs. Gladys Williams gathered clothing and nonperishables from their poor black community and churches to send to places like Haiti to help the foreign missions efforts. Dallas' Saintsville COGIC Church Mother Beatrice Johnson "lent to the poor" wherever she found she could whether in Home Missions or supporting those serving on foreign soil. The Harmony Ministry in Haiti and Beatrice Lott in Africa were two of the beneficiaries of her love in action. "Once we [Texas churches] sent so much to Haiti they told us to stop until they could get it all unloaded."[147] A young Elder Carlis Moody, who would become the international president of missions in 1976, purchased a van for the Liberian Mission Station.

Mother Coffey was a phenomenal woman and commended these early individual efforts across the country. Ever the organizer, Coffey wished a more consistent way to furnish nonmonetary items. Mother Coffey wrote "On August 1, [1949] the contract was completed for the shipment of two refrigerators (operated by kerosene) to be shipped to Africa. . .Mother Collins is now soliciting funds for two Dynamos that we might light up the jungles."[148] Dynamos were vessels run by kerosene that brought light to the compounds. This was very important as Lott shared with the Haynes family and others that the light protected small children who were vulnerable to animals who would sometimes snatch the smaller children in the dark.[149] Mother Mary

---

[147]Kyle's statement confirms decades long complaints that for whatever reason offloading in Haiti has been problematic and continues today.
[148]Butler, 144
[149]Kyle interview

Kennedy prayed that her adventurous oldest son, Charles, would not be snatched as he and other boys his age ventured deep into the jungle. To further strengthen support for missions Coffey organized a powerful but often overlooked unit, the Burners for Africa, a fundraising organization established to provide electricity for the Mission Stations and schools. Mother Ola Mae Haynes was appointed the first Chairman of the Burner's for Africa. Mother Pernella I. Nelson served as Assistant.

Church Of God In Christ national leaders and educators, bishops, national supervisors, pastors, individual members, denomination churches serving in close proximity, the missionaries themselves and beginning in the 1960s Peace Corp volunteers who bought into President John F. Kennedy's idealism provided support, funds, foodstuffs and medical supplies. The volunteers were welcomed by Pearl Page who wrote "Until God blessed us with Peace Corps teachers...I taught all subjects to all [through eighth grades]...and the dedicated Peace Corps Teachers and I [also] made the childrens uniforms." Throughout the brotherhood a cry was made for missions both home and abroad. In a message entitled *"The Multiple Meaning of Missions,"* the gifted orator and Missions Field Secretary Bishop F.D. Washington, encouraged missions support by proclaiming that missions is the heartbeat of God. Many people like Mother Lillian Coffey (built a home for Abraham Brown at Manolu), Supt. Harvious Green of Detroit, MI (who donated funds for a church) and innumerable others supported international missions work through this present day. A partial list of names given to the school or facility in honor of those providing funding include

- *J.S. Bailey Vocational School* (Manolu)

- *C.H. Mason Elementary School* sponsored by Mrs. E.W. Mason and Mother Lillian Coffey (Haiti)
- *Odessa Newman School* (Haiti)
- *Pearl Page Medical Clinic*
- *Roy and Mae Winbush School* (Haiti)
- *Ella Deans School* (Haiti)
- *Do-re-thea Orphanage* (Haiti)
- *M.M. Jackson Mission School* (Tugbaken)
- *Elder J. Austin Gospel Train* (truck at Manolu)
- *O.M. Kelley Industrial Arts Building* (Manolu)
- *J.S. Bailey Christian School* (Manolu)
- *A.W. Brown Vocational Institute* (Manolu)
- *S.M. Crouch Mission School* (Kakata Township, South Africa)

Consistent funding was needed for day to day activities as the work in foreign fields expanded making it necessary that networks be created. The missionaries welcomed everyone to their stations and were not ashamed to receive assistance from a network of government, nondenominational or denominational missionaries operating nearby. Amilcar Exume reports that in the early 60s as many as 200-250 Americans ventured into Haiti representing all ethnicities and denominations. Those from the Mennonite Church donated and brought friends or even farmers stayed at their home for as long as six months rehabilitating the orphanages and schools. Fronz Exume shed further light on how these networks operated.

> A phenomenal network was established between the missionaries. And not just in terms of the missions groups. A lot of the churches and individuals outside the COGIC helped mom financially: the Mennonites, the Summers helped mom with a lot of the work she was able to establish, the Hellman family out of Bradenton,

> Florida and a number of others as well. Mom had relations with the Baptist missionaries in Haiti. Church World Service was a non government organization who helped as well as the Episcopal Church. The missionaries were mutually supportive. They not only helped financially but also physically. Some had masonry skills or medical training and they rolled up their sleeves and came and worked on occasions.[150]

When advanced medical attention was required in Mission Towns like Tugbaken, 30 miles into the interior, there was no quick way to rush into the emergency room of a hospital. By the time Martha Barber arrived, urgently needed transportation was provided by Rev. Crabaugh, an AG missionary who made his plane available. It may have been useful when in 1963, according to a report from Bishop S.M. Crouch to supporters, "Sis. Naomi Lundy and Sis. June Blackwell's car went off the road and turned over three times.[151]"

Missions support had its heyday through the 1960s with some predicting diminished support at the demise of Bishop Mason. But for now early COGIC leaders were especially vigilant in promoting missions activities. Bishop Samuel Crouch served as President of the Home and Foreign Missions from 1937 through 1968 and his great love for missions was a good fit with the work Coffey was doing in this area of ministry. Dr. Lillian Brooks Coffey, Second International Supervisor, founded the Women's International Convention with one of the prime stated objectives to financially assist the work of missions and education. Coffey was very proud of the

---

[150] Fronz Exume interview
[151] International Outlook, October-December 1963, Bishop R.L. Fidler, Editor, 1

work the partnership accomplished. One of the factors in the first Women's Convention being held Los Angeles, with its emphasis on providing financial support for missions ministry and education, was Crouch's interest culminating in his invitation to host it. Plans were finalized for the first historic convention. The site would be California with both Los Angeles (Southern California April 25-29, 1951) and continuing in San Francisco (Northern California May 1-3, 1951) as hosts. The aim of the convention was to raise funds for the Mission Department of the National Church. Each delegate was asked a fee of $100 in return for free board and housing...the goal was 100 women. The famous educator Dr. Mary McLeod Bethune was keynote speaker for the first ever civic night. Although missions' fundraising was in competition for a finite amount of resources in the church and community, Coffey was a savvy businesswoman who knew how to drum up support for her projects. When the Women's Convention was held in Kansas City she made sure Bro. Abraham Brown had a seat on the charted plane that would take them. She took him to the pulpit, sat him next to Bishop Mason and in front of the entire delegation informed Mason that Brown represented the fruit of the abuse, the lying and everything he suffered as Brown was "an African filled with the Holy Ghost." Bishop Mason laid hands on Bro. Abraham and blessed him, saying "Praise the Lord." The publicity from this type of activity almost assured a stronger support base from the founder.

Bishop Crouch went on to represent the COGIC in forty-eight countries including Okinawa, Japan, China, England, Nigeria, Seoul, Korea with Pastor Paul Hong; Jamaica, where the Jamaica Outreach was established with Bishop Ivor F. Rowe; Puerto Rico, C.H. Mason

School in Port Au Prince, Haiti; Bishop S.S. Mainela at Tsienjane, Rakops Botswana, Africa; Ghana, West Africa; Hawaii, Virgin Islands, South America, and the Philippines. He purchased vans for the Tugbaken Mission Station and his Emmanuel Church Of God In Christ pulpit welcomed foreign missionaries from all parts of the world who received financial assistance for their work including Bishop Richard Fidler's work in Cuba, Mother Dorothy Webster Exume and Mother Eleanor Workman (Haiti), and Eld. Richard Griffith (Guyana). He and Emmanuel built and maintained orphanages and schools including the S.M. Crouch Mission School in Kakata Township, South Africa.

The foreign fields were not for the faint hearted or those afraid of negative spiritual encounters. Mary Beth Kennedy recalls living "way back in the hinterland in an area so remote that even the Peace Corps thought it was too dangerous to put their people." When the rains came in the tropical forest each year, Kennedy says no one could get to or from Wissikeh except by swimming made difficult by swift currents. Cut off and isolated they found that the missionary networks served as community and were a relevant source both of financial and social support in shoring up those serving on the field. God placed them there to be His witness for, they said, the harvest was ripe but the laborers were indeed few. The women visited leper colonies observing men and women without toes and with very few fingers. Mary Kennedy says the Lord had to help her when a man left the colony and arrived at Wissikeh seeking medicine. She overcame her fear, ministered to him and later souls were saved at the colony. By the time Pearl Page arrived in Africa,

National Minister Brother Jeremiah had organized the Church Of God In Christ at the Leper Colony on the French West Ivory Coast. Marva Nyema would accompany Mother Kennedy to the colony in the 1980s.

The missionaries did not have much money and relied on donations from the Home and Foreign Mission Board of the Department of Women. Faulkner notes that 1928 minutes records monthly stipends of $50.00 per month were allocated to early missionaries.[152] They shared what they had and God blessed them. Ester Boley tells of a wounded man stumbling out of the jungle who asked for food at the Tugbaken Mission. Mother Lott ordered Ester to go and set the table. She immediately responded that they did not have anything. Lott wanted to teach Ester to have faith and insisted that she set the table. The man enjoyed the meager fare they had to share. As they were eating they heard an airplane overhead. They had been waiting for money from the States and going to the window they spoke excitedly of traveling to the Coca Cola plant in Monrovia where mail, supplies and money was delivered. When they looked back to share their hope the man had disappeared never to be seen again. Mother Lott declared it was God that they had lent to and taught Ester that sometimes angels are entertained by the saints. They survived hardships through the goodness of the saints and received funds from individual pastors, burdened with soul winning, who led their congregations in realizing the vision for missions at home and abroad.

> Mom would leave the orphanage without knowing how she was going to feed the girls. She'd say I'll be

---

[152] 1928 minutes of the Church Of God In Christ assembly recorded by Elder John Earl Williams, National Secretary from 1928 until his death in 1934 provided by daughter Dr. Juanita Faulkner

Chief Niswah Presenting
Land Grant to Mother Barber

Bro. Abraham Brown   High Priest and
                                     Elder W.J. Taylor

Cape Palmas Church and Girl's Dorm
Built by Lott and Barber

Light Burners for Africa

Mrs. Ola Mae Haynes, Co-Chairman(left front)
Organized 1959 by Mother Coffey (center)

Haitian Orphanage
Dorothy Exume, Director
Polly Anna Stewart, Ass't

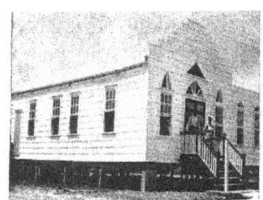
COGIC British Honduras

Grace Yancey Pioneer
Missionary to Thailand

COGIC Leper Colony

Foreign Missionaries at Holy Convocation

(1) L-R: Missionaries Beatrice Lott, Betty Kennedy, Martha Barber, Mother Annie Bailey, Naomi Lundy, Missionary M. Bennett

(2) L-R Missionaries Elizabeth Scott, M. Bennett, Naomi Lundy, Beatrice Lott, V.E. Bickford, Martha Barber, Nell Terry

> back and go to the post office sometimes twice a day looking for a letter from one of the saints. The mail wasn't regular and sometimes the letters would take 6 weeks or a month. Mom wouldn't panic or fret. She'd look to God. One of the missionaries from another denomination would say Dorothy we have an extra whatever. I never knew of a day when the children at the orphanage would not eat. There were occasions where we'd go out. As a kid I didn't understand the gravity of it. Whatever dollars we'd have had to go into the tank to get from point A to point B. The saints were really, really nice and God used the saints. Some would send may be $5 or $12 and it would be just what mom needed.[153]

Additional help was on the way with churches such as the Roberts Temple Church Of God In Christ lending a hand. In her book *My Life with Brother Isaiah* Mother Alva D. Roberts reveals the sentiments of her pastor husband in a letter where Elder Isaiah Roberts lifted up the importance for members to send needed funds. Addressing them as "members of the sweetest place this side of heaven," he stated "For a long time I have heard about conditions in our foreign fields and for a long time I've wanted to do something about them. I wanted to visit these lands where people are underprivileged...[and] I'm not in a position to go so far away...I'm not financially able to send much but with the help of a few people like yourself, I could do some things like clothing for a family, food for some orphans, a small salary for a young preacher..."[154] It is not known to which mission he earmarked the funds and clothing to receive but his October 10, 1958 letter included an invitation to his home to make plans to raise the funds. Other churches and

---

[153] Fronz Exume interview
[154] Roberts, Alva D. *My Life with Brother Isaiah: A Tribute to Bishop Isaiah Leon Roberts,* 2009: Faithday Press, Hazel Crest, IL, 99-100

jurisdictions earmarked funds from $25 to $75 per month with senders instructed to purchase cashier's checks and send them registered to ensure the funds would arrive safely. Yet others went beyond sending funds and purchased clothing: shoes, shirts, suits, socks, trousers and hats for national workers, washable clothing for girls, boys and women; equipment: typewriters, kerosene; appliances: refrigerators and bathroom fixtures. The clothing further identified mission workers and students as part of God's kingdom *and* the Church Of God In Christ. A plea was also made that the clothing be clean and not worn out. Missionaries kept meticulous ledgers of their income and expenses, from women's department or church contributions to expenses paid to local carpenters, sending financial reports to the national church as required. (See Appendix 2:7 for image of ledger.)

COGIC youth remaining in the U.S. identified with the young international missionaries and rallied for their cause. One Youth Congress Souvenir journal included the following appeal to youth: The story was told of a native of a foreign country after having heard a missionary's account of the provisions made by Jesus for his redemption wanted to know when was is that Jesus died for him. His query—"Did he die yesterday?" Upon learning that the scene of Calvary had taken place over 1900 years ago, the native wondered somewhat forlornly, "Why are you just coming? My ancestors have died in heathenism not having heard that Jesus saves."

Inspired by personal accounts and stories like these, the Youth Department joined forces with those across the brotherhood of saints to address the needs of missionaries in a tangible way. In the early 1940s the National Youth

Congress (National Youth Department annual convention) formed a special committee for the "REDEMPTION AND RELIEF OF AFRICA AND THE WORLD" and by 1946 the interest must have been strong since that year the Youth Congress proposed to set up a missionary station in Liberia. In 1949 the Congress assumed responsibility for providing a truck or station wagon for use on the foreign fields and held a special testimonial banquet for missions to raise funds. This project was successful.[155] Missions work was an integral part of the 1952 Youth Congress with an International Forum dedicated to *What Non-Americans Expect from American Christianity* and an International Youth Report session on *The Church's Youth Work Abroad with Countries Reporting: Liberia, Hawaii, Haiti, British West Indies, and Alaska.* An entire souvenir book page was dedicated to the Youth Department's Missions and a *Commission on Youth Participation in Christian Mission Work* was part of a Special Working Commission. Included were updates on foreign missionaries: Miss Beatrice Lott, Miss Martha Barber, Mrs. Francena Wiggins and Overseer Ozro T. Jones, Jr. (Liberia), Mrs. Lucille Kates (Kingston, Jamaica), Miss Effie L. Bright, Miss Dorothy M. Webster (Haiti), Mother Elizabeth White (Africa), Mother Katie Frazier (Bahamas), Mother Willie Holt (Hawaii), Mother Poole (Africa), Overseer Sadler (Hawaii).[156]

By the early 1950s some progress was being made in equal employment and housing in the North. During that

---

[155] 28th Annual International Youth Congress Church Of God In Christ June 26-July 2, 1963, Denver, CO, Bishop O/T. Jones Senior Bishop – Founder/International President, 22

[156] 17th National Youth Congress, Church Of God In Christ, Philadelphia, PA Year Book in Session June 26-July 1, 1952, Bishop Ozro Thurston Jones, D.D. National President, 22-23

1952 Youth Conference pleas were made for additional foreign workers and the University of Pennsylvania where the Congress met was a prime location to make such an appeal for those professionals with evangelistic leanings. Mark Hyman of the *Pittsburgh Courier* compiled the following statistics from the 1950 U.S. Department of Commerce: In Philadelphia Negroes accounted for 2.8% of the city's professional and semi-professional workers including City Councilmen, Civil Service Commissioners, Assistant District Attorneys, City Magistrates, Ward Leaders, Municipal Judges and others. Philadelphia Blacks had a history of organized activity with the city being the birthplace of the African Methodist Episcopal Church and Headquarters for Missions work of the National Baptist Convention. Among the 800,000 blacks living within the corporate limits the Church Of God In Christ represented a large percentage of the total number of Black congregations of the city. Among COGIC professionals listed as needed for foreign missions were those "trained as nurses, practical or registered, doctors, carpenters, teachers, aviators, stenographers, linguists."[157]

Youth across the nation assisted mission efforts even if they could not journey to faraway places. In the early 1960s when electric lights were needed in the church built by Lott and Barber the youth of Cleveland, Ohio sent $1750.[158] Mother Lott requested that Rev. Washington of Fairbanks, Louisiana send Bibles for eighty of the Tugbakeh Mission students. Requesting that International Outlook readers help, Washington explained "This

---

[157] ibid, 12-13
[158] Cornelius, Lucille Cornelius, The International Outlook, The Official Organ of the Church Of God In Christ Home & Foreign Mission Department, *Minutes of Mission Day, November 11, 1965 at the 58th Annual Holy Convocation of the Church Of God In Christ in Memphis, TN, Bishop S.M. Crouch Presiding.* 2-3

appeal is to YOU. They need these Bibles to be able to meet their daily demands at the Mission School" and further stated that "Bibles can be purchased in Liberia for $1.15 each.[159]"

Individuals converting to Christianity upset the tribal way of life with a new found sense of purpose outside village customs, Western sensibilities and the priority given to preaching that the American's God was the only true God. However, caring for the villagers' emotional needs along with practical applications of the gospel through providing a point of contact for medical care caused additional villagers to eventually join them. The American women brought further change in customs as giving portions of their meager income made from farming to the church, teaching that God was high and mighty but also a friend. With this increase the need for extra supplies or medical aid was needed and now the missionaries demonstrated how unity and teamwork could help everyone. For example, when villagers began sending their children to missions or attend the church the average annual per capita offerings were only 39 cents. The missionaries taught them that giving their first fruits and tithes to the church supported the work. This showing of unity allowed the self-worth and sense of achievement of native Liberians to further increase in this new way of experiencing life. These offerings supplemented funds sent from the U.S. and they built the M.M. Jackson Mission School at Tugbaken.

---

[159]Fidler, R.L., Editor, *The International Outlook, Official Organ of the Church Of God In Christ Home & Foreign Mission Dept.*, July-September 1964, 5

Initial concerns by Maryland County officials regarding the school's standards were eventually straightened out. (See Appendix 2:6 for a letter from the Mission School Board to the Inspector of Foreign Missions concerning this.) They were rewarded when on November 17, 1963 Lott preached the sermon at the dedication service and anniversary of the new church. (See Appendix 2:9 for program cover of the dedication.) Native Pastor Toe gave the Act of Dedication, Chief Harry T. Ragland, Chief of the Mission Town presented the church's history and the Paramount Chief of Tugbakeh gave remarks.[160]

> After the bus, we built a school with six rooms and a spacious auditorium. We have taught the African to contribute. We have brought them up from the offerings of just 39 cents to giving the "first fruit and tithes to the Church and in this way we are able to carry on. We have 14 cement block buildings on our station. Sis. Barber built a small clinic on the hill. We use it now for a teachers' cottage and call it the Barber Teachers' Cottage.[161]

Threats from attacks by wild animals were real, early workers were wary of those who practiced cannibalism, and the disappointments from continual financial shortages menaced their spirits. Nevertheless, winning Benjamin (Bwhwae – let it be so) Jabbeh and other native Liberians, they translated English into Gblo-wi, the tribal language of the Nyambo tribe. Jabbeh says that the Kennedy's turned his entire life around. He first met Mother Kennedy when he sought help after an infected

---

[160] Faith Temple Church Of God In Christ, *Service of Dedication of the Extension of the Church Of God In Christ and the 24th Anniversary of the Founding of the Church Tubakeh, Maryland County, Liberia* Sunday November 17, 1963, 4, 7
[161] The International Outlook, February 1966, 3

sore would not heal. He could not use his right foot and leaving the family's farm early one day he hopped to the mission and entered the Kennedy's home. Assessing his wounds Mother Kennedy immediately cleansed and dressed his foot, fed him and gave him an injection. One of their crowning achievements was the founding of the Lee Elementary School (Lee was Mother Kennedy's maiden name) which served students from kindergarten to eighth grade and the Wissikeh Academic High School located at the Wissekeh Mission Station.

> The Anglos, serving with the Assemblies of God, sent their children to mission's schools far away. Chuck and I were educated and felt that we were equipped. I taught school while we were in Puerto Rico and later Charles taught at Howard [University]. People didn't know that we had a high school out in the jungle where we provided not only our children but the native children a superior education.[162]

Some results were outstanding. Jabbeh is called the "first fruit" of the Wissikeh School when he graduated November 28, 1960. Like other international missionaries the Kennedy's attempted to care for every facet of their students' well being. When Jabbeh prepared for his graduation he was to give the speech and his parents could not afford the luxury of buying the suit he wished for. The Kennedy's, wishing the day to be exceptional, purchased his graduation suit. He did not inform his parents that he had a suit but after bathing at home he stated he would finish dressing at the Kennedys.

> Elder Kennedy taught me how to tie the tie. My graduation speech was *Perseverance Conquers* and when I marched in and looked at the faces of my

---

[162]Kennedy interview

> parents wearing that suit they were so surprised. Following the speech Mother Kennedy announced that I would go to the United States and attend college. I was so happy that I went back to the boy's dorm and cried.[163]

Following graduation Jabbeh taught English at the Mission School from March through May 1961 and returned to Tugbaken until Elder Kennedy drove him to Harper County July 12 to take a flight from Monrovia to New Orleans, Louisiana. He arrived in the United States August 28, 1961. The high moral and educational standards required by the missions benefited the Liberian government tremendously. Former missions school students are found among the highest ranking in Liberia holding the positions of Chief of Security, Marshall to the President, Chief of the Police Department and Chief of Immigration. Another student, Benjamin Moses (Gbosio Gbuffua) returned from college and established a school in Monrovia for students up to grade 12. Along with Dr. Charles Kennedy, Moses translated portions of the Bible into native languages including Psalms 23 and The Lord's Prayer causing adult men to cry upon reading the Bible in their own language. The Kennedy's served at Wissekeh for seven years and also founded a clinic and other needed ministries.

Thousands of miles from home and naturally at some disadvantage, international missionaries further relied on each other and used their survival skills to assist their sisters with necessities, companionship and spiritual strength. Cross cultural learning also helped and the Americans learned much from the Liberians. Mary Beth Kennedy's recollection of workers constructing mud huts

---

[163] Nyema/Jabbeh interview.

in the summer heat from January through May was such an experience. They would live in these huts until building made of cement (protecting the structure from termites that ate all the wood and papers) was completed.

> It's wonderful how ingenious many of the people are. When I first heard about mud houses I was intrigued because I wondered how they could make a house with mud. If it would stay up if it rained and all that sort of thing. They are careful [to make the] framework of wood first. They go into the bush, into the jungle and cut down trees and they have the wood posts that are about 6 inches thick. And first they put that down and they make the place where the roof will be and then they go in and get vines and they interweave them among those posts so that they are like holes 8 or 6 inches square. They prepare the mud and put the mud into the holes and let that dry for several weeks, then plaster it again with black mud. They go somewhere where the earth is black and they put the black mud there. And then the cracks that come when the mud dries are a lot finer than when the brown mud cracks. Some of them, [who] really want it nice, go to a place where they have to move the water. They call it baling water, move the water out of the bottom of the creek and they have white clay [which] they smear on. Then the cracks are very, very fine and it looks as if it's been painted white.[164]

Sometimes their hands would bloody as they helped clear the tropical jungle to expand the compound as the need for boarding or educational buildings increased. The native African Liberian children were taught English and about Christ, convincing the Liberians the missionaries' activities were good for them. They walked or were carried on hammocks to villages to bring medical aid,

---

[164] Kennedy interview

encouragement and the gospel of Jesus Christ. As mission towns grew the meager stipend sent by the church was not enough. A look at President Bishop S. Rudolph Martin's 1969 Home and Foreign Missions Financial Report the total grants to Missionaries on Foreign Fields, Foreign Workers, Travel to Fields, Missionary Travel to Convocation and grants to retired missionaries totaled approximately $18,000. These funds were allocated to missionaries, missions' stations and churches in Liberia, Mexico, Hawaii, Honduras, Haiti, Jamaica, Bahamas, Columbia, Panama and India[165] Others in the U.S. would come to their aid.

Bishop E.E. Hamilton along with others at Stateside made large contributions or rallied churches to assist the missionaries. When Beatrice Lott needed a bus after walking for many years or borrowing transportation from nearby denominational organizations she contacted Missions President Bishop Crouch who referred her to a source then sent her $2,000 of the $2,400 needed for its purchase. At Bishop S.R. Martin's urging the districts of Northwest California held "Missions Day" the first day of their conferences sending as much as $1000 for the support of missions in the early 1960s. Northwest California also purchased needed items—a refrigerator and even a car for Sis. Pearl Page (Brown), a member of Bishop Martin's church at that time. By the early 1960s the jungle had grown into a city. Under the Lott/Barber administration 223 acres of land was purchased for the Church Of God In Christ. The missionaries were never sure what they would get into and experienced a constant

---

[165]Church Of God In Christ, International Home and Foreign Missions Department Financial Report Fiscal Year ending September 10, 1970, Bishop S.R. Martin, President

re-invention of themselves performing whatever duty necessary for the missions to succeed. For example, they worked as carpenters and climbed on ladders to build houses themselves when they did not have money to pay workers, wearing slacks under their dress to respect the tradition of the church.

According to Lundy denominational churches opened their doors. The United Holy Church of America operated a guest Mission Home, met those arriving by boat or air and greeted visitors of any denomination. Upon arrival in Monrovia COGIC Home and Foreign Mission Executive Secretary William J. Taylor was met by Miss Edyth Johnson, Officer Richard Brown, Melvina Harris and others who "attended my desires as though I was in America." If for any reason COGIC missionaries did not arrive for transport to missions stations visitors stayed at temporary housing built for rest and replenishment. As the Mother Overseer Lundy was expected to operate the missions smoothly despite limited funding for the needs they encountered. The mission had a nice school where she recalled receiving help from a young Caucasian Peace Corps volunteer, Teacher Dick, when the work at the school, medical clinic and girl's dorm proved to be too much for her to handle. "His mother used to send him things for the children."

While it is unfair to judge or measure earlier generations by today's standards some situations are germane to human nature. Disagreements and misunderstandings fall into that category. Those entering foreign service were necessarily spirited but sometimes strong wills clashed in the day to day work and the Barber/Kennedy dispute rose to such a level that headquarters sent a representative to mediate. The definitive reason that

Liberian missionaries were not getting along is not known but the situation did not lend itself to constructive missionary work. Executive Secretary Taylor "being authorized and impowered by the President of the Women's Convention" visited Liberia in 1956 to review the work and settle the dispute. In a letter dated August 8, 1956, Subject: Missionaries Barber vs. C.H. Kennedy, Taylor said that although "accusations hurled backward and forward [and] through cross examinations it was proved beyond a shadow of a doubt Sister Barber had said some things to the family of Senator Wilson and to Mr. Rogers...it was further alleged that the Kennedys had done some talk to the local nationals." He further stated that looking at the situation "through the eyes of Christianity, I feel and still feel, as Missionaries, these indiscretions can be dissipated and no further alarm be given to such charges again."

Whatever the debate, all parties agreed with his decision "That Missionaries Kennedys and Martha Barber will serve in this field of Christian endeavor to the best of their abilities. As Missionaries who have been granted passports by the State Department of the United States Government their protection must be insured." He counseled them to discuss all domestic, educational, and problems that may develop where more than one missionary is serving among them. "Maladjusted individuals give a magnified picture of adverse elements in our Culture that bear down on the total population. With this thought in mind, there is no reason for workers, especially those who are laboring for Christ, to not get along as the Bible has declared. Therefore we cannot accept each rumor from fields as being documentally correct. The encroachment in the rights of a Senior Missionary naturally will cause disturbance and prevent the efforts of the general program and even stopped in some occasions." Admitting that he had limited orientation of the customs, cultural patterns, and economic conditions which gave rise to the situation, he nevertheless secured the signatures of Martha Barber and the Kennedy's that they would work together for the kingdom of God.

Dr. Arenia Mallory's contributions to Africa were outstanding. Her unfulfilled expectations of travelling to Africa as a missionary did not deter her from providing the means of educating African youth. She became interested in Liberia, West Coast Africa, during a six weeks' tour of the country as a special guest of President V.S. Tubman at his fourth inaugural celebration. While in Liberia she toured the Manolu Mission Station on a hammock built by Abraham Brown.

> Dr. Mallory was about 6 feet something. And she was really heavy. She didn't believe I could fix something that could hold her up. I said yes I can. She was there when I built it and I put her in it. I said now don't be afraid. I am the bodyguard who is here in the back and if we have anything they tell me about. And I'm going to take you there. Sixteen people carried her, four people at a time. I took her to Wissikeh where the mission work of the COGIC started.[166]

After studying the Liberian school system Dr. Mallory organized the "Friends of Liberian Youth (FLY)" in 1960. FLY's volunteer group of American women with headquarters in New York City, specialized in providing transportation to bring students from the rural areas of Liberia to America for advanced educational

---

[166] Abraham Brown interview

opportunities.[167] Among those students recommended to come to America were Annie Wah, Peter Davis (father was a Catholic so he didn't use his native name), Willie Pokolo, Ethel Brown, Peter Nimely, Alexander Gbayee, Benjamin Jabbeh and Sam Boley. Coley, born in 1938, worked with his father on the family's farm and explained that the government did not build schools in the interior. His father Willie and Mother Hedoe allowed him to join others who ventured out of their Doloke village to work, yet the individuals they stayed with did not have an interest in educating the children. After meeting Beatrice Lott and Martha Barber when he was 12 years of age, they allowed him to live in the boarding school. Although he had to work hard on the mission's rice farm and, due to the lack of money students and missionaries had to eat lots of bananas, he was happy to because they taught him to read and write. The missionaries provided balance for the children and he remembers spirited soccer games. Baseball became a favorite past time after Missionary Barber taught them how to play. In a 2010 interview he explained how God worked through Dr. Mallory so that he could further his education in America:

> [It was a] miracle for a group of us to live in America. During President William V.S. Tubman's time at one of his inaugurations Arenia Mallory went to Liberia at the invitation of Mother Martha Barber. After [leaving the inauguration] we went up to the interior. Mother Barber requested if Dr. Mallory could bring three of the students to the United States. Later on she added two more. I

---

[167]Lashley, E.M *Glimpses into the Life of a Great Mississippian and a Majestic American Educator 1926-1976*, 1977 and *Down Behind the Sun – The Story of Arenia Conella Mallory* by Dovie Marie Simmons and Olivia L. Martin, Riverside Press, Memphis, TN 1983, 29

> was one of the ones that were added. We [traveled] on one of the ships they used to carry the iron ore, the *Darrel Campbell*.[168]

Benjamin Jabbeh story is one of the outstanding examples of the success of Mallory's FLY initiative as a starting point for those who began their education in missions' schools established by the missionaries. He arrived on the Saints campus August 28, 1961. There he met fellow Liberians Elder Abraham Brown and his wife, Jessie Brown. (Brown had been sent to Saints after Manolu founder Mother Francina Wiggins heard the voice of the Lord telling her to send him to America to be educated so that he could return to take over the mission.) The school was closed but students returned on September 1, 1961. After graduating from Saints in 1963 he transferred to Western Michigan University and lived with Elder Mike Russell pastor of the New Jerusalem Church Of God In Christ. He received a B.S. in Economics in December 1967 and a Master's Degree in Management in 1968. Before returning to Liberia in December 1969, he successfully interviewed with the Firestone Company in Akron, Ohio. He began work at the Cavalla Firestone Plant as General Services Manager on February 5, 1970 with a salary of $600.00 per month, twice that of the $300 per month paid to Liberian government employees. After working for the company six years he found employment at the Liberia American Mining Company (LAMC) and worked there for five years before transferring to Sweden for advanced training making $1,050.00 per month, an outstanding salary in Liberia. In 1980, he joined the Liberian government People Redemption Council as Assistant Superintendant for Development and was eventually

---

[168]Sam Coley interview

promoted to Superintendant. He was terminated within eleven months and went back to Tugbaken and worked on his farm until 1983 when he gained employment at Harper County's William V.S. Tubman College of Technology. He taught there until the 1989 Civil War erupted. From 1991 until 1996, he served as Community of Caring National Director for Mother Kennedy in Liberia.

Other students transferred from Africa to Mississippi included Abraham Brown, Jessie Brown, Ester Lott, and Sophronia Chesson (Iotka) who wrote a moving tribute upon the occasion of Mallory's kingdom promotion. (See Appendix 2:1)

Many women were going to and from missions stations around the globe. Some other women who served and mentioned in the International Outlook prior to 1970 were:

Evangelist Elizabeth Scott, Nigeria – 1960s
Sis Yearwood (founded Zion Temple COGIC in Barbados, B.W.I) – 1960s
Dr. Rebekah Bonner – Haiti
Missionary Nell Terry – The Azores – 1960s

The COGIC had limited funds for domestic expansion, less for foreign missions work and though dollars were stretched thin women like California Supervisor Mattie McGlothen were active missions' supporters. In an early Missions meeting she proclaimed that she "love[d] Mission. It is a part of my life, day by day." In 1938 she requested and received assistance from Mother Lizzie Robinson and the International Women's Department to build a home for missionaries in the Bahamas. When she became International Supervisor her support continued as evidenced by providing her personal funds to international missionaries to purchase clothing upon their return to the United States.

Lillian Brooks Coffey, a genius of organization and administration, met COGIC Founder Bishop C.H. Mason as a girl, worked closely in the inner workings of the church, and was a woman to be trusted. During her administration additional auxiliaries were added to the women's work: Young Women's Christian Council, Huldah Club, Volunteer Counselors, Missionaries, Hospitality Group, Usher's Unit, Editor's and Publisher's unit, Religious Education Club, Ministers' Wives Circle, Bishops' Wives Circle, Stewardess Board, Church Mothers' Unit, National Evangelists Unit, and Secretaries Unit.[169] These addressed every professional, educational and civic level of leadership needed to engage women in their role of wife, mother and businesswoman. However, Coffey's keen eye turned to finding a way to assist those women involved in the work of global missions. Explaining early budgetary limitations International Supervisor Coffey stated that the COGIC was a "collect as you go church….Our churches are rich in property and income, true enough, but the executives are often poor as they receive a low minimum for living. We have no salaries; we all go by freewill offerings which vary from person to person."[170]

She persuaded Mason and other leaders that a convention dedicated to recognizing women's ministry done on

---

[169]Butler, 141

[170]Calhoun, Lillian S. *Woman on the Go for God*. May 1963, 78-88, 81 Ebony Magazine, 1953

behalf of the Women's Department would be a worthwhile endeavor, having conceived it during the 1950 Holy Convocation "on Monday morning, between 9:30 and 10:30, it was begotten by the Holy Ghost."[171] In 1950 Mother Coffey and her staff chose Los Angeles, the city where Pentecost fell in the 20th century, as the site of her first National Convention of the Women of the Churches of God in Christ International (the name was later changed to the Women's International Convention). Renowned for her ability at fundraising, she planned a system for consistent financing of those things dear to women. Butler notes that Coffey long desired a way to have the women meet together to support the mission activities of the denomination, and in order to do that, it needed to be away from the convocation. An article appearing in the first Women's Convention souvenir journal by Elder Robert E. Roberts, General Secretary of Northern Illinois supports this. Stating that 200 women heard the call to fund Missions, he wrote:

> The Great Dreamer, National Mother Lillian B. Coffey…goes before you fortified in spirit. For the issue of the day has been fully arrived. As a Dreamer this great meeting has come into existence [for] a "better way." This "better way" so illuminated those interests in Mission that you and you forming this Great Cavalcade are facing the stark realities of an awakening…ONE purpose through every act and expression to abolish slipshod methods, and indifferent attitudes toward Missions in this first meeting of its kind.

The Church Of God In Christ departments (Sunday School, Youth and Music Departments) and Women's Department auxiliaries (child evangelism, Sunshine Band;

---

[171]Butler, 145

Purity class, teens; Prayer and Bible Band, women) afforded members the opportunities to serve and receive training in diverse areas. Each area equipped members to understand the power that receiving the Baptism of the Holy Ghost offered in order to live a sanctified life. Through her Department Mother Lizzie Robinson's strong spiritual base and organizational leadership created a team of female leaders and laid the groundwork for mobilizing women across the country. Beginning in 1945 Mother Lillian Coffey's Women's Department supported 12 mission posts in Hawaii, the West Indies, England, Africa and Haiti. Their widespread network fanned out raising funds for the building of the Elizabeth White Clinic in Liberia, shared in the purchase of land with Sister Elsie Mason for the Mason School in Haiti, and the purchase of the St. Juste residence, purchased lands for the L.B. Coffey School at Petit Grove, Haiti and supported missionaries in myriad mission endeavors.[172][173]

The women's support of Missions continued through Coffey's tenure, into Mrs. Annie Bailey's administration and both National and State Mothers were keen to assist. Mother Bailey is reported to have given thousands of dollars supporting missions. She and her husband were the first to purchase a car for Mother Elizabeth White and ship it to Africa. Mother Bailey and the Women's Department would support Pearl Page Brown's first trip to Africa along with purchasing most of her supplies. The November 1965 Missions Report shows that the Mother Annie Bailey and the Department of Women reported $10,475 (along with a special offering of $3,000 to

---

[172] Winbush, Dr. Roy L.H. 1982 The Living Heritage Calendar *Profiles of Dynamic Saints in the Church Of God In Christ,* Memphis, Tennessee

[173] Williams-Goodson, Glenda *Biographical Profiles of Early Church Of God In Christ Leaders*

purchase a bus) to Missions followed by Bishop S.M. Crouch and Supervisor L.O. Hale with $8,344.62, Bishop O.M. Kelley and Supervisor M. Payton with $5,860.00 and Bishop E.E. Hamilton (Bishop S.R. Martin) and Supervisor Mattie McGlothen with $5,230.71.[174]

Under Bailey's administration the Women's Department funded trips to the Women's Convention for furloughed missionaries and also provided money for health examinations. The Lord received a harvest of souls in Belize under the ministry of Missionary Pearl Page but the work took its toll. "When I returned to America, my health was not good, and Precious Mother [Lola] Young took me into her home and nourished and nursed me back to health." Mother Lola Young, the State Mother of

---

[174]The International Outlook, *Annual Report of Financial Receipts for Missions November 1965, Memphis, TN*, 8-13

Ohio North Jurisdiction, also intervened for Page when upon her arrival in New York to board a ship sailing into Africa she found that the ships were on strike. She was stuck in New York for two months before Mother Young called and offered her round trip airfare to visit her mother and family back in California. Mother L.O. Hale of Southern California received the support of Bishop Crouch and led the women in purchasing a gas stove as well as $800 electric and manual mimeograph machines used in Tugbaken to spread the word to multitudes. This type of support occurred throughout the States with State Mothers supporting international missionaries in key areas of their lives.

California Supervisor Mattie McGlothen succeeded Dr. Annie Bailey to become the fourth International Supervisor of Women of the Church Of God In Christ. A missions supporter since the 1930s, upon her ascension she too led the Women's Department in their continuing support of Missions. In 1984 she built a pavilion for senior citizens and unwed mothers in Port-au-Prince, Haiti. Mother Mattie McGlothen was guest speaker at the dedication of the C.H. Mason/Mattie McGlothen Pavilion. The program also listed headquarters guests Rev. J.W. Denny, Executif Secretary of the Department of Missions, Mother Irene Oakley, Special Project Director of the Department of Missions, Bishop Carlis Moody, International President of the Department of Missions, joining Pastor Vanes Datus, Bro. Prospene Brice, Bishop Lopez Dautruche, Haiti Supervisor of Women Mother Mary Gullick joining in the great celebration and unveiling of the cornerstone.

As the COGIC continued to expand across the globe emphasis was placed on private donations and increased innovations for the foreign missionaries to support their work. As they went about their day to day activities spreading the gospel, teaching, interacting with indigenous peoples they networked with other church organizations in the agrarian economy as well as government officials to help where they could. Wissekeh missionary Mary Beth Kennedy's letter to Bishop D. Lawrence Williams found in Appendix 2:8 offers a glimpse of appeals for assistance in providing government mandated books for her proposed high school. Government officials were also contacted on behalf of students and others they served.

The Holy Ghost was falling, spiritual and cultural barriers were broken, the missions grew under the leadership of the missionaries and land was needed. Tugbaken founders Lott and Ragland were the first to request land but for unknown reasons the Mission Land Grant had not been settled. These women were ambassadors of God but were also the face of COGIC operations with the appearance of success or failure of the church within their hand. Their main mission was the church and souls. Education in reading was important because if the African Liberian could not read, he or she could not understand the Bible. Churches were modeled after Stateside services and they trained and appointed pastors, organized districts and when it was time for holy convocations they kept the order.

Home and Foreign Missions Secretary W.J. Taylor visited Mother Martha Barber and the Liberian work after which she was determined to acquire land in the name of the Church Of God In Christ. Demonstrating savvy in both social interaction and negotiation skills, even in the midst of opposition due to Liberian politics, she writes confidently in the December 1955 Whole Truth Newspaper that she had gained the assistance of powerful players Attorney A. Dash Wilson, Liberia's 11th Chief Justice and the Honorable and Mrs. W.A. Rogers, in surveying land to be obtained for the mission's work.

> I was quite pleased...In 1950 the Tribal grant was signed and Hono. Rogers prepared and mailed it for preparation for The Legislature. Upon my return having been asked to ask for a larger plot of land, I started before I reached the mission or even Cape Palmas so as to forward to our Board the necessary documents. The land was properly surveyed and paid advance by our good friends the Rogers. While awaiting the time for the House of Legislature to open, there came an awful blow to us all that there had been an attempted assassination (but failed) and the surveyor's name was entailed. This is the reason for any question of the present situation of our church mission land grant in Tugbake. I then enclosed $10.00 for which Senator has never indicated he wanted, but knowing one can't go too far on friendship alone, I so did and again ask his kindness to see what was to be done, and this he did and is doing.[175]

Everyone was welcomed at the missions' stations with native Liberians as well as their children living in the mission towns. In the tropical rainforest summers lasted from January through May. While the rains held up students and missionaries alike planted rice. After the rains came in August, the townspeople of Harper or Catholics working close by allowed the missionaries, initially without transportation, to borrow their cars to

---

[175]Whole Truth Newspaper, Volume XXIII, No. 92, November 1955, Church Of God In Christ, Memphis, TN

visit other missions' stations or conduct business at the nearby Firestone Rubber Plant. The harvest came after the rains of August. Mother Lott allowed older missions boys and girls to help townspeople cut rice and they would receive great baskets as part of their pay. According to Beatrice Nah natives, city and government officials knew the missionaries were there for altruistic work. Even with land the missionaries needed the support of government officials. Liberian President V.S. Tubman allowed the American women leeway to build the missions at Cape Palmas which grew from a membership of 40 to over one hundred; from a few native huts and churches to 2 mission homes of cement with 10 rooms each, a dormitory for girls which accommodated 30 girls; a compound for the missionaries and board students; a dormitory for boys, a large school building; and a spacious cement church with seating capacity of 400. The results of the hard work performed by the missionaries caused the Church of God in Christ to be held in high esteem by the larger community. There were great celebrations when townspeople presented Mother Lott with a fat goose![176] By the time the program for the August 1965 dedication of the Lott and Crouch building, program participants included native African Liberian pastor J. Hney, Assistant Supervisor of Schools for Maryland County Mr. Giko, Rev. Father Gray with the message preached by Rev. Bolton Williams, D.D., PhD, Supervisor of Schools for Maryland County.[177]

In Haiti, Marlil Exume along with her brothers A. Anthony and Fronz watched as their mother scouted

---

[176]Nah interview

[177]Program for the Dedication of the Lott and Crouch Building, Church Of God In Christ Mission School Tugbake, 8/15/65, Cape Palmas, Liberia, West Africa, B. Lott, W.C. Ragland, Founders

areas to help the children of her Mission Station needing food, housing assistance, and prescriptions filled. For those needing housing assistance Webster-Exume would send someone to pay rent. She found that CARE, Church World Service and on rare occasions the U.S. Embassy provided food for those gathered early mornings. Periodically U.S. Marines brought MREs to the mission.

The actual profiles and commentary in the next chapter will inspire and encourage those who have left possibilities: these pioneers were educated and left possibilities of successful careers in education, entrepreneurship or stateside training; they were young and for the most part left possibilities of marriage and children; they were organizers who left possibilities for upwardly mobility in the church's hierarchy. The sacrifices they made cause reflection then humble us as we see few who are willing to leave the comforts of the familiar to go into the everywhere to win the lost for Christ.

The stories of the following great women of God provide accounts of Black women who served as pioneers in the foreign fields as they represented God and the Church Of God In Christ through sacrifice, ingenuity and results oriented strategies.

Dorothy Webster Exume

CHAPTER NINE

International Trailblazers. . .Instruments of Power

God called both women and men to Himself through Jesus Christ. COGIC international missionaries experienced Holy Ghost fire burning deep within to go out and win souls wherever He chose them to work. As a result of their determination to serve on foreign soil they received an education that an individual cannot get anywhere else. We must not diminish what they accomplished but take their work seriously as they did operate under the leadership of the Holy Spirit. In the vicissitudes of their representative roles ninety-nine percent of the time they kept pressures down and all the balls up in the air – shining orbs of light within the local missionary community, negotiating with government officials, reporting to and receiving assistance/advice from their sending organization (H&FM), contacting supporters, and learning to effectively minister and serve the host country. God used their educational and life experiences in diverse ways to make them champions in the field and refined them as coal pressed into dazzling jewels. The following profiles contain core ideas of self-determination in remaining faithful to purpose. They communicate in their own words through personal interviews or "speak" through the writings they left behind. Though frustration peeks out in some correspondence, their words are simply elegant and will inspire. For the remainder I have built the profiles from recollections of family members or caretakers and have been careful to substantiate the memories by interviewing two or more of these individuals.

MATTIE McCAULLEY — MISSIONARY TO TRINIDAD; CRISTOBAL, CANAL ZONE; COSTA RICO 1926 - ?

Mission Stations: Trinidad; Cristobal, Canal Zone, Costa Rico

Place of Origin: Tulsa, Oklahoma; though her husband is not named records list her as "Mrs." McCaulley

Appointed to Missions Work by: First foreign missionary sent after the establishment of the International Home and Foreign Missions Board

In the following account Mother Mattie McCaulley provides a report of the work in Trinidad. The report is found in the 1926 Year Book of the Church Of God In Christ, compiled by Lillian Brooks Coffey.

REPORT OF THE CHURCH OF GOD IN CHRIST

Port of Spain, Trinidad, B.W.I. – House of Prayer, International Home and Foreign Missions Band

Greetings in Jesus' name. I beg to be allowed to submit the following report:

I sailed from California on the 2nd of February, arrived in Christobal, Panama, on the 14th of February. Had to wait 11 days for the next boat, so I inquired as to whether there were any Christians there. I found some said to be the Assemblies of God, so I went in to worship with them and found they were sanctified, so I labored day and night with them. The preacher told the people that he had never heard the gospel as I gave it. I left them all on the altar waiting for the Holy Ghost. I came on to Trinidad and began my work here. Souls have been saved and the sick healed by numbers. Now I have a little church established; Sunday school, prayer and Bible band, Sunshine Band, and Y.P.W.W., all at work and doing nicely. Through much suffering, thank God I can now say victory is ours.

Money received from the board amounted to $85 from saints otherwise $64.50. Total received, $164.50. I paid out for $89 house rent, $22 for chairs and benches, $4 for lamp and $9.80 for oil. Balance left, $39.70. I also thank the board for song books and Sunday school literature. Elder O.T. Jones sent me 1 dozen Y.P.W.W. topics. I also thank God for Elder E.M. Wilson and H.C. Clemmons of Los Angeles, Calif., and also the dear saints and our Mother Roberson. May God ever keep them true and faithful. We are sending $1 to represent the church as a Church Of God In Christ, Port of Spain, Trinidad.

Brother Timothy Brown has been licensed by the board; also Brother J.F. White. We had one baptizing, four were baptized with water and now have more to be baptized yet. All I do, I want God to be glorified. So, saints everywhere pray that this work will stand until Jesus comes, and wherever I go God will get the glory.

Elder J.T. Hurley, Pastor
Sister J.T. Hurley, Prayer and Bible Band Leader
Sister Marie White, Secretary
Mother Mattie McCaulley, General Supervisor

CORNELIUS HALL – MISSIONARY TO TURKS ISLAND, BRITISH WEST INDIES 1926 – 1936

Mission Station: Turks Island

Place of Origin: Turks Island

Appointed to Missions by: International Board of Home and Foreign Mission

About the same time [as Mrs. McCaulley was sent in 1926] Elder Cornelius Hall left the National Holy Convocation to return to his homeland in Turks Island, British West Indies, to minister to his people. He served faithfully for ten years and died at sea while on a voyage travelling to reach his people. After the loss of Elder Hall, the work was carried on by his assistant Elder R. E. Handfield who served in the Turks Island until his death in 1949.

ELIZABETH WHITE — MISSIONARY TO LIBERIA
1929/1930 - ?

Missions Station: First Church Of God In Christ Missionary officially sent to Africa; Founder of Wissekeh, Wrouke, Wuluken Mission Stations

Family: Mother White's marriage was said to have been annulled and the only family she was known to have was a brother.

Appointed to Missions by: Mother Lizzie Robinson

Other highlights: Beatrice Lott remembered hearing the story of Mother White openly challenging a Voodoo priest in Liberia. She began calling on Jesus. The Voodoo priest fell out as if dead, powerless before the name of Jesus.

Elizabeth White served under the Assemblies of God umbrella beginning in 1925. She met Bishop Mason and Mother Lillian Brooks Coffey in Atlanta, GA. The following information is primarily taken from the testimony of Bishop Abraham Brown, former Overseer of Church Of God In Christ Mission Stations at Manolu, Tugbaken and Wissikeh.

Mother White initially went to the mission's field under the Assemblies of God banner; later joined with Sister Hathaway and Sister Wright of Chicago, members of a Black splinter from the Assemblies of God. While visiting an Assemblies of God working with the Tribe of Barobo Rev. William Klorjuo Brown met Missionary White. In 1928 he asked her to come to his hometown of Manolu where he was now Tobou Chieftain, Maryland County, and open a mission. She responded that she finished her rotation, was soon to return to the United States, but promised to return to Liberia.

Before 1929 she was back in Liberia and came as a Missionary of the COGIC, working with the Nyambo people at Bonniken. White said she "found her place in life" in Africa.

Soon she relocated to the hinterland of Wissikeh and established the first Liberian Church Of God In Christ. She promised Rev. Brown that she could make arrangements for another Missionary to come and open a mission at Manolu and authorized him to open a school and serve as teacher until she could provide him a teacher. When Rev. Brown appealed to the chiefs and tribal leaders, they gave him 18 young men to form his first class of Manolu Mission School. Later she opened a mission at Wuluken, Tobou Chiefdom. From there Missionary White sent several teachers to assist Rev. Brown with the school until Missionary Francina Wiggins arrived.

She was revered among the people she served. Prior to the Liberian Civil War, Bishop Abraham Brown made videos of one of the churches in the hinterland where a mural was drawn of Mother White. She spent seven years there before returning to the homeland.

WILLIE CURTIS RAGLAND — MISSIONARY TO LIBERIA 1934 - 1946

Mission Station: Tugbaken

Place of Origin: Columbus, GA; Mother and father Buddy and Mary Hudson

Appointed to Missions Work by: Mother Lizzie Robinson; Founder of the Tugbaken Missions along with Missionary Beatrice Lott

Other Highlights: Mother Ragland was the founder of the Good Samaritan Home for the Aged. The home was later destroyed by fire.
Family: Although the name of her husband is not known the couple had one daughter, Mrs. Curtis J. Day.

Ragland received the call to service on the foreign fields when she was a very young woman. The second missionary appointed to the Board to be sent to Liberia, was Willie Curtis Ragland, who did not know Mother White, nor did she know that the Church had a missionary in Africa. Mother Lizzie Robinson informed her. In 1934 Mother W.C. Ragland was sent forth to join Mother White in this New Field. Mother White was formerly with the Assemblies of God and Mother Ragland was formerly a member of the Seven Day Adventist Church.

She gave up her work in Africa and returned home to care for her aged mother.

Ragland had the help of Mother Lizzie Woods Robinson who entreated the saints to assist her in going to serve in Africa. The following article from a 1931 edition of the Whole Truth shows Robinson using her power as international supervisor:

MISSIONARY NOTICE

To the Overseers, Pastors, and State Mothers. Greetings

This is to notify you that we have appointed Miss Willie C. Ragland of 455 Berkley St., Camden, NJ to the foreign fields.

She is to be the next missionary to Africa to help Sister Elizabeth White while in Africa. Sister Ragland was at the general meeting and we asked her to get out into the world like Sister White and get up all she can, also her fare to Africa. We are asking you to receive her and asking that she send all monies collected to Elder C.G. Brown.

Overseers, pastors, and State Mothers, please assist her and help all you can, as we want to send her as soon as possible as Sister White needs her help.

Please receive her as she comes to you.

Mother Lizzie Robinson, General Supt. of Women's Work.

BEATRICE S. LOTT — MISSIONARY TO LIBERIA
1939 – 1962

Mission Station: Tugbaken

Place of Origin: Born February 13, 1907 to James and Savannah Lott in Hearne, Texas; retired in Cleveland Ohio

Call to Missions: 1937; During a revival service called "The Time of Refreshing," I was caught away in the Sprit for three days and nights and could only speak in unknown tongues. The Lord readily gave the interpretation: "You've been called to Africa now. Go! Go! Go!"

Appointed to Missions Work by: Mother Lizzie Robinson in 1939; Founder of the Tugbaken Missions along with Missionary W.C. Ragland

Tours: In 1939 Missionary Lott and Missionary Ragland boarded the *S.S. Andamia* in New York with the voyage taking 34 days after layovers in Liverpool, England. Left in 1942 by command of U.S. during WWII; Returned to Tugbaken in 1944; Left Tugbaken in 1952 bringing two girls, Lillian and Esther, with her. Accompanied by Martha Barber in 1955 and her niece, Rosiland Jones, whom she raised. Made another trip November 1960. According to Bishop Abraham Brown she made her last trip to visit her work in 1994. Also served as short term missionary to Rio de Janeiro and other countries outside the U.S.

Other Highlights: Along with Sis. Martha Barber built a girl's dormitory, house for missionaries, built a church in 1963 and then added extension; played a steel guitar.

National Office: National Chairman of the Advisory Committee of the Home and Foreign Missions Department

Died: November 9, 1996 with services held November 16, 1996 at the Williams Temple COGIC, Cleveland, OH

The following account of her call is from an interview with her caretaker Dr. Lisa Peeples.

This is an amazing story. Mother Lott was in her late 20s or early 30s. She was working in the church and had not gotten married. She was at Bishop Page's church in Dallas, working with the children and she said she was bored. She was sitting in church one day and there was a missionary who came and ran a revival. During that revival she received a refreshing from the Lord. The Lord filled her. She was only able to speak in tongues for 3 days. People were coming to see this girl who could only speak in tongues for 3 days. The missionary interpreted the tongues and said "Go to Africa."

When the interpretation came her tongue was loosed. Bishop Page saw that she was to go to Africa. Many of the saints came and brought everything she needed and put it on the stage. One of the saints said "girl look at my knees I've been picking cotton to send you to Africa." They brought a sewing machine, her bed. They could see the move of the Holy Spirit upon her. The saints brought money. She needed to do nursing training. I have her papers where she took her exams. It seems that during that time the Department was very organized and very powerful.

In 1939 she went and there were already missionaries of the Church Of God In Christ there, the pioneer Mother Elizabeth White and Missionary Martha Barber.

See Appendix 2:2 for excerpts from a booklet Mother Lott,

Embracing the World, which offers her worldview and the importance of Missions.

MARTHA BARBER – MISSIONARY TO LIBERIA – circa 1946 -?

Mission Station: Tugbaken

Place of Origin: Chicago, IL

Appointed to Missions Work by: Mother Lizzie Robinson

Sometimes after returning to the United States Missionary Martha Barber is supposed to have married Elder Otis G. Clark of Oakland, California. He was the first male preacher to stay at the Lillian Brooks Coffey Rest Home at 154 Arden Park in Detroit and served as Mother Coffey's "unpaid chauffeur." He may have met Barber there, nevertheless when they married their reception was held in Mother Coffey's home. Barber shares her arrival in Liberia with Whole Truth readers:

Cape Palmas, Liberia, W. Africa

To Christendom and friends everywhere, we greet you.

Since our arrival March 28th on a rather bright day about 6:30 p.m. we can truly witness His Marvelous acts among us. Our double chores have about shut off our communication by correspondence.

Leaving you in New York March 17th, we arrived in Liberia's Air Port (Robertsfield) March 18th, about 9:30 p.m. G.M.T.

There waiting the planes to return to the States was Bishop Jackson and Party who had attended the dedicatorial services of The College of West Africa, which has been recently completed.

Annie and Tutu, (alias) Mary Ella Carnita Barber, soon accepted their disembarkment from that splendid Air Craft to the soil of their nativity. This never to be forgotten trip was made possible by the grand Leaders, Officers of The H&F Board, members and friends of the COGIC.

In the flood lites of that gorgeous Airport of the P.A.A. Co., after leaving from the commitments and agreements of our Board, I also demounted to the grounds of my labor. As upon the walk way each passenger trekked to their emissary, was drawn amiably to my solemnized emissary— For my desire was also to characterize St. Matthew 20:4.

Having been rushed to the relief of Sister Melvina Harris, who had such a marvelous job in holding the school with Teacher Sampson Janafo, she also with Elder Robert Kman, had oversight of the yard. The Station showed definite signs and marks of devoted and faithful guidance. Sister Harris, certainly according to her write up to the Whole Truth some years ago while she was yet at home in Monrovia, desiring to be a missionary, proved worthy of being a missionary. For she did the job of a missionary. I therefore recommend her for license. She was indeed weak and frail in body. I thank the church and friends for your help and encouragement to her. After a very few days of care before she was on her way home feeling and a little better.

One of said trips was made possible and with our Ex. Secretary W.J. Taylor. Sect. Taylor, visit was shared between Mother E. White's Station and people. Monrovia and Tugbake. As well as being a very special guest speaker at two of the outstanding churches in Monrovia. It was exciting and sad to see plump Elder Taylor, fall from the hammock and walk up hills and down as we returned from an interesting visit with Mother White and her people who received their guest (The Big Man). Having the same Paramount Chief, Mother White's reception as well as our own was graced with the presence of the noble man. The many gifts to The Big Man consist of goats, cows, chickens, jewelry, and rice. These certainly displayed the joy the people had at his coming.

During Sec. Taylor's visit to Liberia, I was quite pleased after gaining an interview with Senator and lawyer A. Dash Wilson, who had been employed along with Hon. And Mrs. W.A. Rogers in 1949 to negotiate the surveying and settling of Our Mission Land Grant. Therefore they guided us to first get the Tribal agreement for a parcel of land for Mission Work. Similar steps had first been taken by Missionaries Ragland and Lott, in 1939 when they opened the station, Tugbake. In 1950 the Tribal grant was signed and Hon. Rogers prepared and mailed it for preparation for The Legislature, which was set to open at that time. Being near inauguration there was the usual tie up on things.

Upon my return having been asked to ask for a larger plot of land, I started before I reached the mission or even Cape Palmas so as to forward to Our Board the necessary documents while this meeting is on. The land was properly surveyed and paid advance by our good friends the Rogers. While waiting the time for the House of Legislature to open, there came an awful blow to us all that there had been an attempt assassination (but failed) and the surveyors name was entailed. This is the reason for any question of the present situation of our church mission land grant in Tugbake.

I then enclosed $10.00 for which Senator has never indicated he wanted, but knowing one cannot go too far on friendship alone, I so did and again asked his kindness to see what was to be done, and this he did and is doing.

However if you will help us in this case I will be too glad to again forward the list. You might also enjoy a sample of a partial monthly operative cost, for such a station. All right I'll note a sample for you.

   March—$25.90, 22.75, 1.92, 6.00, 128.
   April—$26.25, 22, 90, 1.99, 6.00, 2.32
   May—$97.95, 22.80, 1.96, 6.00, 1.74
   June—$23.85, 22.50, 1.92, 6.00, 2.12
   July—$17.75, 18.60, .62, 6.00, 1.08
   August—$3.50, 17.75, .42, 11.20, 1.96
   Sept.—$20.00, 11.85, --, 1.20, 1.48

October—$26.40, 12, 80, 2.38, 18.00, 2.14

Well! We did agree for a sample, so before you decide it must be complete, I will leave off there. The missionaries' food is not there, as you will notice, plus several other things.

To our Sunday School Publishers kindly send our books much sooner as of now the quarter is always in the last month when they arrive, as we are quite a distance, Thanks. We need Please 8 Church Banners, 100 of each class of books, 8 year books, 20 Teachers Quarterlys, a supply of record and minute books, and whatever you would like us to have.

It was a sad day when our Precious Mother White was rushed to Tugbake with her family of nine, spending a few days and on to Monrovia, into the hospital for a week (being critically ill) finally home. It was a pleasurable duty for me her daughter to accept whatever she desired of me to do. Beloveds I know God hears and answers prayers. One morning when it seemed mother could not make it, I called the Christians and we touched God on the throne. Then I sent to a neighboring town for a hand victrola and played Our Greater Leaders Prayer Record, and again we felt His virtue, as well when we played The Arrangement of the "Gay Sisters," "God Will Take Care of You." Thank God for you who taped Bishop Mason Praying, and all these good benefits.

May I thank you and you all for all and everything? THANK YOU.

As I close, we beg forgiveness, until we shall make for your enjoyable account more detailed.

We joined in the opening fast of the meeting, and the Lord did bless, and we are expecting more.

Pray for Our Convocation at Christmas time—While you are shopping and enjoying those near and dear do not forget us away out here. Have a GOOD CHRISTMAS IN CHRIST. We all greet you all. Pray for us as we do likewise for you.

Yours in foreign Christian service, Martha M. Barber.

DOROTHY WEBSTER EXUME — MISSIONARY TO HAITI 1947-1977

Mission Station: Haiti

Place of Origin: Born August 10, 1922 in Cleveland Ohio to Fred Daniel Webster and Mary Webster (Doll)

Stateside Profession: High School French Teacher

Education: Dual degree in French and Sociology with English minor (Case Western); Master's of Religious Education (Interdenominational Theological Center 1972); Doctorate with emphasis in Christian Education (Union Graduate School 1982)

Call to Missions: Between the ages of 8 and 12, Dorothy heard a message about African missions at Liberty Hill Baptist Church and said, "When I grow up I want to go and help them." After praying about serving in foreign missions the Lord gave her a dream which was interpreted by Mother Elizabeth Bracy to serve in Haiti. She assigned and arrived in Haiti in 1947 accompanied by International Supervisor Mother Lillian Coffey and Bishop A.B. McEwen.

Appointed to Missions by: Mother Lillian Brooks Coffey

National Work: Founder, COGICs Mason School and Orphanage in Haiti; Secretary to Mother Lillian B. Coffey; Staff Member of Planning Committee of First Int'l

Women's Convention; Founder of Aides to the President, a prestigious group of women, recommended by their State Supervisor to serve the Women's Convention, name later changed to Task Force; Along with Mother Anna Crockett Ford Dr. Exume served as broadcaster for Women's Convention radio programs; First Supervisor of Haiti under Bishop Esau Courtney and briefly under Bishop D'atrouche; Instructor, C.H. Mason Theological Seminary, Trustee Board Member, C.H. Mason Theological Seminary

Died: January 4, 2011

Missionary Dorothy Webster Exume was an unusual woman and unusually gifted. She established missions, approximately twenty churches, a number of schools, a multi-family housing project, feeding programs, launching new programs for arriving missionaries and micro-financing self-sufficiency for entrepreneurial single mothers.

FRANCINA WIGGINS — MISSIONARY TO LIBERIA 1949-1961

Mission Stations: Manolu (sometimes spelled Monolu)

Place of Origin: Michigan

Appointed to Missions Work by: Mother Lillian Coffey

Mother Naomi Lundy recalls Mother Wiggins as a woman of order and an educator. The following is taken from the testimony of Bishop Abraham Brown, former Overseer of Church Of God In Christ Mission Stations at Monulu, Tugbaken and Wissikeh.

Rev. William K. Brown prayed for a Missionary for his hometown of Manolu for over twenty years. His prayer was answered on August 17, 1949 when a young Missionary arrived in Harper County, Liberia. Her name was Francina B. Wiggins. After resting at the Bethel Home, a missionary home in the coastal Harper City, she moved on into the interior to meet Mother White at Wuluken Mission. Joseph Brown, a student at Manolu notes that the missionaries received their assignment from Mother White as she was the oldest missionary. From Wuluken, Missionary Wiggins received her assignment to move to Manolu to establish the Manolu Mission Station.

Rev. Abraham W. Brown served as her interpreter as she did not speak the language. With determination Missionary Wiggins built the Manolu Mission from "nothing" but served the Lord in Liberia until 1961 when she returned to the U.S.

She gives a report of her work in Liberia in the Whole Truth.

Cape Palmas, Liberia, West Africa

Greetings to the entire Convocation from the missionaries of The Churches of God in Christ in Cape Palmas area Liberia, West Africa.

The Church Of God In Christ has three established missions in this section. At Manalu where I am in charge we have a membership of fifty. We have served in this town for the past five years under Mother White who supported a day school here. When I came over I began the mission buildings and organized the church. We have operated a full mission program for the past year.

God is blessing our labor. Many of the young people came and accepted Christ. The young saints and the school children are now engaged in our first permanent school and church building. Prior to this we used temporary mud huts for services and school. We also operate an elementary mission school. The present enrollment is 45 students. Fifteen of these are boarding students. They live on the mission premises supported wholly by the grants sent from our board. Applications are in hand for receiving twice this number, but we do not as yet have the accommodations. One other native teacher and myself make up the faculty and staff.

We have an outdoor clinic which is operated by your missionary and supported by medical supplies from one Sister Ida Burrell in Princeton, New Jersey. May God ever bless her efforts. One twelve year old Alfred Weah who was dying of spinal meningitis was touched by God. A baby choking to death of intestinal worms was healed; A fourteen year old was dying from a poisonous snake bite was healed. Another young woman suffering, was unable to get off her mat for several months, was healed. She now does all her farm work. We are praising God for his great works among the people here. Pray for us that we may gather in the harvest of the Lord.

We have just received into our organization another church in a town about ten miles from here. They are heathens turning to Christ. They have never been in any other organization. We have carried several Evangelistic services into that town, also to every surrounding town within fifteen miles of our station. We stay overnight sleeping and eating among the heathens that they might hear the gospel. We are soliciting for pastor, school teacher and two deacons, four pairs of men's shoes, size eight; four used dress suits; four shirts and four pairs of trousers. They are faithful and loyal to the work serving as unto God.

We are happy to make honorable mention of our dear friends of this church Mr. and Mrs. Wm. Rogers who visited our convocation in 1949. They have gone out of their way and made every possible effort to assist your missionary in this field. May God ever smile upon them.

Francena Wiggins

PEARL PAGE BROWN — MISSIONARY TO HAITI 1962-1963 AND LIBERIA 1965-1968

Mission Stations: Honduras, Haiti, Liberia

Place of Origin: Born in Mississippi, raised in Sykeston, MO; currently residing in San Jose, CA

Marriage: To Elder J.D. Brown (1976), pastor of the Temple of Prayer Evangelistic Church Of God In Christ after returning from Missions Field

Education: Bachelor's and Master's Degrees from San Jose State University; Doctor of Divinity, International Seminary

Stateside Profession: Educational Counselor, Student Personnel

Appointed to Missions: by Mother Annie L. Bailey

National Work: President, International Sewing Circle and Artistic Fingers; Served under every International Supervisor from Mother Lizzie Robinson to Mother Willie Mae Rivers

Mother Pearl Page Brown was saved at five years of age at St. Louis' Kennerly Temple where Elder Samuel Jones served as pastor. She is a self described Masonite. She received her first license under Mother Lola Young, State

Mother of Ohio North Jurisdiction, in 1951. She relocated to California in 1959 and worked her way to Belize, British Honduras in 1960. The church sent her to at least three countries; however, she has ministered in twenty-seven. In 1962 Mother Lola Young accompanied her to Miami and put her on a ship to Haiti where, she served until she returned home in 1963 because of political unrest in the country. In the Holy Convocation she teaches in the O.T. Jones Training Institute and is a favorite among convocation delegates.

The International Outlook Magazine was the official organ of the COGIC Missions Department and was a communications tool for stories from the missions' fields, requests for assistance, updates on conferences and news from the foreign missionaries themselves. Below is a story written by Mother Pearl Page Brown:

On My Way to Liberia – International Outlook 1964

It has been a pleasure serving and ministering to the Lord's people in America, Honduras, and Haiti. I do mean to work until the day is done.

Once again I am saying, "Here am I, Lord, send me." I shall be leaving for Liberia, around the first of the year, to serve the Church there.

This time I will embrace a new phase of missionary work: that of clinical practices. The Lord blessed me to recently graduate from a school of Missionary medicine in Los Angeles, where I learned a smattering of just about everything from pulling teeth to the study of tropical diseases, public health, and sanitation, laboratory sciences, pharmacology, and therapy, etc.

Since God's divine love is so precious to me, I owe Him and my Church my life, for the cause of Missions.

I want to do all within my power to lead the lost, dying and suffering to Christ. With this thought in mind, we plan to minister to the physical needs and win the soul. In addition to this, we will train for vocations, instruct in the art of sewing, and pass on my "Instant, medical training."

Last, but not least by any manner of speaking, I will be praying always in the Holy Ghost, trusting God to supply all our needs through you. Relying upon and teaching the Bible every minute of the day.

I am depending upon your prayers and financial support to help me secure medical and other necessary supplies to take with me.

It is my sincerest desire to get acquainted either personally or by letter withal who will be prayer partners and helpers.

There are many specific supplies and needs that must be secured before I leave. If the Lord will put on your heart an interest to do something in this great Missions Work, especially in Liberia, I shall be happy to give you further information at the Memphis meeting, or through my Ohio mailing address—3717 East 147th St., Cleveland, Ohio, c/o Mother Lola C. Young—or Box 45, Cape Palmas, Liberia, Africa, after January.

May God bless you as you help us to help others. I am gratefully yours for Christ and Missions.

Pearl Page

ABRAHAM BROWN, OVERSEER AND JESSIE BROWN – TEACHER, LIBERIA

Mission Stations: Manolu, Tugbaken, Wissekeh

Place of Origin: Born in 1934 in Maryland County, Cape Palmas, Liberia, West Africa; Son of the Grebos people;

Mother Brown born in Maryland County, Cape Palmas, Liberia, West Africa

Call to Missions: After leaving Mother White's Station the Lord called him to Manolu in 1947 saying *Somebody needs your help*

Appointed to Missions by: Mother White (Manolu) and Bishop Samuel Crouch (All Maryland County)

National Office: Jurisdictional Bishop, Ivory Coast since 2007

Bishop Abraham Brown was saved in 1939 in Liberia. Shortly after that he met Mother W.C. Ragland at the Tugbaken Mission Station where he helped cut bush. He began missions work in 1947 with Mother Elizabeth White. At that time she operated an orphanage, taking in infants whose mothers died in childbirth. He also served as an interpreter. As her mail boy he walked thirty-five miles one way to Cape Palmas to get the mission's mail. After a disagreement over the handling of a teacher he left the mission for a time. Upon his return he walked up a hill toward the Wrouke Mission Station where Mother White was building a new work, knowing that he had to pay respect to her and make straight paths. Mother White welcomed him and sent him to work with Missionary Francina Wiggins (1949) through whom the Manolu Mission in Cape Palmas was founded and established.

She recommended him as a carpenter and asset informing her that with his help Mother Wiggins would get the Mission Town running. He was licensed as a minister in 1949.

In 1960 he was one of the Friends of Liberian Youth brought to Saints Junior College in Lexington, MS by Dr. Arenia Mallory. Missionary Naomi Lundy remembers when National Mother Lillian Coffey and Dr. Mallory discovered Brother Abraham had a wife in Liberia. "Mother Coffey said young man you have to have your wife here. Dr. Mallory and Mother Coffey sent for his wife Jessie and made them get married again in America." Actually Brother Abraham was bethroed to Sis. Jessie and when she met him in America Bishop John Sheard, currently Chairman of the COGIC Board of Bishops, married the couple.

During his stay at Lexington the COGIC Founder Bishop C. H. Mason died. Brother Abraham was well known as a prayer warrior and most days began prayers from 4 – 5am. Saints President Dr. Arenia Mallory was ill and she did not seem she would attend Bishop Mason's funeral. During the services Dr. Mallory shared how Bro. Abraham came to her bedside and prayed and the Lord raised her up with strength to attend the Memphis funeral. He was ordained as an elder by Bishop B.S. Lyle in 1963. In 1965 Bishop Samuel M. Crouch, President of the COGIC Missions Department appointed him as the Superintendent of the Cape Palmas District. Mother Jessie Brown served as a teacher at the Manolu School for twenty-four years and some former students hold high ranking positions throughout Liberian society.

Brown was a master carpenter and did well overseeing

the work of the COGIC in his country. After an assassination attempt upon his life during the Liberian War which began in 1989, he fled his country. Before becoming a refugee he saw the Manolu Mission Station destroyed and observed the saints killed, wounded and scattered into the forests. Bishop Carlis L. Moody, President, COGIC Missions Department sponsored him and his wife Jessie to come to the United States on resident visas. He has traveled to and from Ivory Coast where many of the saints from Manolu and Liberia held church outdoors with palm branches as a roof until the strong rains came. Afterward the COGIC helped build churches of stone with roofs and altars in which they held Sunday School, YPWW, prayer meetings, choir rehearsals, district meetings and annual convocations.

JULIA M. BURTON — MISSIONS SUPPORTER, SUPERVISOR OF WOMEN, JAMAICA

Place of Origin: Texas

Education: Teaching Degree

Call to Missions: After rededicating her life to God Julia M. Burton, while in prayer, she was the recipient of one of the great visions she had ever witnessed.

As I knelt in prayer and supplication to God, in the midst of many adverse circumstances I was lost in the Spirit of God. I had never seen a foreign missionary. But as I prayed, I beheld myself on a large steamer, and as we neared shore I could see thatched huts and many palm trees. I have yet to see a more beautiful sight. Yes, beautiful because the place where God has for you to work is beautiful when you surrender to his will. As I turned to ask my friends, "where are we going?" no one answered, and little wonder, because heavenly visions can only be answered by heavenly agents. And the still small voice spoke expressly three times; and said Africa, Africa, Africa. This same morning my landlady had said, "move out of my house." But I didn't mind because I had been touched by God. She stated she could not stand the noise of prayer. I walked only one block before God had opened another door. But as I walked these words came to me "birds of the air have nests, foxes, have holes, but the son of man had nowhere to lay his head." I was deeply grateful and encouraged. Many days and nights through the years brought back this same vision. I heard Elder St. Juste, Missionary Webster speak of Haiti, and again I was stirred. I heard missionaries Lott and Barber speak of Africa and again I was torn inside. I talked with Mother [Maude] Jackson of Temple, Texas, who had direct contact with these two and always answered their call for aid. I sat through the years and listened to many foreign workers, and each time the weeping and wailing would take hold of me.

Following is an excerpt from a souvenir book with Mother providing further details of her work with missions.

Involvement dates back to the year 1945 when Mother Lott and Mother Barber were engaged in Liberia. It was a pleasure to meet and listen to the Late Mother Maude Jackson of Temple, Texas, who was almost as much inspiration as our foreign workers were to me. She shared letters received from them with me. It was during this time that I had received a real vision from God about the foreign field and Africa: I have told the story over and over again to the late Supt. J.L. Haynes and Mother Lanell Haynes Lee, late Bishop R.E. Altheimer, and his widow, Mother Berniece Altheimer (Nana). These individuals all have a special love for missions. And lest I forget, Missionary Lou Ivy Littlejohn and (mama) the Late Missionary Jesse Ganaway and Mother Sweetie Porter.

I started to Africa once only to be blessed to return home before going. I say blessed because God had other things in store for me. I was hurt, but I told God if He ever wanted me to return and make another attempt to go again, open the college door for me and He did just that. I graduated in three years with a five year teaching degree. My first trip cost me $300. Our Dean of Travel at Pacific Lutheran University wanted me to go, to be reinsured to work there. I saw the long vision come to pass. The pastor said to me there, "The white man's day is over and that now is Our time!" I went in 1976 with Sister Margaret Harrison of Chicago, Sister and Maggie Bowden of San Francisco. We taught doctrine, Red Cross first aid, Bible and had a great revival with many souls being saved, bodies healed and Saints encouraged. We laid ground for a school (McGlothen-Porter Elementary) but due to lack of funds, this died in its embryonic state.

Upon her retirement she served as hospitality person to the Board, seeing that foreign delegations were housed and fed in Memphis in April and November, and as Secretary to the Board. She also worked at Grand Rapids Junior college, served in the jails and medical facilities.

ELIZABETH COPELAND — MISSIONARY TO HAITI AND THE PHILIPPINES 1955 - ?

Mission Stations: Mother Copeland has worked in Haiti; currently serves in the Philippines

Place of Origin: Calls Daytona Beach, FL home

Marriage: July 1955 at age 17

Education: Begin attending the Chicago School of Design at age 13

Stateside Profession: Fashion Designer; client list included Sammy Davis, Jr., Fats Domino and The Supremes

Call to Missions: Her first assignment as an international missionary began when she traveled to Haiti for a design project and ventured "to the wrong side of the country." Appalled to see individuals sleeping in the streets she vowed she would never return to Haiti. She changed her mind and from the mid 1950s to 1968 she traveled across the Caribbean helping people to help themselves.

Like other women who became international missionaries Mother Copeland's acumen was developed by her work in foreign service and as a home missionary. In 1968 she was diagnosed with cancer and doctors gave her up to die. But God had other plans for the woman who refused to call herself a missionary. As she lay alone one day God told her to get on her knees and pray. Instructing her to "look up" He healed her instantly. Soon after her healing another crisis would catapult her into her calling. A group of young men burglarized her Ft. Lauderdale home were scheduled to become part of the prison system when God spoke to her to form a group to minister to them.

Through the *I Care Ministry*, later renamed the *Yes I Can Ministry* she taught young people the art of craft making and her work took her to the Governor's Mansion and the White House. But she yet had to accept her full calling. In 1988 after years of good health she fell immobile on the floor and listened as God told her that she had done many good things, but had not answered the call. He said He would give her blessing all over the world if she would say 'yes.' When she said yes she was able to get off the floor and since then has returned to Haiti. With the help of engineers from the University of Florida, she built PVC pipes that delivered water to villages. In 1997 she began working with the Aeta people of the Sapang Bato village in the Philippines setting up factories to manufacture the Aetas' unique wood carvings and intricately woven fabric. By paying them $10 per day (compared to the $3 most workers get) Mother Copeland ministry opens doors for the gospel to be preached to these aboriginal Filipinos.

CHARLES AND BETTY KENNEDY – MISSIONARIES TO LIBERIA 1956 – 1964

Mission Stations: Tugbaken, Wissekeh

Place of Origin: Pennsylvania

Call to Missions: While living in Puerto Rico she had a vision of a man in Africa asking her to come. She and her husband prayed and found it was the will of the Lord for them to sell most of their belongings and save to go to Africa.

Appointed to Missions Work by: Mother Lillian B. Coffey

National Office: Supervisor of the Democratic Republic of Congo; Elder Kennedy served as Treasurer-Auditor of the International Home and Foreign Missions Board

While Bro. Abraham Brown and Mother Jessie Brown were appointed missionaries in their native Liberia, Mother Mary Beth Kennedy and Father Charles "Chuck" Kennedy were the only couple documented to have been sent by the COGIC to the mission field prior to 1970. Having informed Bishop O.T. Jones, Sr., he was delighted with their interest in the work of missions. Returning home to Erie, they lived with her mother and made plans for Africa. The couple contacted Mother Martha Barber and asked if she needed help at Tugbaken. She responded that she would love for them to come and they were approved by Mother Lillian Coffey and the Home and Foreign Missions Department for service in Liberia where two of their children were born.

After working for almost a year Tugbaken assisting Mother Martha Barber, a group of villagers came and asked Elder Kennedy to come and explore the abandoned Wissikeh Station where he found the missions station in ruins. After spending one year at Tugbaken, they relocated to Wissikeh and spent seven years there. They were a true missionary team working as a single missionary unit. They rebuilt the station and reopened the school up to the high school level. The Kennedys traveled throughout Africa and the third world ministering in Zambia, Ivory Coast, Dominican Republic, Haiti and other countries. They built a school in Erie, Pennsylvania which celebrated 42 years of existence in 2010. Father Kennedy also pastored in Erie.

Missionaries relied on assistance from individuals and churches to supplement their monthly stipend from the Missions Department. See Appendix 2:8 of a typical letter appealing for assistance which appeared in the Whole Truth, written within a short period after the Kennedy's arrival in Tugbaken.

GRACE YANCEY — MISSIONARY TO THAILAND
1954-1973

Missionary Yancey taught in the private schools of Bangkok as well provided private lessons. Although it was hard for her to take the gospel to a wider audience because of the modes of travel the work of the Church Of God In Christ grew.

Bishop B.J. Crouch was appointed as Bishop of Thailand in 1955 (see Appendix 2:11) and sometime in the late 1960s Bishop Samuel Crouch visited Thailand to encourage her that the headquarters had not forgotten her. As a result she reported in 1970 that Sis. Sarah Green and the Women's Mission Circle of his Emanuel C.O.G.I.C. constantly remembered her with love gifts as well as Elder and Mother Jessie Condy. Bishop E.E. Cleveland was also a great supporter of the Thailand work.

MATEAL MC COY— MISSIONARY TO THE
BAHAMAS 1958 – 1973

NAOMI LUNDY — MISSIONARY TO LIBERIA
1962-1966

Mission Station: Manolu

Place of Origin: Emporia, VA January 26, 1920; family relocated to Philadelphia where she was raised. Saved in 1938 in a revival conducted by the famous evangelist Elder Utah "Two Wings" Smith; was baptized in a river.

Married to: Briefly married during World War II

Call to Missions: The Lord gave her a vision of a harvest field. A "little short man" stood in the field holding a sickle but she could only see his head. She asked the Lord the meaning of the vision of Africa. He answered "this man needs all the help he can get." After sharing the vision with her pastor, Bishop O.T. Jones, Sr., she was interviewed by Mother Lillian Coffey and Mother Arenia Mallory in Memphis, TN.

Appointed to Missions Work by: Mother Lillian Brooks Coffey; left New York for Liberia on the *Pilot* Steamship. Her last trip to Liberia was 1985.

Other service: After returning home, she evangelized in New Jersey, New York, Philadelphia, Arizona, California, and Mexico. She has worked at the Community Center in Gloassboro, N.J. assisting in teaching children the Word.

One of the guiding principles in the life of Naomi Lundy is Proverbs 30:5 *Every word of God is pure; He is a shield unto them that put their trust in Him.* The child of the Depression, she found that God took care of her during challenging personal tests and while on the foreign fields. The first of six children of Bro. and Sis. Lundy, she was an example to her five younger brothers and sisters in Christian character, duty to their parents, faithfulness in performing chores such as cleaning the coal room after the coal man dropped it off and otherwise helping her mom Effie keep their home spotless. As a product of the COGIC she gained spiritual and biblical knowledge from her pastor Bishop O.T. Jones, Sr. Bishop Mason visited the mother church often and would touch the children and youth in blessing them. Not long after he touched her shoulder as he passed she was saved at 17 or 18 and became what she describes as a worker for God. She married a handsome young man by the name of Peter but soon found that some of the girls who chased him caught him. She promptly got herself a divorce and had her name changed back to Lundy. During World War II she wanted to do something and after meeting Mother Lillian Coffey and Bro. Abraham Brown in Memphis, Tennessee became interested in foreign missions work.

I was inspired by God to be a Missionary Worker in Africa. Incredibly, there was a need for a worker at Monalu Mission Station and I was appointed by Mother Coffey to serve. I left for the bush of Africa and worked for 3 ½ years at the Manolu Mission. I served as a missionary in the church, clinic and school. On completion of my tour of duty at Monalu, my successors were: a pastor, missionary couple, Rev. and Mrs. [Abraham] Brown who were former students of the mission. The Brown's were educated by the National Church School [headquartered] in Lexington, MS. The National teacher who assisted me during my administration was sponsored to the states through my efforts to further his education. Rev. Nyema returned to Africa as a missionary to his people and has established two church works as an evangelist and teaches High School for his government.

Since my return home after I recovered from a severe illness, My current work in the Philadelphia area is with the "Women's Christian Workers and Foreign Missionaries Fellowship." I serve as a member of the Sunshine committee and Co-chairperson of "Ways and Means" committee.

EVANGELIST ELIZABETH SCOTT — MISSIONARY TO NIGERIA 1960

The Church Of God In Christ was first planted in the free nation of Nigeria by Bishop F.L. Grier of New York City. Through Bishop Grier and the sacrificial labor of Mother Scott "on the spot" the Church Of God In Christ developed. (For the expansion of the COGIC in Nigeria see Chapter 11).

JUNE BLACKWELL — MISSIONARY TO LIBERIA 1962 - ?

ROSETTA GRAHAM — MISSIONARY TO GHANA

In addition to the above, the following were included in the 1954-55 Yearbook of the Church Of God In Christ

MISSIONARIES
Miss Effie Bright

Mrs. Mary St. Juste, Haiti

SUPERVISORS OF FOREIGN FIELDS

Mrs. Kattie Frazier, first missionary to the Bahamas

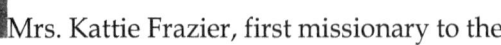

Mrs. Willie Holt, Hawaii
Mrs. Selma Lockett, Jamaica
Mrs. Ernestine Beatrice Washington, Haiti (1967)

OVERSEERS/BISHOPS OF FOREIGN FIELDS
Bishop Samuel Crouch, South Africa
Bishop A.B. McEwen, Bishop of Foreign Fields
Bishop W.G. Law, Bishop of Foreign Field (1947)
Bishop Charles Pleas, Africa/Liberia
Bishop W.A. Kates, Jamaica/Turks Island

49th Annual Convocation in 1956
Bishop O. Freeman, Transjordan
Bishop I. Favors, Egypt
Bishop G.B. Pickens, Cuba
Mrs. E. Lee, Bermuda

OTHER PIONEER MISSIONARIES AND SUPPORTERS
Bishop W.H. Reed, Hawaii
Elnora Lee, Bermuda
Jewel McKenzie, W.C.A.
Winifred Holder, Supervisor of Panama
Elder Richard Griffith, Guyana

June Blackwell

CHAPTER TEN

Missions Beginnings and News from Whole Truth and Other Media

Media reports of global missions provide a wider understanding of as much of the activities as possible.

The Western Voice, July 1943

Excerpts from Our African Correspondent, Rev. J.M. Mutshweni, Church Of God In Christ, 328 Fortuin Street, Ladyselborne Pretoria, Transvaal, South Africa

Dearly beloved, Rev. Crouch, we hope you that you are enjoying God's blessings in the Gospel work as we do here in South Africa. Dear, we pray always for our Brethren over there in the USA. We don't know each other but we shall see each other in the Great City of God in His Throne of God. Only the Work needs Support here in South Africa, as all the Ministers and Evangelists need some help for the Work of God as I have been writing to you about this Work. The work is very Great here in South Africa. We need some Missionaries (Missionary) to come here in Africa to help us in the great need of Gospel. We pray that the Lord may send one of you here in South Africa, to help us as we need some Church buildings and church schools. All our Ministers are suffering from lack of support for the work of God. Please pray for our Church Work here in South Africa. Here in Africa there are many native tribes, speaking about 31 different languages. They are scattered far and wide throughout the Western Transvaal. We reach them by pushing bicycles as far as 96 miles from the Home in the hot sun and on rainy days. Pray for this work for God to give us something quicker than bicycles. We need here at Ladyselborne Pretoria, a HEADQUARTERS for the whole work of the Church Of God In Christ our (feelings) feelings in this; we want you Elder Samuel Crouch to take charge of the work and help us, that is our prayer for you.

Give our greetings to all the brethren and sisters in the Church Of God In Christ. We are glad that we belong in this great Church Of God In Christ. My wife sends her love to you all in that far land.

Dear beloved Bro. Crouch, will you be so kind again to send me some Church Certificates for my helpers and also some Baptismal Certificates and Evangelist Appointment Certificates.

I have received a letter from Sister Mrs. E.J. Dabney of 29th and Susquehanna Ave., Philadelphia, Penn, USA.

I reported to you that we have a very, very good work in our church at Bechuanaland. We have about 300 members in that country of Bechuanaland. Pray for them and many of them are baptized by the Holy Ghost. Also in the East Transvaal at Lydenburg Tvl, the work is going on well. The pastor is Bro. Philip B. Maimela. Also at Pokwanimiddleburg Yvl. God is blessing our pastor, Bro. John N. Molemane. Tell all the brethren to pray for them. I praise God for being in the Work of the Church Of God In Christ as the Lord has called me in the ministry. I preach the Gospel for 23 years now. Don't forget to send me these papers please: 60

Ordination Certificates, 22 Appointment Certificates for Ministers, 18 Evangelist Appointments, 100 Baptismal Certificates for church members. Also some Church Magazines of the Church Of God In Christ.

Whole Truth – November 1952, Vol XXIII Number 56

LONDON, ENGLAND

Greetings in Jesus' sweet name. We are yet reporting victory over sin and shame.

"Why do the heathen rage, and the people imagine a vain thing? The Lord said Ask of me, and I shall give thee the heathen for thine inheritance, and the uttermost parts of the earth for thy possession." Psalms 2:1-2

The Cottage Prayer Band of the Church Of God In Christ, London, England, opened its first session October 10, 1952. Evangelist M. White, presiding; Mother Mary McLachlan, church mother and treas.; Sis. Marjorie McLachlan, Y.P.W.W. President; Brother Lawrence McLachlan, acting deacon and also Brother Ken Gordon acting deacon. The number present at our first sitting was nine, and we are glad to report that one soul was won for the Lord. Friday night is our regular meeting night.

Evangelist White, Foreign Field Missionary

Whole Truth – December 1955, p. 2

ALASKA

Except the Lord build the house, they labor in vain that build it. Except the Lord keep the City, the watchman waketh but in vain. Psalms 127:1

Greetings to the Saints of God everywhere. We are happy to report victory over sin and shame through the blood of Jesus. The Lord has done great things for us whereof we are glad.

We truly thank God for the work in the Territory of Alaska through the help of God and our Pastor Elder C.D. Williams and wife who has worked untiringly. They being young people it is marvelous that they are willing to make such a sacrifice to work in the great Northwest and the Lord has blessed their labor.

November 1, 1953 he opened a mission with five members, and his wife and the church has grown from five to forty (40) members however due to this city being a Military center fifteen (15) have rotated to various parts of the States and as of today we have thirty (30) adults and a Sunday School of Eighteen (18) children regular attendance.

It was our Pastor's desire to build God a house and we do thank God for our State Supervisor who encouraged our Pastor and she put on the first drive for our church which closed May 29, 1955 raised the sum of Fourteen Hundred Dollars and the Pastor was inspired the more to accomplish his aim. The saints had a mind to work and the Lord blessed us in our every effort for which we are thankful.

On September 4, 1955 we marched from our old church to the new edifice singing "When the Saints Go Marching In." We had a time in the Lord that day. When the Saints entered the building they entered shouting and praise the Lord for this great blessing. We had present with us our Bishop Tolliver, State Supervisor Mother Cotton, Elder Randolph, Elder Hutchinson, Minister Thornton and Minister Thurston and many of the other saints from Fairbanks. We enjoyed their presence and are saying to them, Come Again.

We thank God for our Assistant Pastor, Elder C.W. Williams, and Elder Walker who has worked so faithful with us also our Deacons.

Whole Truth – February 1957, Number 2 Vol XXXII

MONTREAL, CANADA

Watch ye therefore, for ye know neither the day nor the hour wherein the son of man cometh. Matt. 25:13

Greetings to the saints of God everywhere. The pastor and saints of the COGIC in Montreal, Canada are happy to greet you in the name of the Lord Jesus Christ.

We thank God for our pastor and wife who through much difficulties are faithfully laboring with us. We pray God will bless them to do the work in Montreal.

On February 3rd, Bishop Franklin appointed Sis. Gailant as mother of Montreal Church Of God In Christ. We are happy that God has blessed her. Mother Gailant desires all of your prayers that God will grant her wisdom to fulfill her duties as befitting the mother of a church. That she will ever stay humble in God's will, so she may be a shining example of those following.

We thank the Lord for Eld. Crenshaw from Springfield, Mass. Who conducted a two week's revival. Truly he was under the anointing as he gave forth God's word. A few of his texts were "The Wages of Sin is Death," Romans 6:23; "Stand Still, The Lord Shall Fight For You." Exodus 13-15, "Be Filled with the Spirit." Eph. 5:18, "Love."

BELIZE, B.H.

Blessed be the God and Father of our Lord Jesus Christ, who hath blessed us with all spiritual blessing in heavenly places in Christ. Eph. 1:3

We have just closed a one week campaign in the Stann Creek Town under our Dist. Supt. Eld. Laing, Missionary H. Taylor, Ministers G. Domingo, H. Cattouse and Bro. Lloyd

Miguel. We are now establishing a work in the capital of this district. We held our services in the open air, and each night we expounded the word of God to hundreds of folk gathered to listen, and by the indication of upraised hands, and personal contact, we found out that they are really hungry for the full gospel which this church has for everybody who can and will believe.

They want us to stay in their midst, and thus constrained us to secure a building which by prayer and fasting we hope will be a lighthouse in their town. Among the many churches in this town there are none like this great Church Of God In Christ. The people are godly proud that our Founder is still alive, and that he is a Negro, also that our brothers and sisters in America care for us. We are hereby asking you dear saints in America to help us. We need clothing, books of all kinds, Bibles, musical instruments and finance. We are confident that many of you saints have things lying around that could be of much service to us in Stann Creek, more than you would think they would. Therefore, I am asking your help for we are determined to carry out our Lord's command and commission unto the uttermost parts of the earth. Will you heed the Macedonian cry, come over and help us? Please send all donations for the Stan Creek work to Br. Hond., directed to Eld. Melbourne Laing, Dist. Supt. Stann Creek, c/o Calvary Temple, Regent St. West, Belize B.H.

May God bless you all for your open hearts for us.

Eld. M. Laing, Dist. Supt.
Sis. H. Taylor, Dist. Miss.
Min. H. Cattouse, Reporter

Whole Truth – April 1959, page 3

British Honduras

P.O. Box 96, Belize British Honduras, Central America

Dear Christian Friends

Again this month we humbly thank our God that He enables us to minister to the many people here in British Honduras. February 6th to 15th we were blessed to have the 5th Annual Convocation of the Church Of God In Christ; delegates from the United States who attended were: Elder A.T. Turner, Madam Marrie Wiggins, Missionary A.T. Turner from Bridgement, Connecticut, Missionary Alma Johnson of Toledo, Ohio and Evangelist Milton Perry of New York.

This year the services were great and crowds were even greater than former years. Souls were saved and healed. Madam Wiggins thrilled the audience every night with her great Gospel Songs.

The Convocation closed on the 15th, then on Monday night, the 16th we went into the MEMORIAL PARK for a Great City Wide Revival Crusade with the Slogan BELIZE FOR CHRIST. Several thousand came out every night to hear MILTON PERRY of New York, American's foremost young evangelist. The city of Belize was stirred as never before in the history of the Colony. Night after night Miracles of Healing were performed before the eyes of the people, many had read about Divine Healing before but they had never actually seen it in an open area. So many blind eyes open, deaf receiving their hearing and the dumb to speak. Each night hundreds were prayed for and on the last night five hundred and fifty-four people were prayed for, still hundreds sought deliverance and prayer but they could not be prayed for individually. Thousands went away disappointed but we prayed that God in some way would undertake and bring them the deliverance they sought for souls and bodies.

Apart from the Healing many Conversions took place also, some received the Baptism of the Holy Ghost. You should know too that the Old enemy worked very hard to hinder the meetings. Pressure was placed on the authorities to stop the meetings…To continue this Move of God we are needing your financial support immediately.

Mother Gladys Coleman, one of our very fine missionaries, is gone to one of the villages. To keep her there we need at least ten dollars per month for her support, perhaps God will speak to some one of you as you read this to help us in the support of these workers that are going out on faith. We have several faith workers and we are asking you to assist us with $10 per month for one of these workers. If you desire the address of one of these workers so you can send direct let us know. But please help us in the support of one of these that have gone out on faith.

They are toiling daily without proper food and it is you and your support that must keep them alive on the field. Can you afford to give $10.00 per month? That one of these might live and carry the Gospel amidst snakes and other wild reptiles and animals. For heaven's sake and the cause of Christ, Write us today and let us know that you are standing behind us in your giving. God bless you.

Sincerely yours,
Bishop Malchus B. Bennett
P.O. Box 96, Belize
British Honduras

Whole Truth – November 1959, Vol. XXXIII Number 11

Turks Island

Greetings to the Whole Truth Readers everywhere:

O praise the Lord, all ye nations: praise Him, all ye people. For His merciful kindness is great toward us: and the truth of the Lord endureth forever. Praise ye the Lord. Ps. 127(?)

We the saints and pastor of the Church Of God In Christ for thanking God for all His benefits. We are just out of a few weeks revival of which five souls were saved, sanctified and baptized with the Holy Ghost and fire. Many backsliders returned. On Sept. 20th, we marched down to the water and three were baptized by Eld. J.N. Watkins.

We are also blessed to have with us the daughter of Eld. J.N. Watkins, a great missionary for Jesus Christ. The church doing well under the leadership of Eld. J.N. Watkins. Pray much for him and family.

Elder J.N. Watkins, Pastor
Mother Mary Grant, Church Mother
Maycita Simmons, Reporter

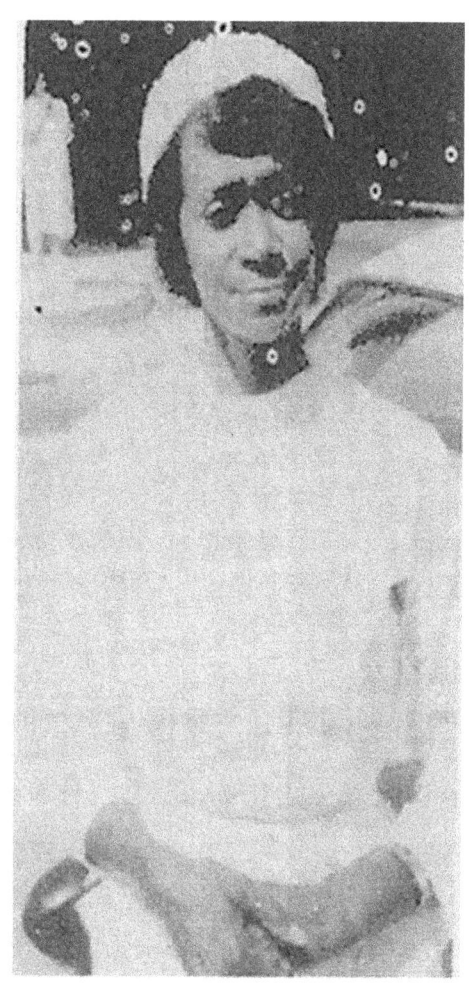

Pearl Page Brown

CHAPTER ELEVEN

Church Of God In Christ International Missions and Church Plantings Prior to 1970

There are reports of unnamed Church Of God In Christ women who have journeyed to countries other than those mentioned in this project. Because a comprehensive treatment of Church Of God In Christ missions history is yet to be written, it is very believable this occurred. I am including a synopsis or at least the dates of origination of those churches outside the United States gathered from women and men I have become acquainted with over the years.

Jamaica
Established 1919

The history of the Church Of God In Christ in Jamaica goes back to the year 1919 when one Elder Alfred Cunningham came to our Shores with the Pentecostal doctrine, and preaching of the Church Of God In Christ.

Since then the church experienced a number of ups and downs under many leaders. Most of the Leaders lived in the United States and were unable to act immediately when problems arose. As a result the church lost as many as 30 churches at one time. These churches broke away to join other denominations.

Bishop Kates was appointed to have the oversight of the churches on the Island. Property was bought at 4 Nelson Road, Kingston 13 that was used as the Headquarters of the movement. After the demise of the Bishop Kates the property was sold to another group that still held the name Church Of God In Christ.

History made mention of one Bishop Driver who came to Jamaica and was for some time in charge of the Churches. During these periods not much mention was made of church growth or expansion. The emphasis was mainly focused on Leadership.

Sometime in the year 1963 the Bishop Ivor F. S. Rowe was sent to Jamaica since he was a native of Jamaica residing in the States, to see about the welfare of the Church. During that same year, another group was in the act of Incorporating Church Of God In Christ. This group however had their charter done with one Bishop Dawkins of Panama.

In 1976 Bishop Ivor Rowe also incorporated The Church Of God In Christ with International Headquarters in Memphis Tennessee. This act was seen by others as an act of rivalry with other groups. This move however did not serve to unite the already fragmented work, but further divide it. There were those who claimed to be the original Church Of God In Christ.

Under Bishop Rowe's leadership property was bought in the City of Kingston to house the Headquarters of the Church. This property was located at 14 Fairway avenue. Because of legal restraints the church had to relocate to the present address, 25 Mountain View Avenue, Kingston 2. Our Headquarters building is now 75 percent completed. Since the Churches were always struggling for survival and financial help, they were always vulnerable to anyone who would come and promise to help. It was this kind of movement which saw yet another break away. Some of the Churches broke away and took on the name Church Of God In Christ United. This move was another subtle plan to divide and gain power by making promises. Jamaica is located in the Caribbean Sea. Every year the Island is exposed to the ravages of Hurricanes. Often times when damages occur as a result of winds and flooding, very little or no help is forth coming, leaving some people to wonder whether or not we do have a Headquarters.

During Bishop's tenure, there was a merger with the Church of God Ground of Truth under the late Overseer S. N. Golding. This merger went on for a while until disagreements arose over where the Headquarters should be located. A division took place which saw some of the churches going back from whence they came, while others chose to stay.

In 1988 after Hurricane Gilbert devastated most of the church buildings the Bishop Ivor Rowe went to be with the Lord. Serving with the late Bishop Rowe as Supervisor of the Women's department was the late Mother Ruth Barren. Mother Julia Burton took over from Mother Barren and served the Jurisdiction until 1993. Mother Rebeca Gordon took up the mantle and became our National Mother until the appointment of Supervisor Beverly Joyner in 2004.

In November of 1989 Bishop Harold A. Haughton was consecrated and given the mantle to oversee the Jurisdiction of the Church Of God In Christ. There are some thirty churches in the Jurisdiction, with seven Superintendents and twenty Pastors. Churches are located in 10 of 14 Parishes on the Island. It is our desire to plant churches in all 14 Parishes, and to uphold the name of the Church Of God In Christ.

Bishop H.A. Haughton

Turks & Caicos Islands
Established 1922

In 1922 after attending the National Holy Convocation Elder Cornelius Hall, a native of North Caicos, British West Indies, volunteered to return (living in California) to his homeland to minister to his people. It was at his return that the Holy Ghost first fell on the island. He served faithfully for ten years. He died at sea while on a voyage traveling to reach his people.

After the loss of Elder Hall, the work was carried on by Elder R.E. Handfield and Hanover Hall who had been assistants to Elder Hall. Elder Handfield served in the Turks Islands faithful until his death in 1949. A few years later Elder Hanover Hall also died. Until approximately 15 years ago when Pastor Courtney Missick was made pastor of Grace Temple COGIC had died.

Ninety one year old Bro. William Simmons stated that he "was about 9 years old when the Holy Ghost first fell on the island but I remember people falling out under the Spirit. Folks came from their farms and out of the woods as the singing and preaching went forth. After the death of Elder Hanover Hall the church died and the Church of God of Prophecy picked up the work."

Pastor Charles Delancy, Pastor Janet Stubbs and Supervisor Spencer took a boat from Providenciales to North Caicos to walk the land where the original Church was God in Christ was built. The foundation is yet there and for the people of North Caicos it is holy ground. Pastor Delancy is the grandson of Elder Hanover Hall so the revival of the original church means much to him. The Church of God on Prophecy has put up a marker across the road giving them credit for the 1922 experience.

This report provided by Mother Clararetha Spencer, Supervisor of Turks & Caicos Islands Jurisdiction, Bishop Charles E. Black, Prelate. May 2011

Haiti
Established 1929

Elder Joseph Paulceus, a Haitian brother who lived in the U.S.A. was saved in the Church Of God In Christ in the early 1920's. In the spring of 1928 he felt led of the Lord to go back to Haiti, his homeland, to preach to his people the Gospel of Jesus Christ, according to the patterns set in the Acts of the Apostles. He went to Bishop C.H. Mason who prayed for him, gave him a tent, enough funds for his voyage and he boarded a boat for Haiti. He arrived in Port-au-Prince, the capital of that country on July 2, 1928.

In the meantime Brother Van Alking, an Assembly of God Missionary from Vancouver, Canada, came to Haiti in 1928 and preached the full Gospel to Brother Joseph St. Juste, who was a member of the Episcopal Church.

Brother St. Juste and his family accepted the words and were baptized in the water. Brother St. Juste, as a baker, was a hard working man. Brother Van Alking who saw him as someone who wanted to help himself, told him, "I want you to be your own boss." He found an old bakehouse with a living quarter, at 167 Rue des Fronts, where we are having now our 42nd Convocation. He rented it with his own money, built a large table and a kneading part and turned everything over with a small capital to Brother St. Juste. He put him to work, left the country and never came back. Brother St. Juste operated the bakery for almost 18 years, taking care of his family and with the profits from his business he later helped the ministers and helped to buy properties for the church.

Brother St. Juste, who was worshipping God in his home, was praying the Lord to send someone who would continue the teaching of the deeper experience with God of Brother Van Alking. Therefore, he received with great joy Elder Paulceus when he arrived in Haiti and made a room available for him and also a place of worship in his living room. Through the teaching of Elder Paulceus, Brother St. Juste and his family received the baptism of the Holy Ghost. And on January 1929, they held the first service of the Church Of God In Christ in Haiti. Later the Church was moved to Bel 'air where the tent given by Bishop Mason was fixed. Meanwhile, Brother St. Juste continued to pay the rent for this property until 1947 when it was bought for the church by Bishop and Sister C.H. Mason and Mother Coffey. It was to be used as residence for Bishop St. Juste and his family.

Bishop St. Juste, his wife, their son Louis, who from 1957 to 1968 was our Bishop, and their daughter Raymonde, passed away. When your humble servant was given the supervision of the work in 1973, he decided to demolish the old building and to erect on this property an edifice which will serve as the main church and the national Headquarters in Haiti of our denomination.

(Excerpted *from "Bishop Dautruche Constructs New Haitian Church Headquarters at Sight of Old Landmark* by Bishop L. Dautruche, The Voice of Missions, Church Of God In Christ Missions Magazine, May June 1978, p. 16)

COGIC Development in Canada Begins in the 1920s

Province	Founding Prelate	Year Established
Ontario	Bishop C.L. Morton	1920s
Quebec	Bishop W. T. Teague	1948
Alberta	Bishop M.A. Givens	1964
British Columbia	Bishop J.A Blackwell	1966
Ontario	Bishop F. Walls	1980's

In the Late 1920's Bishop C.L. Morton Sr. returned to Canada to start the C.O.G.I.C. Branch in Canada. His first church was in the community of Amherstburg Ontario. He converted a Stable into a church after having services in the street and in homes. After this he started a church in Windsor Ont. across the river from Detroit Michigan.

While in an upstairs room that was used for a church he went on the radio with a program called the Dawn Patrol. Later he started churches in Harrow and Chatham Ontario, where they also had another radio program.

During the Great Depression the Mother church, Mount Zion COGIC was built at 795 McDougal St. where it still stands today. It is now pastored by his oldest son C.L. Morton Jr. You have most likely heard of his other sons the most famous in Christian circles being Bishop Paul Morton from New Orleans. Another church was founded during this time period by an associate pastor at the time Bishop A.T. Harrison in Buxton. The churches in Buxton and Harrow no longer exist.

In the 50's Bishop Morton had a dispute with Memphis and he pulled out from under their authority although he still maintained a good relationship with them. During this time Bishop Mason even came to Canada. Bishop Morton died in the early 60's and a split occurred between the followers of Bishop Morton's family and the then Elder Author Thomas Harrison, the assistant pastor at Mount Zion. Bishop Author Thomas Harrison formed another organization and was appointed Bishop by Memphis and the Ontario Church Of God In Christ was formed. In the late 70's Bishop Harrison tried to convince the Bishops in Memphis that Canada was a mission work but they always wanted to include Canada with Michigan. They expected Canada to be able to give like the other jurisdictions and that was not possible. When the Canadian dollar was deflated they still wanted us to give the same amount in US dollars. So when we did our reports say it was $600.00 it would show up as $400.00 because of the exchange our folks would want to know what happened to the rest of the money.

During the early 60's Harrison started ordaining men in major cities like Toronto. These ministers were immigrants from the West Indies. The first being Elder V.T. Channer. Soon they had churches in Toronto, Mississauga and

Hamilton. The late 70's and early 80's was a period of rapid growth and expansion, Harrison soon had the oversight of over 10 churches. However, from 85 onward, troubles began. Issues soon arose over cultural differences and the leadership style of the bishop. Churches either began to leave or split. Bishop Harrison soon cooled ties to Memphis as well. The main reason for this was that he grew tired of paying reports but not getting any support. He would have some ministers who wanted to start their own works and when he asked for money to help them he was told no it was not a mission field. He decided all the money we raised would stay in Canada. We would fellowship with Memphis but all the money we raised would stay home to help our folks.

During the 90's Bishop Harrison asked me to start work on a constitution for Canada. Before it was totally completed he became ill and Bishop Riley was appointed Ass't. Bishop. Although this is not allowed in the U.S. Bishop Ford said it was allowed in Canada because we were a foreign country. Bishop Riley is a part of the C.O.G.I.C. in Memphis.

Bishop Charles Payne

A Brief History of the Calvary Church Of God In Christ in the United Kingdom

The Calvary Church Of God In Christ in the UK was started in 1952 at 57 Navarino Road in London, by Mother McLachlan, her children (Lawrence, Marjorie, Jean, Edward and Aston) and Deacon Gordon from Brixton, who held regular cottage meetings.

In that same year they were honoured with a visit from

the founder of the Church Of God In Christ in the USA, Bishop C. H. Mason. He was accompanied by an illustrious team, consisting of Bishops Watley and McEwen, along with Bishop Driver, Bishop S. M. Crouch and Bishop O.T. Jones, all of whom had come to London to attend the World Pentecostal Conference at Westminster Central Hall. When they returned to America, Bishop Watley met Missionary White who desired to come to the UK to help to establish the Church Of God In Christ. Bishop Watley agreed to finance her mission and accordingly wrote to Mother McLachlan, asking her to receive Missionary White. Missionary White arrived in London shortly afterwards and, together with Mother McLachlan and Deacon Gordon, spread the Gospel of Jesus Christ and also promoted the Church. They found a hall in Sussex Road, Brixton, London and the worship continued there.

Bishop McLachlan
In 1954 Bishop McLachlan (fourth from right) arrived in London to join his family. He soon found another place of worship at Camden Town in London. As the work grew he met Rev. Fred Peacock, of the Dalston Methodist Mission, with whom he had a close friendship, and worship began there. Halls were also obtained in Harlesden (north west London) and Luton, as well as other areas.

The late Bishop and Mother McLachlan attended the General Convocation in Memphis in 1957. During that Convocation, the late Bishop C H Mason consecrated Bishop McLachlan as the first Bishop of the Church Of God In Christ in England and Wales.

Because of ill health Bishop McLachlan returned to Jamaica in April 1963. Before he left he obtained permission from General Headquarters in Memphis to appoint Robert C Bell as the new Bishop and Mother M J Bell as Mother of the Church.

First building purchased
In 1965 we were blessed with our first Church building, in Luton. Other buildings were subsequently acquired including one in Northumberland Park, Tottenham - which became the UK headquarters - and another in Fentiman Road, Vauxhall, south London. More recently buildings have been acquired in Brockley, and Wood Street in London, as well as Mosely and Aston in Birmingham.

The COGIC has grown considerably since it started and now has active Assemblies in nearly every borough of London as well as in Watford, Dunstable, Bedford, Aylesbury, Birmingham, Manchester and Cardiff.

Republic of Panama
Established 1961

It was 1961 and the Rev. Harry A. Dawkins was the Pastor (exhorter) of the Church of God, Cleveland, Tennessee in the city of Colon, Rep. of Panama. A C.O.G.I.C. Elder, who worked on a cargo vessel (*S.S. Cristobal*) which brought merchandise to Panama, was looking for a Pentecostal Church while the ship was in harbor. He was taken to the Church of God and there he met Exhorter Dawkins. (In those days the Church of God did not ordain blacks, the highest position a black person could reach was the title of Exhorter). Elder Green introduced Exhorter Dawkins to C.O.G.I.C., telling him about how the leadership was black and how it gave him the opportunity to work and grow. He also offered to pay his way to attend the Holy Convocation in Memphis, so he could see for himself. That November, he did travel to the United States and attended the Holy Convocation in Memphis Tennessee.

While Exhorter Dawkins was in Memphis, a young minister who had studied in the United States and had been licensed by the COGIC, came back to Panama and wanted to become the pastor of the church where Rev. Dawkins pastored. He brought in the Superintendent to a meeting accusing Rev. Dawkins and other leaders of things that were not true, ending in the removal of Exhorter Dawkins as the pastor for the Church. During this meeting, the Lord gave one of the Church Mothers Psalms 46, and it confirmed his word, Rev. Dawkins called his wife from the United States and told her to tell the saints to read Psalms 46. Eight members left the Church of God along with Rev. Dawkins and for one solid year they met in the living room of Mother Winifred Holder and did nothing but prayed. In 1962 the COGIC officially started and was registered with the Panamanian and Canal Zone government in 1964. Rev. Dawkins then became the Bishop for the Republic of Panama. The church grew and in 1968 we moved from the Living room of Mother Winifred Holder to our first building, and then called First Temple COGIC on 3rd Street between Central and Melendez Avenue.

In 1974 Bishop Dawkins moved to the United States, trying to establish himself and so be a greater help to the church, however, his health failed and he was unable to return home until 1979. In February 1980 he was called home to be with the Lord. His son, who had remained over the work in Panama, became the Mission Administrator. At the time he was only 32, and felt he was too young to be consecrated as a bishop so he accepted to be over the work with the Title of Mission Administrator. In December of that year 1980, Elder Enrique Dawkins also died, leaving us without a leader. Bishop Moody came and conducted the funeral service and I was then appointed as Legal Representative. This position is required by law, and my function is that of a liaison between the government and the church. In 1981, Elder Abraham W. Forcheney was then appointed Mission Administrator by the Recommendation of the National Executive Board, which is the board that governs the Church in Panama. At present I am the Pastor for the Headquarters Church which was renamed Memorial Temple Church Of God In Christ in 1980 after the death of our Bishop. We have a total of 8 churches and 6 missions. All of which are on the Atlantic side of the Isthmus (province of Colon), except one, Vision C.O.G.I.C. which is in the Province of Panama on the West Bank of the canal in Arraijan.

**Nigeria
Established 1966**

The Lord works in mysterious ways. Such was the case when a group of Nigerian brothers sent out a Macedonia call to a man far away in America. They did not know Bishop B.R. Benbow or whether he would respond. But God knew him and also knew that he was the one to assist. The Church of God in Christ started in the South Region about Forty Six years ago at Oboyo Ikot Ita in Nsit Ibom Local Government Area of Akwa Ibom State. In the spring of 1966, during the Biafran Revolution in Nigeria West Africa, Brother S. A. Udo Akpan, and his group of ministers, sent Bishop Benbow a letter as a Macedonian Call ("come over and help us"). The letter read:

Dear Brother Benbow:

I and a group of ministers began seeking the Lord in his fullness according to the Holy Bible. We began receiving much criticism and persecution from our religious constituents.

We started asking the Lord "what shall we do?" While asleep one night, your name and location appeared to me in a dream. So we are following through; we are sending you a Macedonian Call, please come help us, and receive us into your faith".

In 1967, after much prayer, Bishop Benbow, and his wife, Rachel, answered the call. They received into the COGIC, seventeen churches in Nigeria, West Africa. He was appointed Bishop of Nigeria, West Africa, by the late Bishop O. T. Jones, Sr., at the time, Senior Bishop of Church of God in Christ. Mother Benbow was appointed Supervisor of Women for Nigeria, by the late Mother Annie Bailey. Under the leadership of Bishop Benbow and the work of hard working Church of God in Christ saints in Nigeria the work expanded rapidly with missions, churches, an elementary school, the Bennie Roberts Benbow Bible College and each quarter, the church's Sunday School literature was sent to Nigeria. However, the growth of COGIC was soon stagnated due to poor leadership and support from the International Church mainly due to poor communication between the International Headquarters and Nigeria. However events took a different turn when in the September 1999 Bishop Mishael Itoro Akpan was appointed the Bishop of Nigeria having brought over 40 churches into COGIC by Bishop Chandler David Owens during the Atlanta Bishop's Conference. Since that time the saints have been refreshed and COGIC Nigeria has experienced a tremendous growth both numerically and spiritually.

Bishop Mishael Akpan was born on the 26th November 1964 to Pastor Asuquo and Mrs. Bella Akpan in the Village of Afaha Ikot Ede in Nsit Ibom Local Government Area of Akwa Ibom State in Nigeria. He had his primary education at Afaha Nsit Primary School and his secondary education at Etinan Institute, Etinan. He studied French and earned a diploma in French. Having worked for about a year he answered the call to ministry after more than two angelic visitations. He went to a Bible College and earned his Masters degree in Theology and a Doctorate degree in Christian Counseling/Psychology from Victory Fellowship International Bible College, Brighton, Iowa after which he was also awarded a doctorate degree in Theology. His ministry is that which all and sundry knows to be extraordinary, power packed with great miracles signs and wonders.

His unusual ministry has taken him to more dreaded mission fields like United Arab Emirates, Kuwait, Oman, Qatar and Bahrain in the Arabian Peninsula where he also oversees several Churches. His passion for the Arabs is unusual and persistent with the goal of winning more Arabs to Jesus than ever recorded in the history of evangelism in the Arab Nations.

Information was taken from interview by author with Bishop B.R. Benbow in 2000, from the COGIC Nigeria Website and Dr. Gloria Johnson Rodgers, Regional Supervisor of the Nation of Nigeria.

The Korean Church Of God In Christ

Dr. Paul K. Hong, Ph.D. D.D., Overseer of the Korean Church Of God In Christ was visited in May 1970 by Elder Archie Buchanan (later Bishop), the pioneer of Japan. As the Deputy Field Secretary, South Pacific, Home and Foreign Mission Department Overseer Buchanan was sent by the Department to conduct the meeting. Following is his report.

The historic meeting included a number of firsts: The first time The Korean Saints had seen a COGIC minister; the first time the Department had sponsored such a trip to Korea; Pastor Buchanan became the first clergyman of his race and church to have been invited to Korea. Many of them there were wondering what God could say and do for them through a black minister. God proved that He has no respect of persons, as the GOOD NEWS was preached each night for 5 nights; as scores of people were prayed for and many miraculously healed instantly. When the meeting was over, the Korean people were sad to see Evangelist Buchanan leave and invited him back to Korea for the 1971 Campaign. Dr. Hong interpreted the messages in the Korean language. Evangelist Buchanan laid hands-on dozens of people as he prayed for as long as 1½ [hours] each night for the sick. The Young People's Choir rendered beautiful music each night of the 1970 Campaign. Each night's service was taped by Evan. Buchanan. The recording of the first & second nights was sent to Bishop Martin, President of the Home & Foreign Mission Dept., for playing in the 1970 Int'l Missions Conference in Oakland, California held in July 1970.

This March, the Department sent Overseer Buchanan back to Seoul to investigate the properties which Overseer Paul Hong desires to purchase for a Mission Headquarters and Revival Center. The trip was also to conduct a religious retreat for the Korean Saints. Although it was bitter cold (12 degrees on Sunday!), the people filled the churches to see and hear the GOOD NEWS as preached by Evang. Buchanan.

The 1971 EVANGELSITIC CAMPAIGN will be held in late June; Int'l Evang. Buchanan will for the 3rd time return to Seoul to be one of the two Evangelists in that meeting. The Church in Korea is growing under Dr. Hong's leadership. Other churches and schools desire to affiliate with the CHURCH OF GOD IN CHRIST and it is my pleasure to help foster this growth-through annual trips and preaching the GOSPEL.

Bishop Archie Buchanan made the report taken from the Church Of God In Christ, International HOME AND FOREIGN MISSION DEPARTMENT report, Bishop S.R. Martin, President 11/7/70

Naomi Lundy

CHAPTER TWELVE

Where Do We Go From Here?

Pentecost establishes our prophetic vocation...the development of a critical alternative consciousness. – Bishop Ithiel Clemmons

Early Pentecostal members were filled with zeal to tell the world about the soon coming return of Jesus Christ. What is amazing about many of these individuals was that although they lived in an environment sometimes hostile to sanctified individuals, to Blacks, and to women they did not view themselves as victims. They called one another *saints* of the Most High who were on a *mission* for their King. As they labored both in the United States and abroad they built churches, homes for the aged, transformed communities, constructed entire mission towns and built lives. That is to be celebrated. An inquiry was made to the late Bishop A.T. Moore for the reason he attributed to the phenomenal success of early pioneer Church Of God In Christ members causing exponential growth, power to deliver souls from sickness or building Mason Temple during the war years. He responded both simply and powerfully, "we focused on the greatness of

God."[178] That response spoke to the impetus for the church's prophetic vocation in ensuring that God's plans are fulfilled in the earth.

Most organizations begin with a strong sense of purpose and naming is important to purpose. Rev. C.P. Jones, Rev. C. H. Mason and others held a strong sense of purpose when in Arkansas God directed Mason to give the organization the name Church Of God In Christ. The heavenly edict was accepted and the church's objective solidified as members carried out the prophecy through home missions. After its reorganization in 1907 as a Holiness-Pentecostal body the Church Of God In Christ's evangelism geared up in Southern cotton fields, along railroad tracks and later Northern factory towns as blacks migrated. They passed along the biblical principle that an individual could be saved, sanctified and filled with the Holy Ghost. The vision to go out and persuade others of that fact was the mission. Bishop C.H. Mason further espoused and modeled the doctrine that the sanctified church would cause missions both home and abroad to proliferate and was said to have sent out missionaries as early as 1911. The prophecy that there would never be a place large enough to hold the saints was realized as adherents proved that a mission minded church is a growing church. Mother Lizzie Robinson would be instrumental in moving in purpose as she organized the missions in her home.

What is the mission of the Church of God today? Is there a hunger to go into the entire world? Eighty nine year old Mother Gladys Williams oftentimes quotes the following:

---

[178]Patterson, Bishop G.E., Foreword in *The Making of a Legend* by Glenda Williams Goodson, 2006: Lancaster, TX

"There is a child in our midst, what will we do about him?" Missions is the child of the church so what will we do with this child in the 21st century? The intent of this chapter is to again commend the work that has been done by those Royal individuals who have served as single mothers or surrogate fathers to nurture the church's child as well as those who have followed their lead. Secondly to urge others to get involved through research, writing or serving on the field.

Some individuals have the misconception that nothing valid happened on the Black Pentecostal foreign missionary scene until recently. As a nontraditional undergraduate it was my passion and, I felt my mission, to seize opportunities to provide factual evidence of my church's contributions to the world. In my creative writing cluster I broached the subject of writing a short story on the work of the first COGIC missionaries to Africa beginning in the early 1900s. The professor confessed that he was unaware Blacks served in that arena during the period. I challenged him with what little evidence I had of Methodist, Baptist and later COGIC members taking tremendous risks to first of all bring the story of Jesus and His saving grace to indigenous people but explained their successes on foreign soil. He acquiesced that Baptist and Methodist churches perhaps sent Blacks but with very little knowledge of the COGIC he was very surprised by the latter organization's involvement.

The full marketing potential, if you will, of the Church's Missions Department has yet to be realized. I do not use the term marketing in a commercial sense but here it means that The Church Of God In Christ Missions story of how the pioneers survived and thrived must be *told* in order to *inspire*. The Department has evolved in more than eighty years of kingdom service. Missions and churches have been planted in more than 60 nations with an increase of Third World countries seeking affiliation each year. Recently Bishop Carlis L. Moody stated he has joyfully served the people of God prior to and during his tenure and President of the International Home and Foreign Missions Department. In fact, since his appointment in 1976 he has led the Department in new levels in leadership with the assistance of his Vice President the late Bishop J.W. Denny and current Vice President Bishop Bobby Henderson (the latter has been interested in missions since a teen). According to Moody, the work of missions was so important to current Presiding Bishop, the Honorable Bishop Charles E. Blake, that during the infancy of the West Angeles Church Of God In Christ Blake initially sent support of $25.00 (with less than fifty members) each month to the Department. Blake's *Save Africa's Children* organization has a goal of creating 1000 orphanages on the African continent.

Yes, the COGICs Missions Department is active and vibrant. The Department's Youth on a Mission (YOAM), in partnership with Habitat for Humanity and other organizations, annually visits Third World countries repairing Church Of God In Christ schools, orphanages and churches or operating medical clinics on U.S. Native American reservations. Husband and wife teams like the Vincent Matthews family in residence in South Africa operate mission schools and orphanages yet single female missionaries still make up the majority of the church's international rosters. Led by Bishop Moody training sessions are held in International Holy Convocation, Auxiliaries in Ministry Conference, and the International Leadership Conference. And missions pioneer Mother

Betty Kennedy now holds a Missions Training Institute each August in Erie, PA. Each of these venues provide opportunity to explore cutting edge strategies for greater penetration into the darkness to bring souls into light as well as sharing living history.

History informs. History misinforms. Most information regarding non-European peoples was culturally and religiously biased even to the extreme of powerful media forces referencing indigenous individuals as heathen, barbaric or buffoons. In the words of George Santayana, "those who do not learn the lessons of history are doomed to repeat its mistakes." Not even the most destitute refugee or homeless individual welcomes condescension. The majority of these women did not perform in this manner toward anyone but presented holiness as a lifestyle that could be lived out through the power of the Holy Ghost. Indeed Pentecost says that the word we teach of the Spirit's baptism is a call to holiness. Pentecostals, and Black Pentecostals particularly, must not lose our prophetic voice. There are some absolute standards that the holiness church should attain to. As the writing prophets of old we must document this great religious tradition of Holy Ghost fire causing individual believers to build and uplift. If this is not done we are guilty of perpetuating misinformation with future generations less wise. An African proverb says something like until the lion has its own storyteller, the hunter has the best part of the story. There's a call and response number sung within the lively COGIC tradition which says *You Can't Tell It Like I Can!* Recognizing that some things individuals have done will not be recognized until we all get to the other side, until Jesus returns each generation must be evangelized. And while everything will not be recorded, with the COGIC a reported 6 million strong more books such as *Humility Before Honor* by Bishop Carlis Moody, *A Visit to Wissikeh* by Mother Mary Beth Kennedy or *Lord Send Me* by Chaplain Marva Cromartie Nyema should be written. I envision reading of the stories in these forthcoming books to be likened to those unnamed biblical characters who heard exploits of past victories. Pointing out the importance to purpose in telling these stories, one commentator says Joshua had the foresight to tell followers, stop right there! Pick up that stone and share your identity, your God given purpose, so that generations to come will not be lost but can forge a more comprehensive future.

In 2011 legitimate and pressing issues require attention: Crack addicts need to be saved, sanctified souls need the fullness of Holy Ghost baptism, demons of perversions cast out, complacency and backslidings of the saints prayed for, the diminishing of basic Pentecostal teaching of repentance, salvation and seeking Spirit baptism addressed, making clear the line of what it means to be in the world and not of it, children to get through school, and jobs to be found. But there have always been tensions. Could it be that today the saints are so enamored of trying to make it economically or focusing in unbalanced ways on educational, employment or retirement goals that we are guilty of leaving weighty matters undone? It is my contention that reflecting upon those who blazed trails through jungles or climbed mountains to bring the gospel should compel believers to not only research and write but to preserve our Pentecostal heritage with integrity and commitment.

A 2007 statistic claims that there are 4,600 Christian mission sending organizations placing missionaries in countries other than their own. Parsing through souvenir books and journals I read accounts of these brave individuals but had a problem in that I found zero books on the exploits of female Church Of God In Christ international mission workers. I am not a theologian and do not hold that I articulate through that lens. Grants were absent in underwriting this work and, not being a member of the academy, there were no fellowships but like the pioneers before me I had faith that whatever He brought me to, He would take me through. Since there were no stones documenting the lives of these courageous soldiers I had to write because they too lived, they too sacrificed, they too labored. In building this story I hoped to illustrate their love for God and humanity. Just as they were willing to journey thousands of miles, suffer extreme hardship, and experience misunderstandings to offer hope so should that person who the Lord has called today.

If an individual believes it is God's will for them to evangelize in a country other than their own, they are on the road to understanding the historical implications of the work of these women, then personally take pride and grow. But again, their voices must be heard. Their lives should be studied and recorded so that individuals who may have real apprehension about accepting their kingdom call will be affirmed and not distracted by material wealth or a quest for position or power. Everyone should attain to achieve a goal greater than themselves. I take to task those individuals within the denomination who have been called to write popular books such as *Royalty* or scholarly articles on the history of a subset of this formerly marginalized segment of Protestantism and have not answered the call. I challenge others to examine the work and write articles, books, plays, films or documentaries. In the stories to be written are answers to many of today's problems.

Finally, a verse in an old school choir number made popular by the late Ron Winans says *"Where do I go from here/make my pathway clear/lead me and I'll follow/wherever I go let your Spirit follow me."* In the first 50 years the international missionaries of the Church Of God In Christ held a passion for the world in their hearts. Beatrice Lott said eloquently they were "lost in a task of love." Since they were saved and Spirit filled they followed their calling wherever the Spirit led. We must continue to do the same today.

- *We cannot afford to turn inward.* The harvest is ripe. Whatever the ministry or denomination, heaven's mandate is winning, nurturing and developing souls wherever lost souls are found. Pioneer missionaries felt that souls were so important that they reached out to a troubled world. Today we must do the same.

- *Raise awareness of what contemporary international missionaries are doing.* While emerging countries embrace Pentecostalism the American cultural shift that occurred during the last twenty years finds many of today's young people 19 to 29 years old turning away from Christianity or Pentecostalism. Prayer was the foundation on which the accomplishments made by COGIC foremothers built expansive legacies. Pray that the inclusion of contemporary global missionaries would be more than an afterthought in planning programs.

- *Ask questions.* Jesus asked His disciples questions. Today, research should be commissioned with methodologies developed to ask questions to determine what young people think about the church's role in society: *What do you think of when you hear the word* missions *or what is the first church body you think of when you hear of assistance being given outside the United States? Have you ever met an international missionary? Have you ever met a COGIC or Pentecostal foreign missionary? What do you think they do in the fields to positively impact the kingdom of God?*

During an informal interview one educated, professional and thoughtful twentysomething respectfully explained "at this point in our lives most of us don't really care to know what a jurisdiction does or what [financial] reports have to be made. We want [leaders in] *the church* to [teach us how to] go out and *impact the kingdom!*" You have the answer to their frustrations in missions work, home or foreign. I challenge leaders to allow trusted and bona fide international missionaries access to the congregations over which God has made you overseer. Youth leaders, women's department and ministry leaders, embrace everyone who positively impacts the kingdom. Add short term and full time missionaries, YOAM leaders or participants to your speaking circuit. Within the COGIC denomination infrastructure, District or Jurisdictional meetings, conferences and retreats are prime opportunities to lift Christ up through this area of kingdom promotion. Within the body of Christ all should promote missions as vital to the life of their church. Youth must be taught to unselfishly embrace a goal greater than themselves: Young people could raise funds for YOAM construction projects; American cities adopt sister cities in other countries, so could churches adopt mission stations to provide consistent support as well as an exchange of ideas; change the culture to ensure that young men become involved in missions support and service.

- *Utilize Technology!* Youth today communicate differently. With cell phones programmed as mini computers with cameras and camcorders, our young people are connected almost instantly to the *world*. In order to maximize their involvement we must reach out to them via Facebook, MySpace, You Tube, blogs, Twitter, Skypes, etc. with the message that missions work is fulfilling and they are needed to please God and help their church in this important work. Clips from YOAM teens are already out on Facebook posted by individuals. However, the technology must be harnessed for the greater good. The Spirit filled church should be characterized as an energized church. Just as the new birth brings freshness to families and new souls born into the kingdom add life to local congregations, your members, young and old, will be blessed and energized to learn what God is doing through the international missionaries in every denomination. (See PhD candidate Elder Eric Williams article in the COGIC Scholars newsletter on Bishop Mason speaking into the everywhere.)

- *Realize that Jesus is closer in returning than we think.* We are in danger of losing our prophetic voice by making self, our families or our churches idols. We must have balance in our lives while remembering to put first things first. Ensure that the church's primary purpose is realized in our homes, our communities and our world by focusing on readying for the Second Coming of our Lord. And a good way to realize perspective is through participation in missions activities.

- *Prayerfully revisit the Great Commission.* All are not called to international missions, however, the Spirit has given each believer a diversity of gifts to be used for the glory of God. It is up to today's believer to open his or her heart and listen to the Spirit's call. I challenge readers to become involved in international missionary service or support missions through whatever reformation you are a part. *Missions Needs Your Help!* If each of us believes the "other person" will support, then nothing worthwhile will be accomplished. Somewhere in the world—whether it is a refugee camp in the Democratic Republic of the Congo or a Haitian orphanage—a missions worker has been praying that you will obey the prompting of the Spirit to help. There are corporate and other organizations to offer discounts in freight forwarding, sending nonperishables, or clothing that you can influence if you just make the effort to obey the Great Commission.

- *Celebrate the lessons of history.* The labor of COGIC pioneer international missionaries and countless others are yielding an exponentially rich harvest. Their teaching remains a powerful force and as citizens of emerging countries accept the doctrine of Pentecost in growing numbers, the trailblazers should be respected and recognized for their part in planting seeds. There are more stories to be told and you can ensure that they are. Research can be as simple as taking a recorder and allowing pioneers to tell their story, capturing them on camcorders or even cell phones.

Accept your call to the harvest! And as Bro. Winans sings, let us ask God to make our pathways clear in whatever direction the Holy Ghost leads us to make a contribution in this vital function. Christ has commanded it!

APPENDIX

1-1: World Religions:

Religion	Annual change, 1990-2000 Natural	Conversion	Total	Rate	2000 Adherents
All Christians	22,708,799 2,616,670,052	2,501,396 33.4	25,210,195 3,051,564,342	1.36 34.3	1,999,563,838 238
PROFESSION					
crypto-Christians	1,408,763 190,490,250	703,798 2.4	2,112,561 246,319,348	1.89 2.8	123,726,489 63
professing Christians	21,299,796 2,426,157,502	1,797,505 31.0	23,097,301 2,805,218,484	1.32 31.5	1,875,627,394 238
AFFILIATION					
unaffiliated Christians	1,305,142 125,711,785	-381,603 1.6	923,539 124,655,275	0.87 1.4	111,124,545 237
All affiliated Christians	21,403,655 2,490,958,267	2,883,011 31.8	24,286,666 2,926,909,067	1.39 32.9	1,888,439,293 238
Roman Catholics	13,117,804 1,361,965,255	-355,181 17.4	12,762,623 1,564,603,495	1.29 17.6	1,057,328,093 235
Independents	4,495,891 581,642,120	3,925,017 7.4	8,420,908 752,842,240	2.49 8.5	385,745,407 221
Protestants	4,224,076 468,632,927	341,161 6.0	4,565,237 574,418,922	1.44 6.4	342,001,605 233
Orthodox	750,901 252,715,940	385,410 3.2	1,136,311 266,806,050	0.54 3.0	215,128,717 135
Anglicans	1,071,503 145,983,770	73,897 1.6	1,145,400	1.56	79,649,642 166
Marginal Christians	269,292	153,482	422,774	1.79	26,060,230
Trans-megabloc groupings					
Evangelicals	2,839,602 327,834,735	893,484 4.2	3,733,086 448,862,899	1.97 5.0	210,602,983 5.0
Pentecostals/Charismatics	7,016,903 811,551,594	2,812,254 10.4	9,829,157 1,066,318,949	2.10 12.0	523,777,994 238
Great Commission Christians	6,180,025 887,578,895	2,535,490 11.3	8,715,515 1,097,449,417	1.46 12.3	647,820,987 238

1:2 Black Church Beginnings in Overseas Missions

Year	Missionary	Denomination	Country	Sponsor
1791	George Liele 1750-1800	Baptist	Jamaica	Independent/Self-support; help later came from Britain
1792	David George 1742-1810;	Baptist	Sierra Leonne	Independent
1820	Daniel Coker 1780-1840	African Methodist Episcopal	Sierra Leonne	A.M.E. held by American Colonization; later Independent Methodists
1821	Lott Carey 1780-1828 And Colin Teague	Baptist	Liberia/ Sierra Leonne	Richmond African Baptist Foreign Missions; (White) American Colonization Society
1853	Alexander Cromwell 1819-1898	Episcopal	Liberia	American Colonization Society
1876	Andrew Cartwright	African Methodist Episcopal Zion	West Africa	Missionary Director, A.M.E. Zion in W. Africa, Liberia, Ghana
1883	"First 6 missionaries"	Baptist	Liberia	Baptist Foreign Missionary Convention org 1880; start of NBC, USA
1891	Bishop Henry McNeal Turner	African Methodist Episcopal	Sierra Leonne	Organized conference in Liberia, Sierra Leone, British South Africa

1:3 List of Passengers for Baroque *Azor* bound to Monrovia

Cabin passengers

		Sex	Age	
Curtis, Margaret		F.	40	
Flegler, Rev. P. [?]		M.	35	
Gailliard, Sam'l E.		M.	38	
"	, Ann M.	F.	34	
"	, Lee R.	M.	7	
"	, Truphenia	F.	5	
"	, S.E. Jr.	M.	4	
"	, W.G.M.	M.	2	
Green, Pompey		M.	49	
"	~~, [Lucinda]~~	~~F.~~	~~26~~	
"	, Milley	F.	49	
"	, Fanny	F.	17	
"	, J.	M.	3	
Moultrie, J.W.		M.	23	
"	, Mary	F.	18	
Williams, A.B.		M.	22	[in faint writing next to age, "15"]
		~		
Steerage Passengers				
Adams, Wm.		M.	26	
"	, Haillie	F.	20	
"	, Shelley	M.	2	
Adams, Okra		M.	42	
"	, Isabella	F.	35	
"	, Charles	M.	5	
"	, Faith	F.	17	
"	, Robert	M.	20	
	, Eliza	F.	[3 or 13]	

[faint writing: "24"]

Note: Question marks represent illegible text.

1:4 Interview List

Over the years from fifty to seventy five interviews were conducted. A 50 item questionnaire was developed which included demographics to identify suitable participants. Some interviews with primary sources overlapped. Cross analysis of these reports added credibility to the oral histories. Interviews were face to face or by telephone lasting from 90 minutes to several days. On a number of occasions several weeks of follow up were conducted. Interviews were audio taped or captured by camcorder. Telephone interviews were transcribed verbatim. Some interviews were done to answer specific questions and lasted from fifteen to twenty minutes. Only in depth interview participants are listed below.

Name	Title	Country of Origin or Service	Date interviewed	Missions Highlight
Beatrice Lott	Int'l Missionary	Liberia	Late 1980s	Tugbake founder
Emma Barron	Jurisdictional Supervisor, Texas Northeast	U.S.A.	Early through mid 1980s	Missions supporter; educated many int'l students
Dorothy Webster Exume	Int'l Missionary	Haiti	Numerous 1:1/phone interviews late 1980s to early 1990s	Mason School; orphanage founder
Sophronia Barron Smith	Barron's daughter	U.S.A.	Late 1980s; November 2010	Saints' Student; Classmate of African Students in 1950s
Marlil Provost	Exume's daughter	U.S.A.	Sept-Dec 2010	Lived in Haiti age 1-12
Amilcar Exume	Exume's son	U.S.A.	2011	Lived in Haiti
Fronz Exume	Exume's son	U.S.A.	2011	Lived in Haiti
Annette Lewis	Granddaughter of Annie Bailey, 3rd Int'l Supervisor	U.S.A.	2009	
Naomi Lundy	Int'l Missionary	Liberia	Sept 2009-Jan 2011	Tugbake
Pearl Page Brown	Int'l Missionary	Haiti, Liberia	Late 1990s; Sept 2009	Served in twenty-seven countries
Abraham Brown	Missions Student; Monolu, Tugbaken, Wissikeh Overseer	Liberia	Sept 2009-Jan 2011	Jurisdictional Prelate, Ivory Coast

Name	Role	Location	Date	Notes
Jessie Brown	Missions Student	Liberia	Sept 2009-Jan 2011	Missions teacher
Mary Beth Kennedy	Int'l Missionary	Liberia (Tugbakeh and Wissikeh); Ivory Coast	Mid 1990s; September 2009-January 2011	Along with husband, rebuilt Wissikeh Mission; Supervisor, Democratic Republic of Congo
Charles Kennedy	Int'l Missionary	Liberia (Tugbakeh and Wissikeh)	Mid 1990s	Along with his wife, rebuilt Wissikeh Mission
Sam Boley	Former Missions Student	Liberia	2010	Married Ester Lott, who was adopted by Beatrice Lott
Lisa Peeples	Lott's Caretaker	U.S.A.	2010	
Marva Nyema	Int'l Missionary	Liberia	2010	Wissikeh; Assistant to Mary Beth Kennedy
Beatrice Nah	Former Missions Student during Lott's tenure	Liberia		Cooked, cleaned, assisted Lott. Relocated to Minnesota 2007
Emmanuel John	Attended Mason School through primary school	Haiti	2010	60s French to English Translator; pastors 1 U.S./oversees 2 Haitian churches
Theda Wells	Historian, former State Supervisor, Personal friend of Exume	U.S.A.	Mid 1990s-2011	Haitian Missions supporter
Lee Van Zandt	Saved under Exume; Served in Haiti with Exume	Haiti; Liberia	January 2011	Current Brazil Jurisdictional Supervisor
Alexander Gbayee	Tugbaken Missions Student	Liberia	Nov 2010	Liberian Consul to U.S.

Name	Role	Country	Date	Notes
Vivian Haynes	Missions Supporter	U.S.A.	December 2010	Wife of Bishop J. N. Haynes; visited Haiti
Odessa Newman	Former Jurisdictional Supervisor Texas NE	U.S.A.	Mid 1990s	Missions Supporter; made many visits to Haiti; educated Haitian youth
Romanetha Stallworth	Int'l Missionary	South Africa	Mid 1990s thru 2011	Supports S. African students, schools and orphanages; Supervisor, Kentucky 1st; interviewed Francina Wiggins in 1970s
Debey Sayndee	President, National Director of the African Leadership Bible Training Center for Pastors	Liberia	Nov 10 thru Jan 11	
Nettie Jones Dillard	District Missionary; Washington State Women's Dept. Examiner	U.S.A.	September 2009	Born in 1925, Dillard served as companion to famous prayer warrior Mother E.J. Dabney. Lived in post war Germany
Maxine Haynes Kyle	District Missionary; Daughter of Bishop F.L. Haynes, 3rd Bishop of Texas	U.S.A.	Continuous through 2011	Pioneers visited and stayed in their home including Beatrice Lott and Elizabeth White

Grace Kennedy, MD	Conducts medical missions, daughter of Mother Mary Beth Kennedy	Liberia (Wissikeh)	2009	Born on Mission field in Liberia
Charles Kennedy Jr.	Son (deceased 2010) of Mother Mary Beth Kennedy	Liberia Carried to gospel to various villages as a boy	2009	Born in Puerto Rico on mission; Was 6 when they went to Liberia.
Earlynn Byas McDowell	Daughter of Lelia Mason Byas who was a traveling companion of her father; granddaughter of Bishop C.H. Mason	U.S.A.	Throughout 2000's	Short term international missionary
Juanita Faulkner, PhD	Niece of Bishop O.T. Jones, Jr.	U.S.A.	2011	Close friend of Exume; supported Haitian teachers

1:5 Home and Foreign Missions Board 1956 Financial Statement

The Financial Statement of the Home and Foreign Mission Board of the Church Of God In Christ for the year ending November 1956 shows income of 3239.85 funded by donation amounts from a low of $1.00 given by many individuals across the country. The majority of donations of $100 or more given by Bishops, State Supervisors and Pastors were earmarked for individual Mission Stations or missionaries. For example Elder H.W. Goldsberry of Chicago donated $100 in March 1956 as a special gift for Martha Barber. The same year the National Women's Convention donated $1,000 followed by the Home and Foreign Missions Board with$300. Out of these funds expenses for travel by officials to Africa and Haiti, carpenter tools, lodging, Compensation for Tribal Authorities in Tugbake and Manolu, rights to land for the Elizabeth White Memorial, and surveyor fees were disbursed. The statement lists the following international missionaries receiving monthly support:

Month	Missionary	Mission	Amount
January	Miss Dorothy Webster	Haiti	170.00
	Miss Martha Barber	West Africa	125.00
	Mrs. Norine Evans	Honolulu	50.00
	Bishop W.A. Kates	Jamaica	50.00
	Mr. and Mrs. Charles Kennedy (Transportation to Africa)		300.00
February	Miss Dorothy Webster	Haiti	170.00
	Miss Martha Barber	West Africa	125.00
	Mrs. Norine Evans	Honolulu	50.00
	Bishop W.A. Kates	Jamaica	50.00
	Miss Grace Yancy	Bangkok, Thailand	25.00
March	Miss Dorothy Webster	Haiti	170.00
	Mr. and Mrs. Charles Kennedy	West Africa	170.00
	Miss Martha Barber	West Africa	125.00
	Mrs. Norine Evans	Honolulu	50.00
	Mrs. Katie Frazier	Bahamas	30.00
	Miss Grace Yancy	Bangkok, Thailand	25.00
	Bishop Malchus B. Bennett	British Honduras	50.00
	Miss Ernestine Cleveland	Jamaica	60.00
	Mr. Paul D. Gwagee	West Africa	180.00
April	Miss Dorothy Webster	Haiti	170.00
	Mr. and Mrs. Charles Kennedy	West Africa	170.00
	Miss Martha Barber	West Africa	125.00
	Mrs. Norine Evans	Honolulu	50.00
	Bishop Malchus B. Bennett	British Honduras	50.00
	Mrs. Katie Frazier	Bahamas	30.00
	Miss Grace Yancy	Bangkok, Thailand	25.00
May	Grants same as April with the exception of the following		
	Mr. Paul D. Gwagee	West Africa	35.00
June	Miss Dorothy Webster	Haiti	$170.00
	Mr. and Mrs. Charles Kennedy	West Africa	170.00
	Miss Martha Barber	West Africa	125.00
	Mrs. Norine Evans	Honolulu	50.00
	Bishop Malchus B. Bennett	British Honduras	50.00
	Mr. Paul D. Gwagee	West Africa	35.00

	Miss Grace Yancy	Bangkok, Thailand	25.00
	Mrs. Katie Frazier	Bahamas	30.00
July	Grant amounts same as June		
August	Grant amounts same as June		
September	Grant amounts same as June with the exception of following addition		
	Miss Elnora Lee	Bermuda	$150.00
October	Grant amount same as June		
November	Grant amounts same as June		

APPENDIX 2 – CORRESPONDENCE AND MISCELLANEOUS INFORMATION SOURCES

2:1 A Tribute to Dr. Arenia Mallory by Mrs. Sophronia Chesson Iotka, Liberian student

Dr. Mallory had not seen me and I had not even heard of her, sitting here in Liberia, West Africa. In 1951, a young missionary O.T. Jones, Jr., visited the Church Of God In Christ in Monrovia, Liberia, where I was an active teenage member. He asked if I wanted to travel to the United States to study and I obviously responded in the affirmative. In less than a month after Pastor Jones' departure for the United States, after some arrangements, I arrived in the United States on September 17, 1951; to be with her.

Her reception upon my arrival in the United States was like that of a true Christian. She opened her home to me and accorded me every opportunity and privilege a loving child could receive in a Christian home. I enjoyed her counseling, not only as a mother, but as a friend. She encouraged my participation in the choir, glee club, student council, and prayer band at the Saints Industrial and Literary School. She exuded so much love and care for me, that I thought of my natural mother only because she was such. Through her guidance, I was able to enter and complete my college education and returned to Liberia to render service to my country. I have served as Instructor and head of the Department of Home Economics at Booker Washington Institute, the oldest vocational training institution in the country: and now I am the personnel director at the Ministry of Posts & Telecommunications. In these positions, I have had the opportunity to exhibit the love, care and understanding for which I shall always be grateful to Mother Mallory. Without Mother Mallory I wonder what I would have been like. She was truly a Christian in deed. Although I was the only foreigner, I was not the only one upon whom she showed her Christian love. She enjoyed having many persons to care for and, we were certainly many girls for whom she cared. I am sure that she did well in her past, witnessing for Christ and that she has gone from Labour to reward. May her soul continue to rest in perpetual peace.

Sophronia Chesson Iotka's tribute is excerpted from *Down Behind the Sun – The Story of Arenia Conella Mallory* by Dovie Marie Simmons and Olivia L. Martin, Riverside Press, Memphis, TN 1983, p. 66-67

2:2 Excerpts from Embracing the World, Missions Booklet by Beatrice S. Lott

EMBRACING THE WORLD
By Beatrice S. Lott

The contents of this little Booklet come from hard years of conscientious, dedicated service for the Master.

For many years I have labored in the remote areas of Liberia, West Africa. As a very young person I gave my life to God, and when the challenge came to venture into the uttermost part of the world, with the gospel of our Lord and Savior, I hastily responded to the call. As the Apostle Paul said, "I was not disobedient to the heavenly vision."

So many friends and loved ones have insisted that I would write a book, which I hope to be able to do, before I go home to be with God. I have put it off for years, thinking that at a more convenient time, would get to it. My life has been filled with excitement and heavenly joy in the work of God. Many times my eyes were flooded with tears, or I was so hurt, I couldn't cry. But thank God, I can say, "I've learned to trust in Jesus through it all."

Readers, you'll have to admit that there is no substitute for real experience. Matters not how eloquent one's speech is, or how he can philosophize on the hazardous, missionary journeys and experience of the Apostle Paul, he alone could say, "I was there when it happened." There is no greater joy than that of giving one's self to save the lives of others. The scripture says, "greater love hath no man than this, that a man lay down his life for his friends." When one is lost in his task of love, matters not how dangerous the task is, it is only when the work is done, that he realizes that he was just one step from death. And he asks himself, how did I come through this? The Bible answer to the Believers is, "I can do all things through Christ, who strengthens me." There are many who have done heroic deeds, or given their lives to save others, but no written records have been left behind, no song has been sung, no medal has been given, but one thing is sure, their records are on high, and their witness is in heaven.

We cannot put too much emphasis on the need of Gospel in the most extreme parts of the world. There is a task that the Church must do, and the church alone. We cannot pass by on the other side and expect the Red Cross, the Welfare, the Peace Corps, or any other organization to do the job that Christ commanded the Church to do. The world is your parish. The Bible is your guide. How can the Church say, "let somebody else do our task," in this day, when our barns are overflowing, our closets are full, we are dying from overeating, when the world is hungry, not only for the natural food, but for the Living Bread. The Church has to care for her own under-privileged people. What comes from outside, should be a supplement, rather than a meager means of survival. I realize that I am venturing into "deep waters," but this is my version of Missions. To relieve the oppressed, to visit the fatherless and widows in their afflictions. The early Church was concerned as an example to the Believers today.

THE DEFINITION OF MISSIONS AND MISSIONARY

Webster gives the definition of Mission as "A sending or being sent by authority on some service, or function. An organization for doing missionary work. A passage, errand, or deputation. A Missionary is: One engaged in, or devoted to missions, especially be sent to spread religion.

It seems that most church people underestimate missions and missionaries. It is more or less dealt with, as a distant place to send discarded clothes and a few undies, or the missionaries as a few women, with long outdated dresses, with their Bibles, teaching a few heathen children. We seem to forget that Jesus was the greatest Missionary the world has even known, or, ever will know. It was He who gave the great command to the Church, "Go ye therefore and teach all nations," or "Ye shall be witnesses to me in all the earth." St. Paul, whose conversion to Christianity was the Greatest Missionary of his time. He claimed to be least of all the apostles, because aforetime he had persecuted the church.

It is very essential that home missions come first for without ammunition from the homeland those on the frontline could not survive. The church in the homeland should not be too alarmed today at the great uprise of violence, dope, murder and other crimes that are going on in the public schools. Are we doing all in our knowledgeable power to turn this evil from our homes, our churches and schools? Can we as church-loving people complain about Prayer being taken out of our public schools? The Bible says train up a child in the way he should go. . .We have the solution. Train him in your own schools. In your own kindergarten schools, our own elementary schools, our own high schools and colleges. Give him a good Christian education, from start to finish. It pays off in great dividends. This is Mission.

Do not wait until he reaches adulthood, then expect church

and Bible School to reform him. The gospel will transform him while he's young. Jesus never did put material things above His...He so loved the world, that He gave His life for us. That's Mission. The Bible says, "for what would it profit a man to gain the world and lose his soul, or what would a man give in exchange for his soul?" Our children are precious. They can be saints or devils. It's up to us. Notice the child who gets his basic training in a Christian school. When we do start this great Mission Task? The time is now. We're already late.

CONTRIBUTION OR SUPPORT FOR MISSION

Our support for mission should be systematically and in a real knowledge for the purpose in which it is given. In giving spasmodically when one hears a returned missionary, then soon forgets as soon as the missionary is out of sight causes much grief and pain on the part of those whom you have entrusted to represent our church in distant lands. Whether you are giving money or gifts, give your best. Not that, which you can't use, or have discarded. By faith Abel offered unto God a more excellent sacrifice than Cain, by which he obtained witness that he was righteous, God testifying, of his gifts; and by it he being dead yet speaketh. Hebrews 11:4.

Appropriate time should be given for Mission and reports of returned missionaries who have represented you on foreign fields. They have borne the burdens in the heat of the day. The remnant of time is usually allocated for the missionaries, who have become strangers in their own land and church. Mission should have priority to some of the less-compelling church program. Mission is God's plan for reaching the un-reached. So to give of our best, in money, gifts and time will be accepted with God.

ESTABLISHED MISSION STATIONS IN FOREIGN FIELDS

You have often heard of the returned missionaries speak of "our Mission Stations." Many of these stations have started from what we call "scratch." No members, no church, no buildings, just a humble mud hut to live in and a large parcel of jungle land to be cleared. With a little clearance of the jungle land, then a larger mud house. The people begin to bring their children, (mostly their boys, in times past). The number continues to grow, the gospel is preached, and many converts are added. Schools and clinics are now taking the place of the vast forest.

Because of persecution the native Christians choose to live close to their missionaries. So they forsook the heathen village and built their own town, known as "Mission Town." I have personally witnessed some of the cruel treatments imposed on the native Christians, by their own countrymen, because of the stand which they had taken for the gospel. I have seen them take their clothes away that the missionaries had given them. Have seen them take their goats and kill them and drink the blood while it was yet warm. We have had to go into the villages and stand between the native Christians and their own people. Many unfortunate babies, whose mothers have died at their birth, have been taken to the missions. Many girls have found a place of refuge in these Mission Stations, who escaped childhood marriage. Missionaries have paid dowries to redeem these girls. (The dowry is usually a cow, or its worth). At these established Mission Stations a visitor from the homeland might be a little disappointed when he doesn't find a multitude of people to preach to. You will usually find the foreign missionary in the clinic, where an emergency has arisen: A man attacked by a leopard, or someone bitten by a poisonous snake, or scorpion, or someone fell from the palm tree has a broken limb, etc. You'll also find the missionary in the school room, or planning a building project. You're sure to find the missionary in church, if no emergency calls her away.

These are just some of the duties performed at the established missions. At the established Mission Stations, before the Lord had given us ministers, the missionaries are compelled to bury the dead, baptize the converts and administer communion.

We no longer dwell in mud huts, or mud churches and schools. All of our buildings are now cement blocks. We have electric generators for lights. We no longer have to travel on the heads of the natives, by hammocks like we used to, or walk the many lonely, dusty trails through the jungles. Your missionaries have made possible modern living conditions. For years we were without the luxury of ice, in a land that's hot the year round, but God has supplied that need. And now we thank God who has brought us through these and many other perilous times. In sickness often, much hunger, long seizure of amebic dysentery, malaria, and broken shoulder. When the war-clouds were hanging low over the Republic of Liberia we were commanded to evacuate. Had to fly over dangerous territory. Our beginning was indeed a very humble one. It was God alone that kept us during those trying times.

When I applied for my passport the first time, the Liberian Government refused to issue it, unless the church would assure them in writing, that they would give the missionary not less than fifty dollars per month. This order was given because so many missionaries were paid $____ per month. These small grants had to help towards the support of the Mission Stations and school.

A SUCCESSFUL MISSIONARY

Any missionary going to a foreign field should be sure she is in the will of God. Her purpose should be more than just to wear the name of "returned missionary," or just to bring back a report, or for the praise of men. This is a lifetime journey, not for adventure or fame. There must be a total commitment and genuine love for God's people, matters not how humble their surroundings might be. The foreign missionary must always remember that she is to remain a foreigner as long as she is on foreign soil. The foreign missionary's conduct must be above reproach, if her work is to be effective. The missionary must ever keep before her, "that eternal errand, to seek and save that which is lost."

The missionary should not attempt to break down the culture

of the people with whom she has been sent to work among. Any work of your own, in your own strength, will only serve to frustrate a cause for which you were sent to heal. Seeking Divine guidance in all that you undertake to do. Remember, the Word will find its [mark], when properly applied. First, you trust in the Lord with all thy might, and lean not to your own understanding. Jesus said, "let your light so shine that men may see your good works and glorify your Father, which is in Heaven. Emerson said, "show the people the light, they'll find the way."

The Church has a message to tell the world. Preach it! Sing it! Shout it! Above all live it! Love and respect for your fellow missionary should always have priority in your message and deeds. Never seek to tear down the image of one another, on works nor in deeds. "Remember bricks and stones will soon be past. Only what you do for Christ will last."

St. Paul, our model foreign missionary, said he brought his body under subjection of the Spirit, least by any means after he had preached to others he became a castaway. Jesus had this to say, "Woe unto you scribes and Pharisees; hypocrites, for you compass sea and land, to make one proselyte, and when he is made, you make him twofold more than the child of hell than yourself."

We are very proud of the products which we have been able to present to the government of Liberia. In every walk of life there, you'll find young men and women who have been trained by American missionaries. It is like Ford Motor Company. They take a mass of metal, put it through hot furnace, melt it, then mold it, and assemble it, then paint it. Out comes a beautiful, useful car. The foreign missionary takes the primary native children, cleans them up, rid him of his many tropical diseases, put the first garment on him and teaches him. He's then ready to serve his people. The Honorable William Tubman and the late William V.S. Tubman, Presidents of the Republic of Liberia have repeatedly had this to say: "The foreign missionaries from America have done much towards the advancement of our Great Country, and we are grateful to them."

Liberia is the melting pot of the world, for black people. But it is not the silver, nor the gold, that we are in such of, by my brothers and sisters' precious souls. Pioneer Missionaries who paved the way established our churches in the jungles of Africa:

Elizabeth White
W.C. Ragland
B. Lott
Martha Barber
Francina Wiggins

Those who labored there:
Elder O.T. Jones, Jr. (Bishop)
June Blackwell (deceased)
Naomi Lundy
Pearl Page Brown

Usually when one is preaching about the foreign missionary, Paul and his hazardous mission journeys, it sends our souls into a "state of ecstasy." Now St. Paul was a man and a missionary. There were times when he had to support himself, while on his mission, for God. He was a Tentmaker, by trade, although well versed in the law. More is written about the Mission work of Paul than any other of the apostles.

The foreign missionary is not a popular person. She is more likely to be forgotten when she leaves her native soil. For it has been said, "out of sight, out of mind." The young church worker who in times past had been the idol of her friends and church members in the homeland has now become a foreigner, even among her own. Someone has said she is unbalanced, or a fool, for going so far away from home, among heathens. Missionary Paul readily admitted that he was "a Fool," for Christ's sake. The foreign missionary can answer these accusations better than anyone else can. "Do you hear what I hear, do you see what I see?" I hear a voice saying, "Go tell it on the mountain, that Jesus Christ is born!"

Many years ago a missionary came to America, on a very special errand. He came to bring the Light of God's Word to a country, who knew not God. Before that, nearly two thousand years ago a humble group of Believers were persecuted for sharing their new found Faith and were scattered abroad, but they set the world aflame. Unofficially everywhere they went they did mission work. When the going got tough, these missionaries did not compromise, but chose rather, to suffer and die for the gospel sake.

Mission is not an auxiliary, nor a department apart from the main stream of the church. It is the church itself. It is the Whole Thing. When love and enthusiasm for Mission dies, there goes the Whole Church. From out of the Mission was born apostles, prophets, evangelists, then the pastors and teachers. No handful of women can keep the world aflame with the Gospel. The Whole Church must be stirred to her obligation. This is Her obligation. Not tomorrow, nor a more convenient time. The time is now to go up and possess the land, for we are well able. Out of Jerusalem (home mission) the Gospel must be carried to Samaria, all Judea, then the uttermost part of the earth.

Mission quotes by our pioneers and founders, who have gone before us.

Dallas, Texas, 1935. "If Abraham could offer his only son, whom he loved, I have six children; certainly I can give one to God. *By Mother Savannah Lott (Beloved mother of Missionary B. Lott)*

Dallas, Texas. 1937. "God has surely called her, and we must get her ready." *Bishop E.M. Page*

Dallas, Texas 1937. "Girl look at my blistered knees. I picked cotton to bring this offering to you. God has called you and I am going to stand by you as long as I live." *Evangelist M.M. Jackson, Temple, Texas*

Dallas, TX 1937. "I have witness within, that God has called her." *Returned Missionary W.C. Ragland, Columbus, GA*

During the service in Omaha, Nebraska: "Come on saints, let's give a good offering. I don't want my picked to have to eat monkey meat in Africa." *Mother Lizzie Robinson, Omaha, Neb.*

In Macon, Ga., 1938. "Bea, God has called you and we're certainly going to send you, but when you get everything well established, you're going to run into grave difficulties. *Mother Lillian B. Coffey, Chicago*

Newark, N.J. 1939 [O]h Lord, another young woman whom [Yo]u have raised up, to go to Africa, [pl]ease weed out her life, Lord." *Prayer by Mother Lula Cox, Newark, N.J.*

Philadelphia, Penna. "Sister Lott, you think you are strong enough [to] go up against the rugged situation, in Africa?" *Mother Harriete Ways, N.J.*

1943. The Convocation in Oklahoma City, "Brethren, whenever these returned Missionaries come to your churches, always open your doors to them and bless them." *Bishop C.H. Mason, Tenn., Chief Apostle*

Liberia 1940. "Sister Lott, the people at Wissekeh really love you and want you to come over and work with them, while I'm away." *Returned Missionary, Mother E. White*

1940, L.A., California. "Sister Lott, you are returning to your original work, which you established. You have the respect and prayers here, as well as the people at your mission. *Bishop S.M. Crouch, Former Pres. Of Missions*

"Sister Lott, God gave me a vision, to light the jungles of Africa, I want to get to dynamo for lights for your missions, send me information. *Mother Mary E. Collins, Calif.*

1960. At the Women's Convention, Kansas City. Sister Lott, I visited that station where Mother White established. That Missionary is almost immortal." *Dr. Arena C. Mallory, Lexington, Miss.*

1953. While visiting the mission. "I really love it out here. If I were younger, I'd spend the rest of my life out here." *Mother Mary E.D.*

1975. Cleveland, Ohio. While visiting with her former co-worker, just before going to sleep. "Bea, (Sister Lott), I came to let you know how much I appreciate you, and for giving me the chance to go to Africa and work with you. Had it not been for you, I wouldn't have made it. Don't give up." *Missionary Martha Barber, Chicago.*

These all died in the faith. Now waiting for the general resurrection of our Lord.

2:3 Women's Department Response to Beatrice Lott's Request for Funds

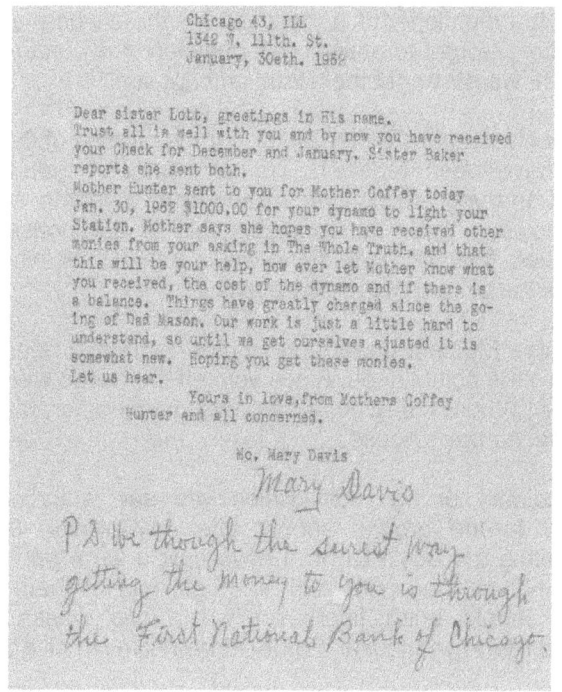

2:4 Transcription of Lott's Typewritten Response to 2:3

Box 45, Cape Palmas,
West Coast, Africa
Feb. 19, 1962

Dear Mothers Coffey, Davis & Hunter

Christian Greetings to you from Africa and may His peace be with you today.

This is to acknowledge with many thanks the amount of $997.00 nine hundred and ninety seven dollars, in reply to my request of you.

This amount received, after the bank's discount. I'm sure you know, that every cent that comes through the bank, a percentage is taken, even a two dollar money order, they get half of it. I mentioned this, because Martha asked me in her last letter, I forgot to answer this question in my last reply to her. No, we never get the actual amount sent.

The monies sent by Sister Baker, for the months of Dec. and Jan., have been received. I'm very grateful that Mother Coffey and you are concerned about the Dynamo, yet you are knowing, that I am applying this to the house, as I requested. You will understand within a few days, when you receive the picture of the new building.

Of course Mothers Davis and Hunter, you have been here, you saw the actual need. Since you left the needs were even greater. When I arrived, there was nothing for a school building, no boy's house.

The country dining room which you saw standing was burned to the ground shortly after my arrival. Besides completing the Boy's Dorm. I have built a large partitioned, cement-block, hog pen, with six hogs, four of them Sows, which should bring [increase] within two weeks. Have planted over five thousand rubber trees. Several acres in cassava, and eddoes, potatoes. Had the road graded again. Built a lovely cement block bath house for the girls, and one for the chickens. We plan to start putting the roof one the new house this week. The doors and windows of the present house, we're in must be repaired, as they are falling out, because of bug-bugs, and dry rot I'm using double precaution this time, as we did not know before just how to preserve the wood material in these building. That is I am treating the material with Carboline, before putting it up.

I am explaining this, not to burden anyone, but all concerned must know where all monies are being used. I have made several appeals through the Whole Truth for the Dynamo, true enough. Have rec'd less than $200.00 on same. Everything that I get now, is going on the new house. Please feel free to make any inquiries of me you desire.

My little family is vacationing with June this week, I do miss them.

P.S. cost of Dynamo 1,640.00, Sixteen hundred & forty dollars

2:5 Transcription of Handwritten Letter from Betty Kennedy to Beatrice Lott

Dear Mother Lott,

Greetings in the Name of the Lord.

This is just a note to thank you for the hospitality you so graciously extended to us when we visited you recently. We appreciate it so very much.

Upon investigation of the charges brought against Matthew and Nathaniel, we found them to be true and are disciplining the boys accordingly. Thank you for letting us know.

School has opened and we are very busy, especially since

the two above named will not be teaching for a while. Seven new students have come from Monrovia, though, and perhaps some of them will be able to help somewhat.

Please tell Lillian "thank you" for the clothes she sent to Annie Nah.

Regards to all,
Sincerely,
Betty Kennedy

P.S. Please pray for the boys and for us too during this time of great trouble on the mission. We have been very burdened and heavy hearted because of this. B.K.

2:6 Transcription of Typewritten Letter to The Honorable Sebastian Bush, Harper County Inspector of Foreign Missions

TUGBAKE MISSIONS CHURCH OF GOD IN CHRIST
Maryland, County, H.L.

The Hon. J. Sebastian Bush, Inspector of Foreign Missions
Harper, Cape Palmas, H.L.

Dear Mr. Bush:

Your letter of July 28, 1960 addressed to Mr. Galloway Gag has been brought to our attention and its contents noted.

We are very anxious that our children at Tugbake should continue to receive their education, and so we have brought the matter before the missionaries of the Church Of God In Christ who are now in Liberia. We have asked them to remedy the condition mentioned in your letter so that the school may meet the proper requirements of the government and be reopened as soon as possible. In order to do our part and take our share of the responsibility in this matter we have formed a school board composed of the undersigned. We are all residents of Tugbake and have a direct interest in the school. We will work under the supervision of the missionaries and especially we will undertake to back up the principal in such matters as attendance and discipline. All arrangements that we may make now are temporary, of course, until Miss Lott arrives. We hear that she is to come in September.

We thank you for your concern for the welfare of the school, for we too want our school to be correct and adequate in every respect. Hoping this will meet your approval we remain,

Yours sincerely,
Tugbake Mission School Board
Jasper Friday, Chairman
Chief Harry Ragland, Chief
Miss Suzanne Johnson
Brown Blawah
Jasper Hney, Pastor

2:7 Ledger Showing Uniform Payments

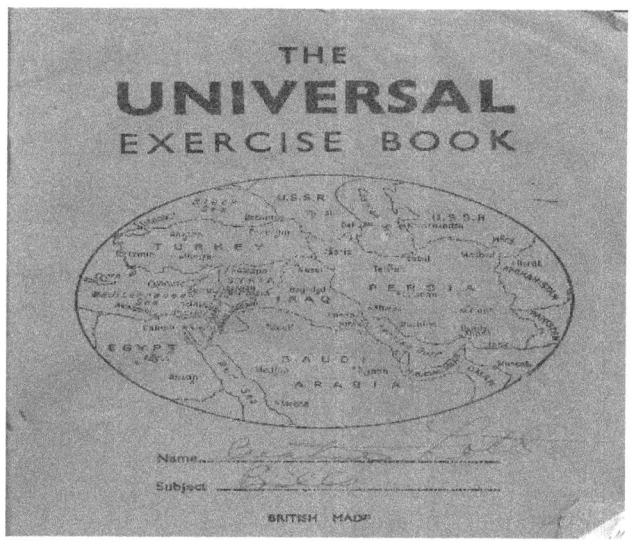

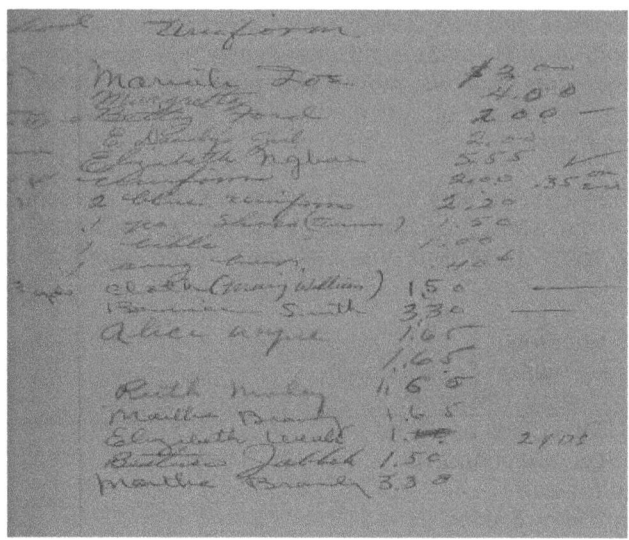

2:8 Letter from Missionary Betty Kennedy, Liberia, in the April 1957 Whole Truth

Bishop D. Lawrence Williams
1201 Merrimac Avenue
Norfolk, Virginia

Dear Bishop Williams,

Holy greetings in the name of the Lord. We have been intending to write to you for some time to let you hear from us and to report on our work over here. God is blessing our labor and is working in a wonderful way out here in the wilds of Africa. It is really a thrilling sight to see the power of God filing those who are termed "aborigines" or "heathen" but whom we recognize as children of a universal Father.

The specific reason for writing to you at this time is to ask you about the possibility of you and your church assuming the responsibility to raise for us $100 for school books.

These books are the ones which the government requires. And so it is imperative that we get them. We would have to have the money by the end of the year, so we could get the books and be ready for the next school year which begins in February. Knowing of your interest along educational lines. I felt to appeal to you for help, believing that you will do all that is in your power.

We have received permission from the government department for instruction to proceed with our plans for an elementary school and a high school. And we are quite pleased about this since we have not yet been here a year and it is an honor for the governmental authorities to recognize us to the extent that they allow us to start a high school. Currently there is not a high school within the radius of about 30 miles. So there is a real need. Ours will be the first Protestant mission high school in the Cape Palmas area (and as far as I know in the entire Maryland County) so it will be quite a boost to the prestige of COGIC in Liberia if we are successful in establishing it.

It is very necessary to have the books that the government requires. The representative of the department of education here has offered to purchase the books for me in Monrovia, so that will save the trouble and expense of one of us going there. The government seems very cooperative and willing to help us. Please do what you can to show us that you back home. Both COGIC clergy, and laity, are standing behind us.

How is your church progressing? You know, I've often thought you should start some sort of seminary to train COGIC young ministers. I think you'd really be good at something like that. And the church needs a denomination theological school.

Pray much for us that God will continue blessing our ministry here. The sick, the dying, the spiritually starved and the seekers for education all come to us and we can minister to them only by the grace of God, and through His mighty power. Pray for us and ask your church to pray for us that we shall submit ourselves to God and follow His divine leading all the time.

Betty Lee Kennedy

2:9 Dedication of Faith Temple located at Tugbaken, Maryland County, WCA

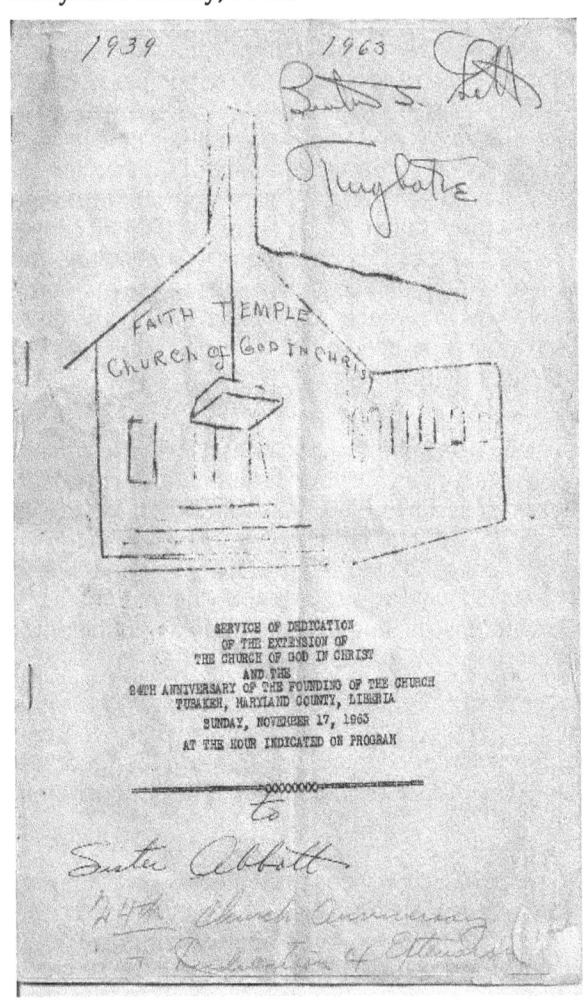

2:10 Letters Typical of Those Requesting Assistance

THE PANAMA CALL IS URGENT

"THE PURPOSE IS TO SECURE THE PROPERTY on which we have our church edifice. Because of the present Military Government under which we are now, our churches' constitutional rights in matters of this kind are not enforced. So all property comes under one commercial status. No exemption whatsoever is given to Churches."

"So a Resolution has been passed on March 9, 1970, that all property owners must purchase their land under two conditions, cash or credit."(The minimum down payment on the said property is $2,150.00). (This letter was referred to the Home and Foreign Mission Department by Bishop J. O. Patterson, Presiding Bishop of the Church of God in Christ

NATIONAL SUPERVISOR OF WOMEN
Mrs. W. HOLDER
Assistant SUPERVISOR OF WOMEN
Mrs. J. J. JOHNSON
National Superintendent of Sunday School

National Y. P. W. W. President

P. O. Box 1401
COLON, R. of P.

Church of God in Christ, Inc.

Colon, Rep. of Panama

Rom. 8:1, 2 Cor. 13:8, St. Jhon 13:35

BISHOP
HARRY A. DAWKINS
BOX 1401 - PHONE
COLON, R. of P.

June 3, 1970

(Contd)

This letter is written as the request of the Saints asking me if Our Head-quarters would not be able to help us with this Down Payment.

The Signatures below are the Officials who requested that this letter be written.

Mrs. Winifred Holder
National Supervisor of Women

Thomas Wellington
National Treasurer

Minister Enrique R. Dawkins
Youth President

Minister Abraham Forcheny
National Sunday School Superintendent

Miss Caroline Deerr
Secretary National Women's Board

Miss Johanna J. Johnson
National Secretary

Bishop Harry A. Dawkins

Respectfully Yours,

In The Masters Service

Bishop Harry A. Dawkins

2:11 Example of Early Missions appointment (1955)

SELECTED BIBLIOGRAPHY

Alexander, Estrelda, *The Women of Azusa Street* The Pilgrim's Press, Cleveland: 2005

Amt, Emilie *Women's Lives in Medieval Europe,* Routledge, New York/London: 1993

Anderson, Allan, *The Azusa Street Revival and the Emergence of Pentecostal Missions in the Early Twentieth Century,* Transformation 23/2: April 2006

Andrews, Edward E. Christian *Missions and Colonial Empires Reconsidered: A Black Evangelist in West Africa, 1766–1816,* Oxford University Press/UK

anglicanhistory.org/africa/lb/missions1928, *Handbook on the Missions of the Episcopal Church*, Liberia, The National Council of the Protestant Episcopal Church, New York: 1928

Bays, Daniel H., *The Foreign Missionary Movement in the 19th and early 20th Centuries*,
nationalhumanitiescenter.org/.../fmmovementcredits.htm

Bonnano, George A. and Anthony D. Mancini, *Predictors and Parameters of Resilience to Loss: Toward an Individual Difference Model,* Journal of Personality: 2004

Bowden, Henry Warner, American Indians and Christian Missions: Studies in Cultural Conflict University of Chicago Press: 1981

Brooks, George E., Jr. *The Providence African Society's Sierra Leone Emigration Scheme, 1794-1795: Prologue to the African Colonization Movement...* from The International Journal of African Historical Studies, Vol. 7, no. 2 (1974) "Courtesy of The New York Public Library. www.nypl.org"

Butler, Anthea, *Women in the Church Of God In Christ: Making a Sanctified World,* The University of South Carolina Press, Chapel Hill: 2007

Calhoun, Lillian S. *Woman on the Go for God.* May 1963, 78-88., 81 Ebony Magazine, 1953

Caravantes, Peggy *Marcus Garvey Black Nationalist,* Greensboro, NC: 2004

Carter, Jessica F., *Known and Yet Unknown, Women of Color and the Assemblies of God,* Assemblies of God Heritage, Vol 28: 2008

Clark, O.G. National Evangelist *The Azusa Street Mission,* 5491 Jordan Avenue, El Cerrito, CA 94530, copyright 1984

Coffey, Lillian Brooks Re-copy of Original Print with excerpts by Elder Jerry R. Ramsey, III Year *Book of the Church Of God In Christ for the Year 1926* Chicago, Ill

Comaroff, Jean and John Comaroff, *Of Revelation and Revolution: Christianity, Colonialism, and Consciousness in South Africa* University of Chicago Press: 1991

Comaroffs', Of Revelation and Revolution: Volume Two. The Dialectics of Modernity on a South African Frontier (Chicago: University of Chicago Press, 1997).

Delaney, Martin R. *The Condition, Elevation, Emigration, and Destiny of the Colored People of the United States,* Published by the Author, 1852

Dubose Hampden C. Rev. John Leighton Wilson, D.D.: Missionary to Africa and Secretary of Foreign Missions *Presbyterian Committee of Publication, Richmond, VA: 1895*

Elbourne, Elizabeth, *"Word Made Flesh: Christianity, Modernity, and Cultural Colonialism in the Work of Jean and John Comaroff,"* The American Historical Review 108, no. 2 (April 2003): 435-59.

Feuerbacher, Haley *How Women's Participation in Christian Missions Over History Has Met Formidable Opposition Based on Gender Issues,* associatedcontent.com/article/58338/...

Fidler, R.L., Editor, *The International Outlook, Official Organ of the*

COGIC Home & Foreign Mission Dept., July-September 1964

_____*Missions in the Local Church,* Church of God in Christ Home and Foreign Mission Dept., Bishop S.M. Crouch, President

Frazier, E. Franklin, *The Negro Church in America*, Schocken Books, New York: 1963

Goodson, Glenda *Bishop Mason and Those Sanctified Women!,* HCM Publishing, Dallas: First Printing 2002, Second Printing 2003

Gooren, Henri, Review *of An Introduction to Pentecostalism:* Global Charismatic Christianity

Hall, M. Elizabeth Lewis, *Married Women in Missions: The Effects of Cross-Cultural and Self Gender-Role Expectations on Well-Being, Stress, and Self-Esteem* in Journal of Psychology and Theology Copyright 2003 by Rosemead School of Psychology 2003, Vol. 31, No. 4, 303-314 Biola University, 0091-6471/410-730

Henderson, Jaquelyn S., *African American Baptist Women: A Study of Missions in African American Churches in Atlanta, Georgia* Publication: COPYRIGHT 2005 Baptist History and Heritage Society

Hiebert, Paul G. *Cultural Differences and the Communication of the Gospel.* www.uscwm.org/uploads/pdf/psp/hiebert_cultural.pdf

Israel, Adrienne *Mothers Roberson and Coffey – Pioneers of Women's Work: 1911-1964,* in *Bishop C.H. Mason and the Roots of the Church Of God In Christ* by Bishop Ithiel Clemmons, Pneuma Life Publishing, Bakersfield, CA: 1996

Johnson, Penelope *Equal in Monastic Profession,* The University of Chicago Press, Chicago and London

Jones, Charles Edwin, *Black Holiness: A Guide to the Study of Black Participation in Wesleyan Perfectionist and Glossolalic Pentecostal Movements* The American Theological Library Association and The Scarecrow Press, Inc., Metuchen, N.J. & London: 1987

Kennedy, Mary Beth, *A Visit to Wissikeh,* 5/28/58

Kenny, Gale, *Reconstructing a Different South: The American Missionary Association and Jamaica in Slavery and Abolition* Vol. 30, No. 3: September 2009

Kalu, Ogbu, *African Pentecostalism: An Introduction,* Oxford University Press, New York: 2008

Langley, J. Ayo *Chief Sam's African Movement and Race Consciousness in West Africa* from Phylon, vol. 32, no. 2 (Second quarter, 1971), Courtesy of New York Public Library, nypl.org

Lashley, E.M *Glimpses into the Life of a Great Mississippian and a Majestic American Educator 1926-1976,* 1977 and Down Behind the Sun – The Story of Arenia Conella Mallory by Dovie Marie Simmons and Olivia L. Martin, Riverside Press, Memphis: 1983

Lutz, Norma Jean, *History of the Black Church,* Chelsea House Publishers, Philadelphia: 2001

McBride, Calvin S., *Walking in a New Spirituality,* iUniverse, Lincoln, NE: 2007

McGee, Gary B. and Darrin J. Rodgers, *The Assemblies of God: Our Heritage in Perspective*
www.ifphc.org/index.cfm?fuseaction=history.main

Moody, Carlis L., *Church Of God In Christ Department of Missions History and Organization,* Memphis: 1996

Moody, Carlis L., *Humility Before Honor,* Just Writers Publishing Company, Evanston, IL: 2000

Nash, Dr. Gary B., Excerpt of *"The Unknown America Revolution,"* presented at the University of Pittsburgh 10/25/05

Noble, Mae *Christianity's African Roots: A Curriculum Emphasizing Aspects of The African Heritage of Christianity,* first published in 1980

Nyema, The Right Reverend Amos K. Sr., *Brief History, Progress*

Report and Needs of the Church Of God In Christ of Liberia to Presiding Bishop G.E. Patterson, October 2001

Park, Eunjin, *"White" Americans in "Black" Africa: Black and White American Methodist Missionaries in Liberia, 1820-1875*, Studies in African American History and Culture, Graham Russell Hodges, General Editor, Routledge: 2001

Patterson, Bishop G.E., Foreword in *The Making of a Legend* by Glenda Williams Goodson, HCM Publishing, Lancaster, TX: 2006

Patterson, J.O., German R. Ross and Julia Mason Atkins, *History and Formative Years of the Church Of God In Christ, with Excerpt from the Life and Works of its Founder – Bishop C.H. Mason* Reproduced, Church Of God In Christ Publishing House, Memphis: 1969

Porter, Andrew, *Religion Versus Empire? British Protestant Missionaries and Overseas Expansion, 1700-1914*, Manchester: University of Manchester Press: 2004

Roberts, Alva D. *My Life with Brother Isaiah: A Tribute to Bishop Isaiah Leon Roberts*, Faithday Press, Hazel Crest, IL: 2009

Saheed A. Adejumobi, "The Pan-African Congress," in *Organizing Black America: An Encyclopedia of Black Associations*, Nina Mjagkij, ed. Garland Publishing, Inc., New York: 2001

Sanders, Cheryl J. Cyberjournal for Pentecostal-Charismatic Research, 1996 PCCNA National Conference, Memphis, Tennessee, October 1, 1996, "*History of Women in the Pentecostal Movement*, Howard University School of Divinity

Simmons, Dovie Marie and Olive L. Martin, *Down Under the Sun: The Story of Arenia Conelia Mallory*, Riverside Press, Memphis: 1983

Smith, Amanda Berry, *The Story of the Lord's Dealings with Mrs. Amanda Berry Smith*: Meyer and Brother Publishers, Chicago: 1893

Smith, James K.A. *Thinking in Tongues*, in Pentecostal Manifestos, with Amos Yong, coeditor of a new book series, Pentecostal Manifestos, Eerdmans personal.denison.edu/~waite/liberia/history/acs.htm

Spann, Billie Roberts *The Role of Women in the Church From the Creation to Modern Day Denominational Practice,* Umoja Community Development Corporation, Baltimore: 2010

Sutherland, James W. *African American Underrepresentation in Intercultural Missions: Perceptions of Black Missionaries and the Theory of Survival/Security,* A Dissertation Submitted to the Faculty in partial fulfillment of the requirements for the degrees of Doctor of Philosophy in Intercultural Studies at Trinity Evangelical Divinity School, Deerfield, Illinois, May 1998

Synan, Vinson, *The Century of the Holy Spirit,* Thomas Nelson, Nashville: 2001

Taylor, William J., Home and Foreign Mission Executive Secretary, Church Of God In Christ *World Mission Digest,* 1956

The Apostolic Faith Mission of Portland, Oregon, *The Apostolic Faith History, Doctrine and Purpose,* Pediment Publishing Canada: 2005

The Columbia Encyclopedia. Copyright © 2001-10 Columbia University Press.

The International Outlook, The Official Organ of the Church Of God In Christ Home & Foreign Mission Dept., *Annual Report of Financial Receipts for Missions November 1965, Memphis, TN,* Bishop S.M. Crouch, President, Bishop O.M. Kelley, Vice-President, Mrs. Elsie W. Mason, Executive Secretary, February 1966

The New York Times, December 17, 1873

The Schomburg Center for Research in Black Culture, In Motion, *The African-American Migration Experience, The Colonization of Liberia* "Courtesy of The New York Public Library. www.nypl.org

Townes, Emilie M., *Womanist Justice, Womanist Hope,* The American Academy of Religion Series No. 79, Scholars Press, Atlanta, GA: 1993

Troutman, Joseph E., Editor, *The Journal of the Interdenominational Theological Center,* ITC Press, Atlanta: 1987

Ward, Kevin and Brian Stanley, eds., *The Church Mission Society and World Christianity, 1799–1999* William B. Eerdmans Publishing Co., Grand Rapids: 2000

Wells, John Miller, *Southern Presbyterian Worthies, Chapter II,* John Leighton Wilson: The Foreign Missionary Presbyterian Committee of Publication, Richmond, Va: 1936

Wells, Theda B., *Time to Remember: 100 Year Anniversary Celebration 1907-2007,* Church Of God In Christ Publishing House, Memphis: 2007

Whole Truth, *COGIC Boys During the War 1941-45*

_____Volume XXIII, No. 92, November 1955, Church Of God In Christ, Memphis, TN

Williams-Goodson, Glenda *Biographical Profiles of Early Church Of God In Christ Leaders accompanying Louis F. Morgan's article "The Flame Still Burns,"* Charisma Magazine, Volume 33, Number 4, November 2007

Winbush, Dr. Roy L.H. The Living Heritage Calendar *Profiles of Dynamic Saints in the Church Of God In Christ,* Church Of God In Christ Publishing House, Memphis: 1982

yale.edu/.../storm/AfricanAmericanMissionaries Revised.pdf
www.lottcarey.org/history

Archives

Dr. Juanita Faulkner, Private Collection, Philadelphia, PA
Emma Clark, The Mattie McGlothen Library, Richmond, CA
Dr. Ladrian Brown, D.J. Young Foundation Archives, Kansas City, MO
Glenda Goodson, The Center for African American Church History and Research, Inc., Lancaster, TX
Janis Echols, Private Collection, Waco, TX
Jerry Ramsey, Private Collection, Gloster, MS
Bernice Abrams, Private Collection, Dallas, TX

Newspapers and Periodicals

Ebony Magazine
The New York Times
Church Of God In Christ Voice of Missions
The Whole Truth
Assemblies of God Heritage Magazine
Charisma Magazine
International Outlook
The News of Haiti
The Liberian Observer

Unpublished Documents

Mendiola, Kelly Willis Ph.D., Approved Dissertation, *The Hand of a Woman: Four Holiness-Pentecostal Evangelists and American Culture, 1840-1930* 2002: University of Texas at Austin

Brown, Abraham, *Missionaries of the Church Of God In Christ, Manolu Mission, Maryland Country, Liberia*, 2006

Other

Philip Quaque, Letters of the Rev. Philip Quaque of West Africa (East Ardsley: Micro Methods Ltd. 198-85). The second is Philip Quaque, The Letters of Philip Quaque, 1766-1811 (East Ardsley: E.P. Microform, 1970s). Originals are housed at the Rhodes House Library, Oxford University

The Marcus Garvey and UNIA Papers Project, UCLA "African Series Introduction: Volume VIII: October 1913--June 1921". UCLA. http://www.international.ucla.edu/africa/mgpp/intro08.asp. Copyright © 1995-2010 Retrieved 3 February 2010.

An Interview with Miss Beatrice Lott, Returned Missionary to Cape Palmas, Liberia, Africa, 35th Annual Ohio State Convocation Church Of God In Christ, August 5 through 14, 1952, Elder U.E. Miller, State Overseer, Mrs. Lola Young, State Supervisor,

Cogswell, 6f. Thompson, 296. The Missionary Herald, Vol. 20, 1844

INDEX

A. Dash Wilson, 195, 210

aborigines, 137, 297

Abraham and Jessie Brown, 218

ACS. *See* American Colonization Society

African Liberians, 19, 83, 111, 138

AG. *See* Assemblies of God

Amanda Smith, 14

American Baptist missionary society, 47

American Board of Commissioners for Foreign Missions, 16, 26

American Colonization Society, xix, 10, 18, 274

American Society of Free Persons of Color, 9

Americo-Liberian.. *See* American Liberian

Americo-Liberians, 19, 86, 111, 137

    discriminatory practices, 111

Annie Bailey. *See* Annie Pennington Bailey

Apostolic Faith Mission, 31, 34

Assemblies of God, 33, 35, 37, 58, 148, 179, 201, 203, 204

assistance, 166, 188, 195, 197, 199, 226

    appeals in Whole Truth, 194

    Baptist missionaries in Haiti., 167

    Church World Service, 167

    Emannuel Temple COGIC, 169

    funds for school books, 297

    Mennonite Church, 166

authority of God over demonic. *See* demonic

Avant vs. Mason, 40

Azusa Street, ix, 30, 31, 33, 40, 56

    William J. Seymour, 31

Baptism in the Holy Ghost, 41

Barber vs. C.H. Kennedy, 184

Bel 'air, 124

Benjamin Crouch, 62

Betsey Stockton, 15, 26

Bible studies. *See* church services

Bishop C.H. Mason, xiv, xxi, xxiv, 39, 42, 43, 46, 48, 52, 57, 58, 69, 71, 122, 157, 168, 203, 211, 220, 229, 247, 253

Bishop C.H. Mason

    visited Haiti, 126

Bishop C.H. Mason
　visited Canada, 250
Bishop C.H. Mason
　World Pentecostal Conference, 252

Bishop A B McEwen. *See* Overseer A.B. McEwen

Bishop A.B. McEwen, 121, 157, 212, 231

Bishop Abraham Brown, xii, xxiv, 102, 148, 203, 204, 213, 219

Bishop Archie Buchanan, 259

Bishop Author Thomas Harrison, 250

Bishop B.R. Benbow, 255

Bishop Bobby Henderson, 264

Bishop Charles E. Blake, 264

Bishop F.D. Washington, 165

Bishop J.W. Denny, 264

Bishop Mason. *See* Bishop C.H. Mason

Bishop Samuel Crouch, 60, 167, 219
　built churches, 60
　built orphanages, 60

Bishop W.A. Kates, 231, 280

Bishop W.H. Reed, 231

Bishops and pastors outside U.S.
　Bishop Amos Nyema, Liberia, 82

Black Americans, 128

boarding school. *See* mission town

broken limb. *See* medical clinic

brush arbor. *See* church building, 293

Burners for Africa
　provided electricity, supported schools, 165

Calvary Temple. *See* Church of God in Christ outside United States

Cape Palmas, 16, 82, 85, 102, 109, 154, 158, 160, 195, 196, 208, 210, 214, 218, 219, 220, 293, 295

Carlis Moody. *See* Bishop Carlis Moody

Carlis Moody, Sr, 62

carpenter. *See* occupation

Cavalla River, 145, 153

celebrations. *See* holiday

cement blocks, 287

charges
　discipline, 294

Charles G. Finney, 24

Charles Parham, 30

Chicago School of Design, 223

Chicago School of Nursing, 73

Chief Harry T. Ragland, 178, 296

childhood marriage. *See* marriage

Christianity, xix, 6, 8, 11, 23, 33, 102

Christmas. *See* holidays

Church of God in Christ Jamaica. *See* churches outside United States

Church services, 116

churches
- Calvary Church of God in Christ in the UK, 251
- Holy Temple Church of God in Christ, 105
- Mount Zion COGIC, Canada, 250

Civil War, 5, 7, 13, 39, 188, 204, 221

COGIC bishops and pastors outside U.S, 121

COGIC bishops and pastors outside U.S., 60, 61, 121, 231, 244, 249, 253, 258, 280

COGIC Dept. of Women Int'l Supervisors
- Annie L. Bailey, 191
- Annie Pennington Bailey, 80
- Lillian Brooks Coffey, 52, 68, 71, 72, 73, 106, 107, 155, 164, 190, 208, 220, 229, 248, 291, 293
- Lizzie Robinson, xxi, 47, 48, 57, 58, 71, 80, 158, 188, 201, 202, 204, 205, 206, 208, 216, 291
- Mattie McGlothen, 124, 188, 192, 193
  - purchase clothing, 189
- Willie Mae Rivers, vii

COGIC international pioneer missionaries
- Lelia T. January, 69

COGIC missions officials
- Elder C.G. Brown, 58

COGIC pioneer international missionaries, 88, 280
- Anna Jewel McKenzie, 145, 231
- Beatrice Lott, xv, xvi, xxiv, xxv, 52, 65, 69, 71, 84, 88, 94, 95, 96, 101, 105, 116, 118, 131, 133, 134, 138, 139, 143, 144, 146, 149, 154, 158, 161, 163, 170, 175, 176, 182, 186, 196, 202, 205, 207, 222, 282, 292, 294
- Charles and Betty Kennedy, xii, 88, 105, 109, 110, 111, 178, 225, 280
- Charles Kennedy, Sr., xii, 61, 73, 110, 114, 120, 225
- Dorothy Webster Exume, xxiv, 68, 71, 94, 96, 103, 106, 107, 121, 122, 123, 124, 125, 126, 128, 129, 137, 138, 151, 162, 169,

175, 197, 212, 213, 276, 280

Effie L. Bright, 175

Elizabeth Copeland, 223

Elizabeth Scott, 188, 230

Elizabeth White, 37, 58, 61, 67, 71, 80, 82, 83, 89, 96, 148, 157, 163, 175, 202, 203, 205, 207, 219, 278, 279, 289, 291

Elnora Lee, 231

Francina Wiggins, 61, 88, 96, 175, 203, 213, 216, 219, 278, 289

Grace Yancey, 227, 280

June Blackwell, 88, 138, 155, 160, 230, 289

Katie Frazier, 96, 175, 231, 280, 281

Lee Van Zandt, 75

Lelia T. January, 88

Lucille Hayward, 136

Lucille Kates, 175

Martha Barber, 88, 96, 103, 105, 106, 107, 110, 112, 114, 115, 118, 133, 138, 144, 154, 161, 167, 175, 184, 186, 194, 207, 208, 222, 279, 292

Mary Beth Kennedy, xii, 73, 107, 150, 169, 178, 294, 297

Mrs. E. Lee, 231

Mrs. W.C. Ragland, 65, 96, 219, 290

Mrs. Willie C. Ragland, 70, 86, 204, 205, 289

Mrs. Willie Holt, 96, 175, 231

Naomi R. Lundy, xii, xxiv, 72, 73, 88, 116, 138, 144, 153, 154, 183, 213, 220, 228, 229, 276, 289

Nell Terry, 188

O.T. Jones, Jr., 88, 120, 175, 281, 289

Pearl Page Brown, xii, xxiv, 52, 53, 88, 120, 124, 145, 154, 165, 166, 169, 182, 191, 192, 216, 217, 276, 289

Rebekah Bonner, 188

Rosetta Graham, 230

Winifred Holder, 231

color, xxii, 57

communication, 208

    Creole, 123, 144, 162

    dialect, xxi, 86, 102

    language barrier, 119

confession. *See* salvation

Cornelius Hall, 201

cultural, 90, 130

cultural boundaries. *See* culture

culture, 142, 185, 287

customs office. *See* customs

D.J. Young, 40, 42, 95

dancing, xx, 32

danger, 145, 178

    man attacked by leopard, 286

poisonous snake bites, 286
scorpion bites, 286

Dawn Patrol, 249

demonic
authority of God over, xxiii
cannibalism, 150
drinking warm blood, 149
human blood sacrifices, 151
sacrifices made to idol gods, 83
spiritual hex, 147
Voodoo, 150
Witch doctors, 147

denominational and non COGIC support network
CARE, 197
Church World Service, 197
U.S. Embassy, 197
U.S. Marines, 197

Department of Women, vii, 45, 50, 54, 170, 191

discipline, 80

disease, 108, 121

doctrine, 90, 223, 243, 271

Doloke, 186

Dorothy Webster Exume, 144

Dr. Arenia Mallory, 79, 147, 185, 186, 220, 228, 281, 291

Dr. Cora Berry, 87

Dr. Willa Battle, 87

drum beating. *See* culture

Dynamo, 159, 161, 291, 293, 294

education, 12, 96, 118, 119, 125, 128, 179, 186, 187, 199

Elder Searcy, xxi, 51, 57

Elizabeth Dabney, 80

Elizabeth Isabelle Smith. *See* Lizzie Robinson

Elizabeth White Memorial, 279

Ella Deans School, 166

emigration, 8, 9, 20, 26

Ernestine Cleveland, 280

farm, 98, 132, 188, 215

farmers. *See* occupations

Father Gray, 196

financial reports. *See* records

Firestone, 84, 145, 187, 196

Florence Crawford, 56

foreign fields, xxii, 34, 87, 93, 95, 166, 169, 173, 175, 197, 205, 285

foreign missions, 33, 100, 157, 162, 188, 212
request for COGIC professionals to volunteer, 176

foreign missions work, 37, 51, 58, 61, 100, 188
Trinidad, 201

forest. *See* hinterland

Friendly Society of Sierra Leone, 17

Friends of Liberian Youth, 80, 185, 220

fundraising, 87, 162, 182, 193

furlough, 87, 139
   health examinations, while on, 192

Garvey. *See* Marcus Garvey

Gasper Hinah, 143

Gaybee. *See* Alexander Gbayee,
Gbayee, *See* Alexander Gbayee

global missions, 57, 157, 189, 233

glossolalia. *See* speaking in tongues

Great Awakening, 3

Great Commission, 80, 143, 271, 273

Haiti, 8
   revolution
      François Dominique Toussaint L'Ouverture, 8
      Jean-Jaques Dessalines, 8

heathen, 6, 22, 24, 36, 137, 235, 265, 284, 286, 297

hinterland, 61, 83, 89, 102, 169, 203

holiness, 125

Holiness-Pentecostal, xxi, 42

Holy Convocation, xxi, 42, 58, 61, 86, 106, 154, 157, 190, 217, 254, 264

Holy Ghost, 30, 40, 47, 66, 81, 96, 144, 146, 148, 151, 194, 199, 201, 207, 234, 239, 241, 265

Holy Spirit. *See* Holy Ghost

Home and Foreign Missions Department, 57

home missions, 50, 284

Hope Magazine, 47

Humor. *See* Black Americans

idol gods. *See* demonic

illness, disease
   dysentery, 145
   intestinal worms, 215
   poisonous snake bite, 215
   spinal meningitis, 215

immigrants, 6, 12, 19, 250

innovations, 118, 194

Inspector of Foreign Missions, 295

International Outlook, 176, 188, 217

J. Austin Gospel Train, 166

J. W. Denny, 62

James Temple, 15, 18

James Theodore Holly, 9, 15

Jane Waring Roberts, 27

January. *See* Lelia T. January

Jessie Brown, xii, xxiv, 187, 220, 225, 277

Jesus' power. *See* power

Joanna Moore, 47

Joseph Paulceus, 81, 121, 247

jungle. *See* hinterland

land purchase. *See* mission towns

leadership, 67
   biblical females, 77

Leatha and Reatha Herndon, 80

ledgers. *See* Financial records

Lelia January. *See* Lelia T. January

leper colonies. *See* leprosy

Liberian Consul General. *See* Alexander Gbayee

Liberian government, 19, 83, 119, 132, 186, 194, 295, 298
   President C.D.B. King, 21
   President V.S. Tubman, 185, 196

Lillian Brooks. *See* Lillian Coffey

local African women selling their girls. *See* customs

Lott Carey, 12, 56, 274

M.M. Jackson Mission School, 166

M.V. Susan. See ships

malaria, 108, 287

Manolu, xxiv, 83, 86, 90, 98, 99, 116, 143, 165, 166, 187, 203, 214, 219, 279

marriage, 137

Martha Barber, 61, 95, 106, 206, 226, 280, 289

Marva Cromartie, 88

Mary Beth Kennedy, xxiv, 95, 145, 179, 194, 225, 277, 279

Mary St. Juste, 96, 230

Maryland County, 89, 110, 178, 196, 203, 218, 219, 298, 299

master carpenter. *See* occupation

Mateal McC oy, 227

MATTIE McCAULLEY, 200

medical clinics, 121, 150
   Elizabeth White Clinic, 191
   Pearl Page Medical Clinic, 166

medical missionary training, 52, 120

Methodist, 88, 274

Methodists, 274

migration, 6, 17

miracles, 153

Mission Station, Mission Stations
   Wissikeh Mission Station, 58
   Wissikieh Mission Station, 83

Mission Station, Missions Stations

    Wissikeh Mission Station, 226

Mission Stations, Mission Station, 133, 135, 164, 165, 197, 200, 201, 203, 204, 205, 207, 212, 213, 216, 218, 223, 225, 228, 279, 285

    Bonniken Mission Station, 85

    grants, 182

    Manolu Mission Station, 61, 96, 185, 221, 229

    Tugbaken Mission Station, 95, 110, 138, 167, 169, 170, 219

    Wissekeh Mission Station, 120, 179

    Wissikeh Mission Station, 95, 96, 113, 143

    Wuluken Mission, 214

mission students, 137

Mission supporters

    Supervisor L.O. Hale, 192

Mission Supporters

    Elder H.W. Goldsberry, 279

Mission Town, 116, 178, 220, 286

mission towns. *See* mission town

Mission Towns, 134, 167

Missionaries, 36, 87, 101, 102, 108, 112, 123, 124, 128, 132, 135, 136, 183, 194, 199

    adoptions, 138

    building projects, 85, 87, 196, 199

    buried the dead, baptized converts, administered communion, 286

    Disagreements and misunderstandings, 183

    distributed food and medicine, 122

    entreprenurial activities, 213

    evacuated from Liberia, 102, 287

    evangelized, xxiii, 82, 85, 89, 181, 228, 265

    furlough, 87, 163

    health, 87, 192, 211, 287

    housing, 113, 181

    orphanages, 142

    overcame fear of leprosy, 169

    planted churches, 103

    planted rice, 195

    planted rubber trees, 293

    preached, 144

    served as overseers, 85

    witnessed cruel treatments of new converts, 286

Missionary calling, 87, 101, 112

    Charles and Betty Kennedy, 226

    Dorothy Webster Exume, 71

    Elizabeth Copeland, 224

    Lizzie Robinson, 47

Naomi Lundy, 228
missionary children, 35, 107, 108, 109, 111, 122, 123, 125, 129, 145, 152, 179, 226

    Amilcar Exume, 107, 123, 147, 166, 196

    Charles Kennedy, Jr., 111, 152

    Eleanor Page, 124

    Fronz Exume, 87, 99, 125, 162, 166, 196

    Marlil Provost, 124, 136, 196, 276

Missionary Society of the Methodist Episcopal Church, 88

missionary workers

    Michelle Dijuste, 123

missions gardens, 147, 294

Missions officials

    Bishop Esau Courtney, 60, 121, 130, 213

    Bishop S. R. Martin, 59, 61

    Bishop S.M. Crouch, 59

    Elder C.G. Brown, 205

    Elder Searcy, 58

    Mrs. Deborah Mason Patterson, 62

    Overseer A. B. McEwen, 60

    Richard L. Fidler, 60

    William J. Taylor, 183

missions students, 86, 98, 99, 102, 116, 117, 118, 122, 129, 130, 131, 132, 133, 135, 148, 154, 180, 181, 186, 214, 219, 220, 281, 286

    Alexander Gbayee, 104, 186, 277

    Annie Nah, 295

    Beatrice Nah, 137, 143, 196, 277

    Benjamin Jabbeh, 118, 131, 186, 187

    Bernice Nah, xxv

    Chief of Immigration, 180

    Chief of Police Department, 180

    Chief of Security, 180

    Emanuel John, 126

    Ester Boley, 138, 170

    Ethel Brown, 186

    Gaspar Hney., 118

    Marshall to the President, 180

    Peter Nimeley, 118

    Peter Nimely, 186

    Sam Coley, xxv, 186

    Sophronia Chesson, 281

    Willie Pokolo, 186

Missions supporters, 43, 70, 88, 136, 164, 165, 182, 186, 192, 193, 194, 216, 217, 222, 226, 228, 290, 291

missions workers, 127, 136

mixed cultural signals, 97

modern living conditions

    progress, 287

Monrovia, 11, 13, 16, 18, 19, 22, 27, 61, 69, 88, 89, 105, 110,

120, 132, 180, 183, 209, 211, 281, 298

Montserrado County, 89

moral code, 97

Mother Barclay, 88

Mother January's. *See* Lelia T. January

Mother Ola Mae Haynes
   see Burners for Africa, 165

Mr. Kofi Asaie, 93

Mrs. W.A. Rogers, 195, 210

mud hut, 286

mud huts, 101, 215, 287

multiple wives. *See* culture

National Convocation. *See* Holy Convocation

native Liberians, 61, 83, 87, 154, 177, 178, 195

Neely Terry, 31

Negro Improvement Association. *See* Marcus Garvey

Negro missionaries, 18

Negroes. *See* Black Americans, *See* Black Americans

Norine Evans, 280

O. T. Jones, Jr, 61

Oknewa Onwuckewa, 62

ordination, 44, 85

orphanage, 90, 99, 122, 128, 136, 152, 170, 219

outdoor clinic. *See* medical clinic

overseer, 70, 270

Overseer of Women, xxi, 45, 48

Pan African Congress, 67

paramount chief, 85, 114

Paul Cuffee, 17

Paul D. Gwagee, 280

Peace Corps, 116, 165, 169, 183, 283

Pentecostal, xviii, 51

Pentecostal movement, xx, 30, 31, 33, 47, 57, 148, 243, 254

Pentecostals. *See* Pentecostal

Pilot Steamship. *See* ship

pioneer African leaders
   Rev. William Brown, 148, 214

Pioneer international missionaries, xviii, 53, 81, 85

Plebo High School, 119

power
   in the blood of Jesus, 147
   of God delivers, 148
   of God over witch doctor, 151
   teaching about God's power, 149

power of God. *See* power

prayer
   Bishop C.H. Mason, 211

prayer services, 99
prayer walks, 99
prayer warriors, 159, 220
success of church growth, 98

President Franklin D. Roosevelt, 85

project. *See* government projects

Protestants, 273

Ramone St. Juste, 151

Religious support, 90

Rev James M. Priest, 18

Rev. Bolton Williams, 196

Rev. C.P. Jones, 39

Rev. Crabaugh. *See* transportation

Rev. J.M. Mutshweni. *See* COGIC South Africa

Rev. John Brooke Pinney, 16

Rev. John Jeter, 39

Rev. W.S. Pleasant, 39

Rice farms. *See* farm

Richard Allen, 9, 14

Richard Griffith, 169

Richmond African Baptist Missionary Society, 13

Robert Kuma, 144

Roman Catholic Church, 81

Rosetta E. Harding, 88

Rosiland Jones

neice of Beatrice Lott. *See* Beatrice Lott

Royal African Society, 17

rubber, 84

S.S. Andamia. *See* ship

S.S. Cristobal. *See* ship

Saints Home Church, 42

Saints Industrial and Literary School, xiv, 131, 148, *See* education

educates missions students, 187

salvation, 148, 266

Sam Coley, xxv

Samuel Crouch, 99, 160, 227, 231, 234

sanctification, viii, xviii, xxi, 39, 46, 80, 105

Sapang Bato village. *See* Mission Stations

Schools, 90, 119, 132, 186, 194, 296

A.W. Brown Vocational Institute, 166

Bel'air, Haiti, 103

C.H. Mason School, 126, 169

Ella Deans School, 126

J.S. Bailey Vocational School, 165

L.B. Coffey School, 191

Lee Elementary School, 179

M.M. Jackson Mission School, 177

Mason School and Orphanage, 212

mission schools, xxiii, 177, 264

Odessa Newman School, 126

Peace corps volunteers, 183

Roy and Mae Winbush School, 126, 166

S.M. Crouch Mission School, 166

Tugbaken school board, 295

Wissikeh Academic High School, 179

Wissikeh Mission School, 179

Selma Lockett, 231

ship, 109, 187

ships, 11, 12, 69, 102, 109, 193, 217, 254

Sierra Leone, 4, 11, 12, 16, 26, 37, 52, 274

slaves, xx, 4, 6, 8, 13, 20, 21, 41

social support, 90, 169

Sophronia Chesson, 188, 282

souls

soul winning, 199

South Africa, 34, 62, 81, 163, 166, 169, 231, 233, 264, 274, 278

Southern Board of Missions, 16

speaking in tongues, ix, xx, 30, 32, 40, 41, 69, 149

spiritual connection, 101

spiritual discipline, 114, 153

spiritual gifts, 78, 87

Sunday School, 105, 132, 211, 221

termites, 113, 181

The Honorable Sebastian Bush, 295

The Honorable William Tubman, 288

Tobou, 22, 23, 83, 203

training

nursing exams, 70

prerequisite to assignment, 88

Translations

Gblo-wi. *See* Bibles

transportation, 9, 107, 110, 112, 133, 145, 167, 182

tribal chiefs, 147

Tugbaken, 61, 85, 90, 95, 104, 106, 107, 112, 119, 143, 149, 166, 177, 188, 193, 194, 203, 204, 205, 206, 213, 218, 226, 276, 277, 299

U.S. Agency for International Development, 127

U.S. Embassy, 123

UNIA, 21

United Holy Church of America, 183

village, 83, 104, 133, 144, 151, 154, 177, 286

   Aeta people, Philippines, 225

   customs, 97

   Philippines, 225

   tribal chiefs, elders, 104

villages, 83, 152

   hostilities, 102, 154

   prayer walks, prayer services, 99

vision, 41, 73, 74, 84, 225

vocational training, 102, 282

Voice of Missions magazine, 62, 249

voodoo, xxiii, 100, *See* denomic

Voodoo priest

   defeated by the power of God. *See* power

W. E. B. Du Bois, 20

wages, 86, 101, 183, 196

Whole Truth, xiv, xxv, 44, 65, 71, 91, 92, 95, 158, 195, 205, 208, 209, 214, 235, 237, 238, 240, 294, 297

Whole Truth newspaper, 91

William and Rosabella Burke, 13

Winifred Holder, 254

Wissikeh, xxiv, 61, 75, 89, 90, 112, 114, 119, 134, 180, 185, 203, 213, 276, 279

Women's Convention, 167, 168, 184, 190, 192, 213, 279, 291

work, 47, 186, 195

World War II, 102, 228, 229

worldwide revivals

   Welsh Revival, Keswick Convention, Korean Pentecost, African revival movement, 30

Wrouke, 83

Youth Congress, 174, 175

Youth Department, 174

YPWW. *See* Youth Department

If you like this book you may also be interested in the following books and DVDs from HCM Publishing

Bishop Mason and Those Sanctified Women!
(2004)

Our Mothers' Stories: History of the Department of Women with live interviews from COGIC pioneers
80 minute documentary on DVD (2004)

I'm So Glad I'm Sanctified: Wisdom Quotes and Treasures from COGIC Pioneering Women 1911-1975 (2005)

P.O. Box 36
Lancaster, Texas 75146
glendagoodson@aol.com
www.glendagoodson.com

www.ingramcontent.com/pod-product-compliance
Lightning Source LLC
Chambersburg PA
CBHW072004150426
43194CB00008B/988